PUBLIC RELATIONS
IN THE 1980's

PUBLIC RELATIONS IN THE 1980's

Proceedings of the Eighth Public Relations World Congress
London 1979

Edited by

SAM BLACK, M.B.E.

Secretary General of the
International Public Relations Association

PERGAMON PRESS

OXFORD · NEW YORK · TORONTO · SYDNEY · PARIS · FRANKFURT

U.K.	Pergamon Press Ltd., Headington Hill Hall, Oxford OX3 0BW, England
U.S.A.	Pergamon Press Inc., Maxwell House, Fairview Park, Elmsford, New York 10523, U.S.A.
CANADA	Pergamon of Canada, Suite 104, 150 Consumers Road, Willowdale, Ontario M2J 1P9, Canada
AUSTRALIA	Pergamon Press (Aust.) Pty. Ltd., P.O. Box 544, Potts Point, N.S.W. 2011, Australia
FRANCE	Pergamon Press SARL, 24 rue des Ecoles, 75240 Paris, Cedex 05, France
FEDERAL REPUBLIC OF GERMANY	Pergamon Press GmbH, 6242 Kronberg-Taunus, Pferdstrasse 1, Federal Republic of Germany

First edition 1980

British Library Cataloguing in Publication Data

Public Relations World Congress, *8th, London, 1979*
Public relations in the 1980's.
1. Public relations - Congresses
I. Title   II. Black, Sam
659.2   HM 263   79-41553
ISBN 0-08-024065 8 Hardcover

In order to make this volume available as economically and as rapidly as possible the author's typescript has been reproduced in its original form. This method unfortunately has its typographical limitations but it is hoped that they in no way distract the reader.

Printed and bound in Great Britain by
William Clowes (Beccles) Limited, Beccles and London

Contents

v

Preface

A Public Relations World Congress is sponsored every third year by the International Public Relations Association and organised on its behalf by the National Public Relations Association in the host country.

The purpose of these Congresses is to promote understanding of current and expected international problems which affect the work of public relations practitioners, and also to examine and debate new trends in public relations thinking, methods and techniques. Attendance is open to all who wish to register and the level of practitioners attending is generally that of senior executives in the profession.

The message of the Eighth World Congress was that in this increasingly complex world public relations professionals need to be fully aware of and understand the shifts in relationships within both national and international societies and to be able to evaluate and use new techniques and methods in a professional manner to contribute to a more harmonious world society.

The speakers were from 16 countries and delegates represented 55 different nationalities, giving the World Congress a truly international character. The programme was very concentrated and covered a great variety of subject matter.

In retrospect, based upon reactions from a large number of delegates, it undoubtedly stimulated new thinking in the field of professional philosophy and techniques and in exposure of current international affairs. And perhaps an equally important dividend was the opportunity for men and women from so many different national and professional backgrounds to meet and discuss, compare attitudes and experiences and hence create more understanding and links between practitioners throughout the world.

DENNIS BUCKLE
Chairman of the Congress

Introduction

The title of this book is "Public Relations in the 1980's" so it would seem appropriate to consider how the profession has evolved and what is currently understood by the term "public relations". This attempt to explain and define the term should be of particular value to all those readers who are not professionally engaged in the field.

The basic philosophy underlying public relations practice is that people matter and that the support of public opinion is of prime importance in all spheres of activity. This truth has been understood by leaders and politicians since the earliest days but the professional practice of public relations as we understand it today dates only from about 1923. In both the United States of America and England, however, there were isolated examples of its use during the early part of the 20th century.

At a world gathering of public relations practitioners from many countries which was held in Mexico City on 11 August 1978 the following statement was adopted:

"Public Relations Practice is the art and social science of analysing trends, predicting their consequences, counselling organisation leaders, and implementing planned programmes of action which will serve both the organisation's and the public interest".

At the public exhibition which was organised in London by the International Public Relations Association (IPRA) during the month of May 1979 on the occasion of the World Congress ten groups of activity were identified as comprising together the full breadth of public relations practice. These ten groups are:

1.   Public Opinion
2.   Public Affairs
3.   Government Relations
4.   Community Affairs
5.   Industrial Relations
6.   Financial Affairs
7.   International Relations
8.   Consumer Affairs
9   Research and Statistics
10.   Media of Communication

These are the fields in which public relations plays an important part, and all of these subjects were included in the Congress programme.

The speakers were from many different countries and the participants from 56 countries. This emphasises the truly international nature of our subject.

If there are ten different fields of activity, there are numerous different ways in which the public relations professional contributes to good "management". The following list gives the main avenues of our professional work but of course no practitioner performs all these functions at the same time.

1.   Counselling based on an understanding of human behaviour
2.   Analysing future trends and predicting their consequences
3.   Research into public opinion, attitudes and expectations and advising on necessary action
4.   Establishing and maintaining two-way communication based on truth and full information
5.   Preventing conflict and misunderstandings
6.   Promoting mutual respect and social responsibility
7.   Harmonising the private and the public interest
8.   Promoting good-will with staff, suppliers and customers
9.   Improving industrial relations
10.   Attracting good personnel and reducing labour turnover
11.   Promotion of products or services
12.   Maximising profitability
13.   Projecting a corporate identity
14.   Encouraging an interest in international affairs
15.   Promoting an understanding of democracy

A typical public relations activity will have four separate but related parts:

1.   Analysis, research and defining problems;
2.   Drawing up a programme of action;
3.   Communicating and implementing the programme;
4.   Monitoring the results, evaluation and possible modification.

To achieve success, public relations must be based on truth and full information and be carried out on a continuing basis. It cannot succeed if used as a fire brigade to be called in when an emergency occurs. It is not merely cosmetic and can never be a substitute for good performance, indeed it is likely to expose any intrinsic weaknesses. Correct timing is also very important.

The success of public relations activity can be judged by the extent to which short term objectives are achieved.

Public relations is the direct responsibility of the Chief Executive or head of an organisation, but it is equally the duty of every member of staff. The public relations professional, however, has the training and experience to play an important role in the discussion and formulation of policy and to visualise and coordinate its implementation.

It follows from this that public relations practice should be an integral part of management and not merely a tool of management as suggested by many previously, nor is it "communication" although obviously communication is a very important part of the operation.

It would be easy to devote many further pages to discussing definitions of public relations since they have been legion, but one thought expresses the very essence of the function. "Public relations practice can be considered as a positive attempt to achieve harmony with the environment". These sixteen words are nearer the truth than the many lengthy and complicated definitions which have been formulated in the United States of America and other countries since the achievement of harmonisation with the environment is such a basic requirement for success in any endeavour.

This book comprises the complete proceedings of the Eighth Public Relations World Congress which was held at the London Hilton 23-25 May 1979, and it will be seen that the Congress followed the traditional pattern of these events by combining plenary sessions which considered problems of world-wide impact with concurrent sessions which dealt with professional problems and practical considerations which affect the everyday professional work of those involved.

The first Public Relations World Congress was held at Brussels in May 1958 during EXPO 58 which was the first world exhibition and gathering after the war. The enthusiasm of that occasion will be remembered by all who were privileged to attend, and while some of the enthusiasm has been dissipated during the vicissitudes of the intervening years nevertheless there is an atmosphere at world gatherings which should never be under-valued. 800 men and women in public relations from 56 countries attended this London meeting in May and while the papers and discussions were of a very high quality - as will be seen from the following pages - nevertheless the lasting impression of the Congress is the wonderful spirit of comradeship and common interest that was displayed.

For the record it is worth listing the eight world congresses which have been sponsored by the International Public Relations Association since 1958:

1st Congress - Brussels 1958   2nd Venice 1961   3rd Montreal 1964
4th Rio de Janeiro 1967   5th Tel-Aviv 1970   6th Geneva 1973
7th Boston 1976   8th London 1979.

We now look forward to the Ninth Public Relations World Congress which will be held in Bombay in early 1982.

It only remains to thank all those concerned with the Congress sessions and in particular to thank the convenors of the sessions who were so helpful in collecting together the material to be included in this book.

SAM BLACK

Chairman's Opening Remarks

Dennis Buckle

On behalf of the Organising Committee which embraces the Institute of Public
Relations of Britain, Public Relations Consultants Association of Britain and the
International Public Relations Association - to all our overseas delegates -
welcome to Britain and welcome to London - and to all the delegates - welcome to
the Congress.

Now just recently I realised that the gestation period of this world congress
exactly matched that of an elephant! And at this point in time I must say that I
feel - as a female elephant must - when she sees her new-born calf, well here it is
and I wonder how it is going to turn out. Certainly we have the encouraging
support of delegates from fifty six different countries of the world and we hope
that we have contrived a programme which is sometimes provocative and always one in
which you can participate because everything depends upon your interest, and your
contributions, if we are really going to extract the benefits that we hope you will
extract from the programme that we have contrived. There are two main
complementary strands to the programme. One which I might call the socio-
political world plane in which eminent speakers will turn our thoughts towards the
international perspective within which we all live and the second the plane of
professional competence and future development within which I am sure we shall all
find much to learn not only within the sessions but outside the sessions from each
other. If we have successfully presented these two strands within our programme
then this world congress will prove its worth as a focal point for the exchange of
new thinking, new ideas, new techniques and professional experiences. Because as
we all know, public relations is not a static science or a static art it is a
profession which must by the very nature of its contribution to society adapt and
keep pace with changes in our society. And that can never be achieved by
myriads of little cells, but by the free and widespread flow of knowledge and
discovery.

I do not want to delay any longer your exposure to Dr Conor Cruise O'Brien, a
person who can rightly claim to be an original thinker, a fearless promoter of
peace and world harmony and a personality of wide renown. But first, I would
like to read the message sent to this Congress from our Patron, His Royal Highness
Prince Philip, the Duke of Edinburgh. This is the message sent from Buckingham
Palace.

Message from HRH The Prince Philip Duke of Edinburgh

"There are two sides to communications. There is the technical business of
sending and receiving messages and then there is the composition of the messages to
be sent. While most people are aware that a major revolution in communication

techniques has been going on for a number of years, there are a great many thinking people who are convinced that the content of the messages has been deteriorating. Truth, reality and exactitude are gradually being swamped by dogma, illusion and vagueness. Ends are beginning to justify the means. The world is certainly changing in many ways, although this is patently not a new phenomenon. If it were, we would still be wearing fig leaves. But human nature does not change. The challenge that faces everyone who deals in ideas and information is to encourage and sustain the best in human nature and to recognise and condemn its evil and destructive features in what ever plausible guise they may appear. The means of communication are changing all the time but truth, honesty and virtue are timeless. It is up to each one of us to decide how to use the means at our disposal."   Signed: PHILIP

With your endorsement, I would like to send a message of appreciation to our Patron at the end of this Congress.

Now I have the very great pleasure of introducing our guest speaker, Dr Conor Cruise O'Brien. It is very befitting that such an international man should be the one to set the backcloth for our discussions during the next two and a half days. But our problem was in which of his many guises to invite him and in the end we decided that it was that of savant or wise man. His life since leaving Dublin University has encompassed three different activities, any one of which would have satisfied most of us for a lifetime career. Starting in his country's diplomatic service he became a prominent figure in the United Nations and for a time in 1962 he undertook the very difficult task of supervising the United Nations operations in Congo, now known as Zaire, designed to bring peace to that very troubled country. It was while visiting Zaire during that time, that I heard a great deal about him and the tremendous effort he was making to achieve - what I know has always been his ambition for the world - a genuine peace. Leaving that service, he then entered the academic world as vice-chancellor of Ghana University and during three years there he inculcated fresh thinking and higher standards on the campus and left an indelible mark on that community. He subsequently was Albert Schweitzer Professor of Humanities at New York University for a further three years but then domestic politics attracted him home. In addition to all this, for the past twenty five years or so he has achieved a significant reputation as a writer of many books that are learned and stimulating. Now Dr Conor Cruise O'Brien has decided to grace another eminent profession, that of journalism and he is now Editor in Chief of one of our most distinguished papers, "The Observer". From such a wide and varied and distinguished life I am sure that the thoughts we are going to hear expounded by Dr Conor Cruise O'Brien this afternoon, will open our minds to the theme of our Congress - Challenges of a Changing World.

1

Keynote Address

Dr Conor Cruise O'Brien
Editor-in-Chief, "The Observer"

I think that in terms of your initial metaphor my speech has to appear on your agenda in terms of the first bleating of a new-born elephant calf. I am very happy to assume that significant and progressive role and persist in it here. I should like - before I go further - to say how reassuring I find it to be addressing an audience composed entirely of public relations people. I have a reason for that, politicians - and I am a partly-sometime-politician - are accustomed to address audiences which may be hostile. When one is talking to a public relations audience one has a cast iron in-built guarantee of an audience that will be polite and will not heckle. So I thank you in advance for your character and for your professional function which I respect.

I would like to say first a few words about communication in general and then something about the somewhat contentious theme of flow of information in the world, that theme which has been much discussed at UNESCO and in other international forums. First about communications. I attended, not long ago a meeting of the Aspen Institute in Berlin on the subject of communication. As you can imagine at a conference of that kind, there were many people skilled in communication who articulated what they had to say very well. But there was one very wise man with a great international reputation there and he was from India and he sat through the whole proceedings of the conference in total, serene, unbroken silence - he did not utter a word. So I wondered in my naive Western way why a man would come to a conference on communication and refrain from communicating. So I asked him, brashly, "Why do you do this?" So he looked at me sadly and he said, "I am surprised, Dr O'Brien that at your age and with your experience you have not yet learned that communication is impossible!"

That at least is one thought which I would like to leave with you as you start your proceedings. Of course, literally speaking it is untrue, communication is possible, only too possibly we may sometimes think. Prince Philip, in those moving words which our Chairman has just read to you put his finger on some of the troubles of communication in what is being communicated. But this is a very old problem indeed.

Plato talks about it in the Sixth Book of The Republic, where he talks about the political man who is accustomed to move people. We are all interested in moving people for one reason or another. But Plato depicts the man who is interested in moving people as himself being moved by them and the process being a two-way one and one which Plato (the aristocratic philosopher) sees as essentially corrupting and degrading to both sides. And that is the picture of which at least we have to take account. We do not have to go along with the total pessimism of that but we should not either think of communications as somehow inherently good, it is not.

3

It is as good as we make it or as bad as we make it.

We have seen in our century people moved to terrible ends by terrible orators from Adolf Hitler to others in our time. I have seen people moved to terrible things in the Congo, in Nigeria, in my own land of Ireland and in New York. I think communication is not impossible but communication about communication may be very nearly impossible because we never know exactly what is being communicated.

As I talk, I can't know what is happening in all of your heads, some of you certainly are not listening at all - are thinking about some other and possibly very much more interesting things - others, their attention comes and goes, others, perhaps listen but then start their own different chains of thought. We don't know what is happening in a room like this *a fortiori* we don't know what is happening in the so-called global village as communication goes on.

It is possible to be pessimistic about communication thinking of evil as more potent than good in the world - an anarchian view - and one thing that we may think of there is this: That in all the centuries since the message of the Gospel, the message of Christ first went out to men. No message has been propagated with greater assiduity, with greater sacrifice, possibly in the world than that one. And after two thousand years what is the behaviour of those to whom that message was addressed. I think of that topic with particular distress and particular shame when I think of the behaviour of contesting factions of so-called Christians in my own country and in particular, in Northern Ireland. One can only console oneself with the thought that if they behaved that badly as Christians how much worse would they behave if they were not Christians!

And there is much also in contemporary facts of world communication to engender some degree of pessimism.

The Flow of News in the World

I would now like to move to my main topic which is the flow of news in the world. The flow of news in the world today which as we know has been the subject of controversy is determined by two different kinds of power, I think we must speak analytically about this before we begin to speak moralistically. It is determined by two different kinds of power. In the Communist world and in much - though not all - of the Third World it is determined by state-power by the government in power - by the government of the day.

In the West it is in conditions of what we call freedom and the word is not meaningless but I am using different terms of definition here. In the West it is determined by purchasing power, the power to buy newspapers, to pay licence fees, to buy goods whose producers can buy advertising space, that is the base of the freedom of the press in the West - a freedom of the press which is a most precious acquisition - but whose material base we should keep clearly in mind.

I am not equating these two kinds of determining flow of information. The first kind, that of state power is narrow and constricting and produces a press which is generally at an unhappily low level. The second is diffuse, variegated, subtle, more nearly approximating of the ideal of freedom of information, it churns out enormous amounts of nonsense with the prodigality of nature in waste and it also makes possible the production of the best newspapers and the best radio and television that exist anywhere in the world. All that goes together and all those are linked together in freedom, the freedom of course includes the immortal God-giving right to make a bloody fool of yourself!

As far as informing the Western public is concerned it is rather hard to see that this system can be improved upon. Those who wield the power being the general public. But if we look at the flow of news in the world generally we see that there is something in the case against the Western version of freedom of information, that case so regularly made at UNESCO and in the United Nations. I may say I don't agree with this case, in fact, I am strongly opposed to it – in its totality and particularly I question the motive of many of those who make it and whose own record in relation to freedom of information in their own countries is so bad. Nonetheless, there is something in the case and I would like to say what the something is in my opinion.

Informing the Third World

The flow of news in the world is determined by the interest of the cash customer, the population of the affluent newspaper-reading-world. News is defined as that which interests those people. That is the way it works. It's not a question of how it ought to work – I am talking about how it actually does work. The news which reaches the Third World is generally a kind of cast-off – a garment of information designed for someone else and in this case someone a lot fatter. Or rather, and these aspects are not generally stressed at UNESCO. The flow of news reaching the Third World consists first of that Western by-product minus, in many cases, in many Third World countries though certainly not in all, minus whatever a local form of dictatorship finds it feasible and opportune to filter out plus the propaganda output of the local dictatorship itself and plus also the propaganda output of the Communist countries if that happens to be to the taste of the local dictatorship.

Again I am proceeding analytically and therefore bleakly because parts of this field have to be surveyed bleakly. And what remains of the Western by-products even those designed for other people remains much the most informative as well as infinitely the most entertaining ingredient in that package and that is the element which the critics at UNESCO have to digest. I have said what I think there is in their case and that is a large part of the reply to their case. Only in so far as the distribution of wealth and of freedom in the World shifts – and there is a relation between those values – can we expect to see a radical shift in the flow of news. Certainly UNESCO efforts to change the flow through further aggrandisements of state power should be resisted unequivocably.

But even within the confines of the existing system and structure of the World there is surely room for some improvement through the growth of consciousness in the Western public that the course of events in the Third World and in particular the progress or the non-progress of development there is a matter of great and direct concern, not only to people in the Third World but to all of us here as it will do much to determine the character of the World in which our children and all those other children will grow up. If Western interest in these matters can be increased then the value to the Third World of what I have called the 'Western by-product' also increases. It is not enough, however, to hope for automatic change. We have to do what we can by deliberate action to improve the situation.

One effort at improving it was made hopefully, with the setting up of a pool of news and information generated in the Third World itself which the Yugoslav News Agency helped to distribute.

Talking to editors who have used that service I must say that they have not found it satisfactory or a good base. Interesting though the idea was, something more real is needed. I have wondered, for example, about the possibility of what one might call a 'quality pool'. That is to say the cooperation of quality news-papers throughout the World wherever such newspapers exist for the collection and re-dissemination of information about Third World development in the broader sense. The barrier to that has generally been the disproportion of the cost of gathering such information to the interest of the subject matter to an affluent public and to the Third World capacity to pay. I am talking again analytically about material bases - these are facts that have to be taken into account - and I think a collective effort of this kind might prove a practical answer to some of these problems.

I would hope that such ideas may be discussed at the forthcoming International Press Institute conference in Athens next month which I shall be attending.

Communication and Peace

Communication is an ambiguous process and I think there is only one thing certain about it. I would like to say that communication is conducive to peace, I am not quite sure that it is - certainly not all communications are conducive to peace and again if we think again of the career in broadcasting of Adolf Hitler we find some confirmation of that theme.

But communication, whatever else it does, represents an abiding need of human nature - its improvement to meet present possibilities and overcome present obstacles is therefore one of the most certain ways in which we can respond to the challenges of a changing world - this vast theme of your Congress this week. In conclusion, I wish your deliberations every success and I am very happy to have been engaged in the beginning of them.

2

Issues for the Eighties

Brian E. Urquhart

Under-Secretary General, United Nations

There has been a steady process of what I can only call 'democratisation' of the international scene. By that I mean that the world has ceased to be dominated by one or two imperial powers and instead there is a growing and articulate constituency of middle and smaller powers who know what they want, who are prepared, either singly or in groups to work peacefully for it and who are increasingly, it seems to me, a very important balancing factor in a world which formerly used to be dangerously polarised between the greatest powers only.

Of course, the United Nations has been a catalyst in both of these very important processes and there is a good deal of complaint still in the Old World about this process. Old club members normally resent new ones and the club of sovereign nations in the world is no exception but, politically, it seems to me this is a much healthier system than any that has existed before and a system upon which – it people only make the effort – a very promising new civilisation can grow. A civilisation with an emphasis on equitability, if not on equality; an emphasis on participation and cooperation rather than on struggle. And also I think, on the international scale, the beginning of a conviction that any society which is worth its name has an obligation to protect the weak and the interests of the weak if necessary against the strong, which seems to me in fact, to be the key character-istic of a successful political society.

Now to come to the negative side. We live in a world of finite resources, a world which has suddenly woken up to the fact that the natural resources of the planet will not go on for ever. At the same time its population has grown enormously and the aspirations and appetites of that population have vastly increased.

So our problem is to try to evolve out of these rather confusing, but not at all unpromising elements, a new and a more or less stable and progressive order and that is the challenge which governments and people have been trying to face in the United Nations and must accelerate their efforts to face.

I think that one of the most important things to try to put across is that this is everyone's business, it is not simply the business of bureaucrats, like me, or politicians, or diplomats or internatinal organisations. Because in fact most of the changes which will have to be made and most of the steps that will have to be taken depend on a serious and acceptable changing of public attitudes. The way people live will have to change in accordance with the times and this is not necessarily bad. There was an incident last week in the United States when Sheikh Yamani, the Oil Minister of Saudi Arabia who was there for the graduation of one of his daughters, was asked what he thought about the current gasoline

7

crisis in the United States and he said in a very kindly manner that he felt that the people of the United States might have to face the possibility of changing their life style. A remark which had the most tremendous repercussions in the United States and I merely quote this as an example of how most people do regard any change, especially in a prosperous society, as being a change for the worse. And it is very important that they should stop doing that. Now all of this is going to take time - but how much time do we really have? If we exclude - and I am afraid we can not quite exclude it - the possibility of a nuclear disaster of one sort or another, we still have to reckon with processes which are already under way, which have come upon us almost unawares.

I have mentioned the exhaustion of natural resources. There are also the threats to the environment which various kinds of technology have produced. There is something which I think we are only just beginning to think about properly now and that is the runaway scale of our society - the size of the units - which now make it up. The erosion of confidence and stability which that process - and also partly the process of over-communication has brought about. I think we have to consider that there are large segments of our society which are quite likely to become quite unmanageable and these are things which have to be faced. There is not any time to be wasted about that, and there is no room for defeatism. It is extremely important to realise that throughout history people have had to face change and if they failed to face it they have either gone down to an ignominious decline or in some cases, ceased to exist: and there is no reason why this should happen to our society. But again I say that especially in such matters as order and manageability public attitudes are the key. You can not, for example, solve a temporary shortage of gasoline in this country or the United States if everybody panics in an irrational manner and proceeds to exhaust the available supplies unnecessarily.

This is a very simple example, but this applies to almost all changes in attitude. Now personally, I have a very strong distrust of doctrinaire approaches to problems. I think that an honest process of discussion and trial and error on a basis of mutual respect is a much more realistic way of tackling problems, which in any case have to be identified properly before you can tackle them.

A great deal of the trouble in the world is - it always seems to me - has come from people who really believe that they know best about other people's lives and this tends to inhibit debate and also usually to promote the wrong kind of solutions. In the United Nations we have an unending debate which is a matter of participation, of trying to identify problems of trial and error and really centres around a number of general propositions. First of all what do people really want? Second, what can they reasonably hope to get; and thirdly, what really will contribute in the long run to a more reasonable organisation of society? Now all of this at the moment takes place within the context of a world of independent sovereign states and it is no good saying that this is an anachronistic context, this is what we have and this is what we have to work with. But it does add a very complex factor to the equation that we have to try to solve. And I think it is one of the things that it is important to try to get across to the public at large if they are to really play the part that I think they should in changing the attitudes as necessary.

There are a number of false assumptions which many people find it convenient to believe. For example, people are really very loath to accept the idea that self-interest is a key motive in almost all transactions. Perhaps the key motive, and really it has to be made compatible with human survival and there is no reason why this should not be done providing we recognise the problem. I think it is very important for people to really understand that governments - no matter how good and wise - are not free, usually, to adopt the course that they really think is best.

There are all sorts of reasons in almost all political systems why governments are inhibited in doing that. Nor in fact are international organisations which are mostly made up of governments. I think it is also important to realise that people who are hungry or frightened or angry will not make good far-sighted choices and therefore we have to tackle that part of the problem all the time.

By that I mean that the gulf between rich and poor which has always existed throughout history, in our time is no longer a humanitarian or an economic problem. It is our No 1 political hazard and our No 1 political problem if we are thinking in terms of trying to create some kind of stable World society. No political order will ever be secure unless that gulf can be shown to be lessening rather than widening. Another thing which it seems almost too obvious to mention is that reason and good will and moderation are at present at any rate not a very powerful factor in most political situations. Fear and pre-conceived ideas and sometimes greed, are unfortunately, much more important immediate factors.

For that reason we need to pay more attention to the management of emergencies and short term crisis while we are looking for long term solutions. Now on the positive side there are a number of things which people really do not often think about. In the first place, as I mentioned before, there is a new and almost limitless potential for improvement through knowledge, through technology and through communication. There is, in fact, some kind of World community slowly emerging and I think one of the evidence of that is that the international organisations and groups like yourselves are discussing now - as if it were perfectly normal and usual - global problems, but really for the first time. This did not happen before. And recognising that there are problems which have to be tackled on a global level, which have to be identified and to which only a co-operative approach can have a hope of succeeding.

I think it is very important to avoid emphasising all the time the possibility of disaster which causes in fact, more often than not, a kind of self-generating deterioration in most situations. I mentioned the situation in California over gas at the moment, and it is a very good example. And I think here, that the media can play a really disastrous role and there is a major duty, it seems to me, not by any outside agency but by the various sides of the media themselves to really consider the effects of some of the approaches they take to problems. Another thing that seems to me to be long overdue is a hearty distrust of ideo-logical, rhetorical and dogmatic approaches. I very much doubt if most of the problems that we are facing now could be solved by such approaches, they merely complicate them and it is good to see that in some of the major international debates now a new spirit of pragmatism is becoming dominant. I am thinking particularly, for example, of the Conference on the Law of the Sea, which is of immense importance to any future orderly conservation of resources, which was widely thought absolutely hopeless two or three years ago and would now appear to be gradually - by a pragmatic approach - overcoming the most complicated long term problems.

Now inevitably in the affairs of humanity groups form themselves. Groups with common or identical interests are formed and they usually are violently resented by people who are not in them. I think there is a lot of nonsense talked about various groups especially by people who are not members of them. The sorts of groups that I am thinking about are not monolithic or self-perpetuating, they simply emerge to pursue a certain set of common interests and then they evolve and change and they can be extremely useful in articulating a serious approach to major problems provided that they do not become too predominant and that they do not exist to the exclusion of other interests.

Dangers of Stereotypes

One of the more dangerous aspects of the groups is that they tend to give rise to a lot of stereotype thinking, which is another hazard of the media. And stereotype thinking gives rise to vague resentment and to great misunderstanding. The use of words like, leftist and rightist and Third World and racist and colonialist are portmanteau words which save a lot of space in newspapers but in fact are usually extremely misleading. And they block understanding and on the whole, in my experience at any rate, they foster a great deal of unnecessary distrust and I think we should beware of them. Because really to make progress people have to make an effort to see other people in their own context not in the context of the beholder. If you do not do that, it is impossible to understand what the problem is. I think we need groups which are <u>for</u> things and not <u>against</u> them. It seems to me for example, that a group for World economic and political order is long overdue - I suppose you could say that the United Nations is that - but it is a somewhat distracted group. It seems to me that we should really not give way to either too much optimism or too much pessimism. After 34 years in the United Nations, preceded by six years in World War II, I must say that I am both optimistic and sceptical. I believe more than ever in the essential decency and the potential of humanity to shape a better future for itself - though I am very sceptical about some of the institutions it has chosen to have to do it and their capacity for living up to the challenge. I think it is really a very simple attitude that needs to be adopted if we are really to make the kind of progress that we have to make in the time that is available. I think we must in the first place believe that we are at the <u>beginning</u> of an era and not at the <u>end</u> of one. I do seriously believe that we are at the beginning of an era if - even if it is a very confusing beginning - and this is the era of World community. We cannot avoid it as we have managed to make the World so small and to make communication so immediate that there is no alternative. And it is not a bad choice to be faced with, it seems to me. You who represent the world of communication have a very <u>key</u> part of play in the healthy and constructive development of that world community and for that reason I am very much pleased and happy to have been here today to share the beginning of this conference with you.

DISCUSSION

Rodney Wheeler (United States of America).   I would like to mention the
recent event at Three Mile Island in Pennsylvania where even after the event had
reached the point where there was no danger to the public the television networks
were still giving the worse case scenario and talking about the possibility of
evacuating 800,000 people. We in public relations endeavour to communicate, to
give facts, to keep things in perspective, but we tend to run into situations
where media people have not really prepared themselves and really do not know
what they are talking about. This is particularly true in the Three Mile Island
case. Do you see any hope, Sir, that we in the communications business and the
media can find a better communication in parts of the world we are trying to
reach?

Urquhart.   I think this is a really crucial problem in any society,
especially a free society. I do not have any doubt that if it is the price we pay
for a free society we ought to pay it, because it is well worth it. But it does
affect the other problem I was mentioning, of manageability. There is a strong
feeling developing in many places now that if things go on as they are, some
countries and some parts of the World will become ungovernable simply because of
the process you mention. Here you have an event which is interpreted and which
causes a reaction - a major reaction. And I think that the only possible way of
dealing with this - and I do see the problem for the media themselves - the only
possible way is to try to develop increasingly a form of voluntary restraint. The
media should consider what is in the long term good of the greatest number and if
they have to choose between having a terrific news story on page one which creates
a tremendous amount of attention or taking a little more trouble and having a much
more balanced story on page six, it seems to me that very often the latter should
be chosen. This is a great problem with news media though because as everybody
knows "good" news is no news!

There are 13 million people living in New York City and you never hear about that.
What is front page news is if one of them falls off a building and gets killed. I
think this is a major problem because it has begun to affect the capacity of
governments and public authorities to make long term plans, to seriously use the
knowledge they have for the good of the people and to really plan for the future.
And I imagine in your profession it is one of your major pre-occupations. I very
much doubt if you can do it on your own. My experience of trying to correct news
stories which are grossly misleading is that you never catch up with them. And
therefore you really have to tackle the thing at its source. And it is very, very
difficult to do this.

Jorgen Gram (Denmark).   Would the speaker agree that to a large extent the
differences in reporting the Three Mile Island case was the fact, as far as I see
- that both scientist and government officers were rather unprepared, they did not
know much about what was going on - so no wonder the reporters did not know either.
I think a lot of dirt has been thrown on reporters in that case and without
justification. Could I put a second question. You seem to think that a lot of
people are fond of running other peoples' lives. Would you not agree that in many
cases certain nations try to hide behind the screen of a barrier labelled 'internal
affairs'?

Urquhart.   When I said that I thought it was dangerous for people to run
other peoples' lives, I was thinking again more of the effort to apply doctrinaire
and dogmatic approaches to problems which really are not susceptible to them and

that really it is much better to admit that you do not know the answer and try to
work it out, than to apply a completely dogmatic system which almost certainly
will not work. I think you are quite right, there is a lot of hiding behind the
internal affairs business. We have a major problem in the United Nations because
the United Nations Charter is contradictory on this point. At one point it refers
to human rights and then at another point it refers to the domestic jurisdiction
of states and the inviolability of that jurisdiction. Now what this means in terms
of the very many human rights cases that come to us from the World, is this: we do
not really have a constitutional basis to get into them but you can still do a
great deal on a much more informal basis, because governments resent, in a human
rights case, being publicly castigated. If you can get at them quietly and point
out to them that they would not only be doing their victims a favour but also themselves by manifestly correcting some abuse of this kind, you can surprisingly often
get a result, in which case it is no news at all, and nobody ever hears about it.

I think there are certain problems, especially of a humanitarian and human rights
kind, where international pressure can be brought to bear by other means and until
we get a much more developed sense of community in the world it will be very, very
hard to change that, because after all the national sovereignty is the building
material out of which the whole structure is made. If you destroy that before
having an alternative - then I imagine the disorder and the abuse will be worse.

D O'Donovan (Ireland).   Dr O'Brien spoke about the UNESCO Report on News for
the Third World and he set up the case and then he tried to demolish it. Sean
Macbride , another Irishman is, I believe, the rapporteur of the UNESCO commission
which drafted a report which sets out the objectives of a system of new transmission
- new to the Third World - which would be fair and equitable and would remove the
obstacles which Dr O'Brien mentioned.   Does Mr Urquhart have a view on (a) the
means and (b) the necessity for a system - a workable system - of transmitting
news to and around the Third World?

Urquhart.   Dr O'Brien is infinitely better qualified to speak on this subject
and he has written quite a bit on it. It just so happens that both he and Sean
MacBride have been close colleagues and friends of mine in the past and it is
interesting the differences of view they have. I have a suspicion, though as I
say, I am not an expert on this subject - that it may be that this very heated
debate that is taking place is not really quite focused on the origins of the
effort to improve the distribution of news in the Third World. And I think again
it is an example of people thinking of other peoples problems in their own context
rather than the context of the other people. It is undeniably true for obvious
reasons that the Western news resources and agencies are very dominant in the World,
for technical and other reasons. And it is certainly true that in many Third World
countries this has on occasion been a source of some resentment. Not least because
there is a feeling that the correct priority is not given to the problems which are
the pre-occupations of the peoples of those countries; that the reporting
inevitably is from the perspective of people from developed countries who may not
really fully have the perspective of the problems they are talking about or even do
not report them at all. I think it has got mixed up with the political dispute
over the control of news.   I have very strong feelings about that - I do not
believe that there is any sense whatsoever in trying to establish governmental
control of news. It seems to me on the whole to be a self-defeating process, but
that is a personal view. I think this whole controversy has mixed these two
problems up and as it always happens in international bodies and especially United
Nations bodies - you start off discussing a perfectly serious problem which exists
and then it gets steadily tinged with the political pre-occupations of the people
who are arguing about it on both sides. And that appears to me to be what has

happened here.   Personally I do not think it is any bad thing that this whole subject should be debated.   It is very important how news is presented to the public - how public opinion, public attitudes can be helped to be strengthened and to be formed in a proper way and a useful constructive way.   I think we shall hear much more about this debate.   I am sorry that I can not give you a detailed analysis of the UNESCO report because I have only read excerpts from it.

Question.   This is the third World Congress of IPRA that has taken a serious look at global problems from the political point of view as well as professional - and in the next few months all of us will be hearing a great deal about the new international economic order and the new international information order as you prepare for the special UN session next May to develop the strategy for the next decade.   My question is whether when governments are developing a strategy for global development for the next decade, whether there is not a process that could be set up by the Secretary General and Governments whereby the communicators of the world and international associations such as IPRA and others, could be consulted - a process of consultation so that we can participate in some way in that strategy planning?

Urquhart.   I am very grateful to you for this question because I think it is really an eminently sensible proposal.   This is not my side of the shop, I deal with the political and peace-keeping side - but it is a very sound suggestion and when I get back to New York tomorrow I will ask the people concerned what they are doing about this.   It is really like leaving out part of the equation if the people who are planning something which of all the activities of the United Nations most requires public understanding and some adjustments to attitudes if we do not make use of organisations like your own.   I will most certainly ask what they are doing.

In some previous exercises it has been done with great success, for example, in the environmental business where an enormous amount of work was done by non-governmental organisations at all levels and extremely effectively.   I must say that I am quite surprised that it is not being done on something of this importance, because this is an immensely complicated subject in which we need all of the help we can get because it is very far reaching.   I will certainly ask what is being done.

Dennis Buckle. (Great Britain).   I think I ought to add at this point that IPRA is in Consultative Status with the United Nations Economic and Social Council and we were discussing in the Board of Management the other day the failure of this relationship to develop into anything really worthwhile - and we are not saying it is the fault of the United Nations.   I think that we came to the conclusion that it was largely the fault of IPRA that having won this status we have not developed it well enough.   So there is a basis there, if we can only develop it further.

Urquhart.   Whoever's fault it is - it is very well worth exploring.   It certainly should be.   We need all the help we can get.

John Paulus (United States of America).   I would like to accept the speaker's invitation to speak on the news coverage of the Three Mile Island situation since it involved my state and I was there.   It was the result, in my view, of a strange convergence of events which made news coverage difficult if not impossible.

First the disastrous syndrome of the news media especially television. Second, it was a first time event of its kind with relatively in-expert operators at the scene. Third there was a new Governor and a new Government and a change of administration newly in office in the Governor's mansion in the state of Pennsylvania in Harrisburg, the site of the accident. Furthermore there was the release and broad publicity of a motion picture, "The China Syndrome", which attracted wide public attention, and attention from the news media. The real story of the incident at Three Mile Island is that the system worked, the materials worked and no disaster occurred.

<u>Dominican Republic</u>.   Small countries, such as mine, feel that they are discriminated against by the international news agencies. It is for this reason that in many parts of London people say: "The Dominican Republic, what's that?" You have to link it with Puerto Rica or with Cuba so that people realise that it is in the Caribbean.   And all this despite the fact that very recently we were participants in a political procedure which should not have been ignored by anyone who is interested in politics. In our country we put into practice the human rights which are supported by President Carter. We were able, through due democratic political processes, to pass from a very dictatorial system, which existed previously, to a democratic system due to a large extent to the geo-political influence emanating from North America for the elimination of dictator-ships. And I consider that such an important matter was overlooked by the international news agencies which tend to give far more attention to such matters as Peter O'Toole's shoes or to Mia Farrow's divorce. I hope the international news agencies will not continue manipulating the news and will give the smaller countries an equal crack of the whip.

<u>Question from Venezuela</u>.   How would you like the function of socio-communications to be faced. There is a crisis if we always talk crisis. It is always <u>crisis</u> never <u>solutions</u>, only hopes and references backwards in time.

<u>Urquhart</u>.   I am not sure how to answer this question. I think you are right, we do deal in terms of crisis more than solutions but from my experience of trying to get the international community and especially governments to look ahead it is something that we are not yet capable of. We therefore deal with things as they come up and this is a great weakness of an organisation like the United Nations. It is something which I think is a very important aspect of establishing a consistent order in the World. At the moment we deal with emergencies as they occur instead of foreseeing them and trying to avoid them which is what most good governments do. And I do not know when we shall get over this weakness. In the United Nations Secretariat we spend a great deal of time suggesting to this or that body of the United Nations something that is extremely likely to go wrong and the action they might wish to take to forestall it. This is usually advice which is not well received. I think we will have to make a lot more progress in the concept of a consistent day-to-day management of human affairs before we remedy this problem.

<u>Question from Nigeria</u>.   From your analysis of the contributions of the United Nations, would you also agree that the United Nations has been relatively effective in promoting international understanding but not so some of the institutions which I would call "supra-national-institutions", the EEC and the organisation of Latin American states. Would the speaker not agree that this type of institution should be reduced or as much as possible discouraged in favour of United Nations type organisations?

Urquhart.   Well I thank the speaker for a very interesting question because
this is really a fundamental political and even constitutional question.Personally,
I do not really believe that regional organisation are in any sense an impediment
to international organisations provided that they are what they say they are. It
is clear that, for example in Europe – which is a political and social grouping of
countries which have a great common tradition and history – it is much easier to
develop more sophisticated supra-national organisations than it is if you try to
do it in the World at large. For example, the European Human Rights Court is an
innovation in International organisations which certainly could not yet exist in a
context wider than in the context of Western Europe. And I think that what one
should try to do is to see these other regional organisations as perhaps the
pillars on which eventually we shall be able to build a much larger World structure.
I think that some supra-national or international organisations like military pacts
for example, are perhaps a hangover from the past and I hope will not necessarily
always be a part of the international scene because I think it is true that while
they do not do any harm to the concept of the United Nations they are not an
active positive ingredient of it.

But I would have thought really that we are still in such an early stage that the
kind of experiment that can be made in a slightly narrower context can be very
valuable. I would say, for example, that in Africa the OAU has done a number of
things – especially in the field of mediation and conciliation – which are
extremely important and which really it is much more suitable to do than the
United Nations.

Question from Venezuela.   As an optimist and one working through the
educational system and through universities to try to achieve a change of
attitude, is there any real point in this?

Urquhart.   I think there is every point in the world in it. If we could find a
way to enthuse young people in politics, in international politics, in international
economics and for all the great objectives – which we know we could tackle if we
had the will to do it. I think that not only would we have a very good chance of
creating a far more interesting and productive World, but also I think the lives of
the younger people would be much more interesting too. And we would be getting the
kind of real participation at the beginning which I believe is absolutely essential.
It is no good educating a whole lot of people beyond the dreams of their forefathers
if they are then going to sit on the sidelines and simply be spectators. And I
think this is a tremendously important thing and I do not see any reason why it is
not practical.

It is essential that we should develop responsible attitudes and the necessary
changes to cope with the various revolutions which we have brought upon ourselves.
If we do not do this, I think we shall decline and that seems to me to be
unecessary and would be very sad.

Chairman.   Brian Urquhart flew over from New York especially to participate
in this World Congress and I just hope it has been as worth his while as it has
been worth our while to listen to his wide-ranging talk on the problems of the
future. He quite rightly highlighted the fact that change is subject to the basic
laws of physics and can be dangerous if not properly handled. Where you have
change you very often have counter-reaction. But, as he said, he has confidence
that the basic problem, the basic factor in this situation of acceptance of change
towards the one world which obviously not only he and his colleagues at the United
Nations – but I am sure all of us would like to see – is that of a change of public
attitude. And that has put a very large ball right in our court. So may I on your
behalf thank Brian Urquhart most warmly for coming from New York to talk to us
this afternoon.

3

IPRA Presidential Address

Sanat Lahiri
President IPRA

One of the definitions of public relations is negotiating change smoothly. Changes are taking place in our society, in government, in educational systems, in business, in technology, in resources, in ecology and in environment - sometimes at a frightening rate. Understanding, analysis and help in adjusting to these changes are essential to the profession of public relations. It is, therefore, most appropriate that the theme of the Congress is: "Challenges of a Changing World".

"The difference between evolution and revolution is the rate of change" said a wise man. Because technology is advancing more rapidly than human relations, society has not been able to adjust itself to the pace of technological advances including those in communications technology. And all these are resulting in maladjustments and tensions.

Today professional public relations is needed more than ever before because public relations enables individuals and institutions to apply principles of the social sciences to achieve understanding and integration with their publics.

Social conflicts caused by differing and changing values are common today. Maladjustments in the field of Government-citizen, employer-employee, manufacturer-consumer and many others are based on the misunderstanding of realities. Professional public relations activity brings to human and social maladjustments the skill and expertise of a specialist of how human and social relationships function in an era of change and prove that conflicts resulting from apathy, ignorance and misunderstandings are avoidable.

But the public relations professional must have a clear idea and knowledge of change and its impact on the public. This is essential before the interpretation, analysis and recommendation for action.

This is the main challenge before us and it is against this background that we must face the reality. For too long public relations has been a fringe profession. For too long it has remained a management appendage. Is it surprising that too many public relations practitioners are regarded as "publicists" - creators of pseudo events - and sometimes as manipulators of people? No wonder our profession in some countries of the world has been suffering a decline and a number of corporations and institutions are dropping the title of "public relations" for "public affairs" or "social affairs" or "corporate communications" and other circumlocutions!

For much of this, we ourselves must face the responsibility. For too few public relations practitioners look upon themselves as true professionals and understand that public relations involves _far_ more than communication.

For the true public relations professional, as our pioneers and the Mexican Statement of August 1978 point out, is an analyser and evaluator of the socio-economic and political environment in which his corporation or institution operates; an adviser and counsellor to his management; a communicator to various publics including his management; and an evaluator of results.

If the public relations people by and large have not won the recognition and respect for this significant role in our society, it is because too few practitioners subscribe to the ideals of a true professional; acquiring knowledge, applying it in practice and dedication towards the profession.

I am aware that we now live in a society where hard work, responsibility, professionalism and pride in one's performance, in short, pursuit of excellence, are considered outdated. In this context, may I quote John Gardener. He says: "We must learn to honour excellence, indeed to demand it in every socially accepted human activity.......The society which scorns excellence in plumbing because plumbing is a humble activity, and tolerates shoddiness in philosophy because it is an exalted activity, will have neither good plumbing nor good philosophy. Neither its pipes nor its theories will hold water".

We who belong to the emerging profession of public relations have a _special_ responsibility. For, we are on trial as a profession. On our pursuit of professional excellence will depend the future growth and development of public relations practice.

We in IPRA are very conscious of this responsibility to develop and encourage greater professionalism. Since our last Congress, IPRA has introduced the "IPRA Review", a new professional journal under the editorship of Sam Black. An IPRA Gold Paper on Public Relations Research has recently been edited by Carroll Bateman for the Professional Standards Committee. Two IPRA innovations are: the public exhibition: "The World of Public Relations", at Reed House and the International Public Relations Development Seminar next week.

These are only a few of the IPRA activities and we have many more plans in the future.

Although IPRA with some 550 members in 54 countries continues to remain a fraternal and professional association of individual members, we recognise the real need for a closer international cooperation and coordination between all of us in the field of national, regional and international public relations practice.

I therefore invited the Presidents of all regional and national public relations association of the world to meet together in London yesterday afternoon. We had a very successful and fruitful meeting and a number of very useful ideas were discussed and agreed. I believe this new development will go a long way in integrating our profession to the benefit of all of us in the field of inter-national public relations.

While on the subject of international public relations, I would like to leave two thoughts with you. In a fast moving world with changes all round us there·is an urgent need for the public relations practitioner - whether international or domestic - to understand and appreciate two fundamental questions: One concerning the spectrum of attitudes towards public relations/communications/information getting and giving that exists in various societies in the World. There is a need on the part of everyone of us to recognise that there _is_ a difference in the attitudes to the work as well as differences in tools, techniques and practice of public relations between one country and another. There is also a need to appreciate the historical, cultural, religious and social and political factors which determine such attitudes in a country or a region. Therefore, to apply only one, known and proved set of practices in say, an affluent, developed, mature country or society will not be justified in a less developed one. It is important to remember this in the practice of international public relations.

The second is even more fundamental. In a world which is getting smaller in the sense of transportaton, news transmission and communications, one can often forget the fact that 60 per cent of the world's population is still poor, often hungry and often disease prone. As public relations practitioners, we must accept our international responsibility of developing a wider vision, of making use of all our skills and expertise, tools and techniques to try to lessen the gap between the developed and developing societies.

In the next two days we shall have the pleasure of hearing many eminent speakers and interesting discussions. I hope you will have a very useful and worthwhile time and I wish the Congress every success.

Let us now drink a toast together to friendship and our profession.

4

Social Aspects of Change

H. E. Shridath Ramphal, Kt CMG QC SC
Commonwealth Secretary General

It is no mere courtesy to acknowledge my pleasure at being invited by the International Public Relations Association to address the 8th World Congress. My work at the Commonwealth's headquarters just a few hundred metres away has important points of reference to your professional pursuits. Ours is quintessentially the work of deepening the quality of relationships between our member states – of enlarging understanding amid great variety, and making co-operation more probable. On behalf of a quarter of the world's states and a quarter of the human race we are in the business of communications – mainly as between member countries, but, in important respects, in the wider context of the international community. This latter dimension, the global one, is inevitable; with a constituency that is so much a sample of the world, it is with global impediments to universal understanding, cooperation and prosperity that we are mainly concerned.

In his message to you the Chairman of the congress, Dennis Buckle, has explained that your theme "Challenges of a Changing World" will "highlight and inspire discussion of the areas of human progress which present (you) with the challenges of the present and of the future to which (you) must adapt (your) professional lives". I hope you will not regard me as deviating from the theme if I suggest that it is not only, or even mainly, the areas of human progress which present challenges to you now, and will in the future, but the areas of human failure also. Indeed, it is becoming steadily clearer that we are only likely to meet with any adequacy the challenges of progress by facing up to the challenges of failure. Let me put it more concretely: the challenge which the silicon chip poses for the rich world may be incapable of answer unless we answer also the challenge which poverty and negative growth poses for two-thirds of mankind. It is about some of these challenges, therefore, that I speak – essentially, challenges thrown up by our failure to respond not only to the implications of man's genius but also to the consequences of his selfishness and his greed.

I see much of our global disparities, for the Commonwealth by being a sample of the world, mirrors its division between rich and poor, or in the euphemistic usage of international dialogue, between North and South. The search has begun for a more equitable international order – for relationships that are more orderly and a good deal more just. That search, whose success is now critical to the future of both North and South – both rich and poor – is, I believe, the central challenge of our changing world. To ignore it is to render inadequate our responses to most of the other challenges of our times and our societies.

As the era of decolonisation, the true post-war era, draws to a close, there is accumulating evidence that political independence is but the first phase of a

19

deeper transformation of the international community - that the norms of equity and
justice which, together, provided a moral mandate for the self-determination of
nations, must now equally provide the ethical basis for economic relations between
nations.   As that era of decolonisation closes, therefore, another has begun -
characterised by a movement from status to contract as the touchstone of human
relationships and moulded by intimations of our world as a single community. For
both reasons, it is an era of negotiation of what Harlan Cleveland has called "a
planetary bargain".

A Period of Transition

The last few years have shown conclusively that we are at a time of transition in
history - transition from a world of political power and economic dominance to a
world more mindful of the limits of power and the dangers of the disparity that is
the hand-maiden of dependency.   It is a transition induced and made inevitable by
the reality of interdependence.   In such areas as food, energy, raw materials,
population and the environment, it is now obvious that peoples and states are
dependent on each other - everyone, in some area, needs another; no one is immune,
sanitised, sanctuarised from acts or omissions anywhere on earth.   And the interrelationship of these areas of material dependency with such other issues and areas
as disarmament, science and technology, the exploration of the sea-bed and outer
space, have made us at once each other's guardians and each other's wards. We are
both trustees and beneficiaries in a world of mutual interests.   But it is a
world not yet won.   Response still lags behind perception.

It is with that response to interdependence that our generation must be essentially
concerned - response to a changed world environment through change in the structure
of human relationships and the global systems that determine them. It is the
management of that change - from a world rooted in an adversary system of winners
and losers to an interdependent world committed to the harmonising of human
interests - that is the true challenge of our changing world - and it is a massive
challenge.

Amid the economic confusions and discontinuities of the last few years one truth
has emerged above all else. It is that tinkering with the existing world economic
system, fine-tuning the machine, will no longer suffice. The machinery, quite
simply, is obsolete.   From the point of view of the developing countries whose
future depends so much on fresh approaches to a global development strategy - but
from the standpoint of industrialised societies as well - every day brings
aggravation.   Each day, the problems become more daunting, more intractable and
more entrenched - as UNCTAD V at Manila even now confirms.

The steady disintegration of the world's economic system, the increasing uncertainty and instability which has long plagued the poor countries but which is
now beginning to affect rich countries as well, the heightening of tensions between
nations as economic insecurity leads to protectionist barriers; all these argue
for acknowledgement of global interdependence; but they derive in fact from our
denial of its imperatives.   They are the manifestations of an old economic order
struggling to reassert itself in tidewaters running ever more strongly the opposite
way.   And those who urge that we postpone action for 'better days' fail to discern
or, while discerning, fail to acknowledge that better days may never come if the
necessary structural changes in the world's economic arrangements are not made now
to ensure that these better days do come for all countries.

It is now a long time since Gandhi warned that "the earth provides enough to
satisfy every man's need but not every man's greed".   Yet, it has taken the
economic cataclysms of the last few years to make us acknowledge the finiteness of
the world's vital resources.   The pursuit of profit which has for so long been the

driving force in the oil business has now conspired to render both rich and poor dangerously dependent on a fuel which is fast diminishing and for which substitutes have been almost callously discouraged.   Amid the profligacy with which a small minority of the world's people (no more than 20 per cent rich) continue to consume its resources (some 80 per cent of them), we have begun to sense the need for greater care in their use, as well as the prudence of searching for alternatives to them, if mankind is to devise a strategy of survival worthy of his claim to both wisdom and sentience.   Yet there are capitals in the West where congresses claiming to speak in the name of the people reject enlightened efforts of just this kind - efforts which themselves represent a modest first step to survival.

Just as OPEC has jolted the world into recognition of its interdependence in the field of energy, so the global food crisis (of 1973) has forced us to recognise the dangers of the present balance between population and food supply. An unequal world which sentences many to a lifetime of hunger is an unsafe world. Oases of wealth surrounded by parched lands of want more than prod our conscience or appeal to our charity. They provoke bitterness and invite conflict. A world of such disparities in the levels of human existence contains within it the virus of its own destruction.

Perhaps it was considerations such as these that prompted Zbigniew Brzezinski to comment in 1978:

> "Previously dormant people have become active, demanding, assertive.
> Under the impact of literacy and modern communications, hundreds of
> millions of people are becoming aware, both of new ideas and of
> global inequity.....If we try to create artificial obstacles to
> change for the sake of the status quo, we will only isolate our-
> selves - and, eventually, threaten and undermine our own national
> security".

And now, this last week, as hard-headed an organisation as the International Institute of Strategic Studies has reinforced these perceptions in the same context of Western security interests.   In its 'Strategic Survey 1978', the IISS warned that:

    (i)   "it is insufficient to apply the East-West matrix to conflicts
            which are largely an out-growth of local conditions";

    (ii)   "the political and economic relationship between the Western
            countries and major raw material producers will have to be
            re-aoooooed";

    (iii) "economic strategies cannot be integrated with the political
            and strategic needs of the industrialised world by ad hoc
            arrangements alone.   A more durable framework will have to
            be found to promote Third World stability and coordination
            in the crises to come".

So there it is.   Development, conservation, the environment - can no longer be dismissed as the obsessions of 'soft' do-gooders.   The hard-liners, blinkered by pre-occupations with power, have failed to recognise its new limits and are turning out to be not the protectors but the wreckers of national (and international) security.   It is to the pursuit of human solidarity - not the shoring up of 'narrow domestic walls' - that communities the world over must look for security and survival.

The Need for Effective Management of Global Change

This much is clear: there is no lack of perception at the highest levels of global
leadership of the dangers facing humanity.   What is not yet evident is the resolve
to act to avert the dangers so clearly before us.   The case for better global
management and for the effective management of global change is unanswerable; yet
the action it calls for remains largely deferred.   One tragic result is the
further widening of disparities - a worsening of the global malaise.

Today's picture of world trade reveals the kind of shadow that falls between
perception and response.   Protectionism, once the safeguard for infant industries,
has become the last refuge of senile and uncompetititive ones; and the cost of
this protection in terms of inflationary prices to consumers is suppressed or
ignored - as is the cost in terms of the falling off in demand for Northern exports
resulting from the forced decline in the export earnings of developing countries.
Protectionist measures do save some jobs; but far fewer than is generally believed.
Forty-eight jobs, for example, were lost in the period 1962-1975 in Germany as a
result of technological change for every one lost to imports from developing
countries.   The world's business community knows better than most that short-term
gains in job protection are being bought at unacceptably high cost to the health
of the world economy.

Micro-processors will probably compel greater structural change within industrialised societies than the attainment by the developing countries of the UNIDO target
of 25 per cent of world manufacturing by the end of the century.   If, in
industrially advanced societies, it becomes, as it might, a privilege to work
amidst a crisis of leisure, it will be a circumstance induced not by the betterment
of the economic lot of the world's poor, but by the dubious triumph of technology
over social management.   Indeed, it is from the broadening of the base of human
prosperity that will come the best prospects for containing that crisis in the West
and enlarging the privilege of work among its people.

And now a kind of semantic camouflage is being used to give protectionism a
'management' image.   "Orderly marketing arrangements", voluntary export
restraints", non-tariff "regulatory measures" suggest, and are calculated to
suggest, better management of the world economy. But management for whom?
Management for what? Protectionism by whatever term it is called is in fact the
antithesis of management; certainly it is the negation of management for economic
growth and human welfare.   It is resistance to change, repudiation of global
interdependence, masquerading as 'management' of the world economy. All this
tragically ignores the enlarging empirical evidence that global change responsive
to the imperatives of interdependence can benefit rich and poor alike; that the
'management' the world needs is the management of interdependence.   I have talked
in these terms to the world management community at their 18th World Congress in
New Delhi - but the issues are of direct relevance for you also as the managers of
their public relations.

In these areas of challenge, governments are not the only actors. Various
institutions, various groups within society, have the capacity to influence the
decisions of governments.   Among these, the business community is particularly
well-placed to create an environment hospitable to enlightened and courageous
national decisions in the economic field.   But it has, also, an autonomous
responsibility, because of its pervasive role in contemporary economic life, to
respond through its own action to the challenges raised by an inequitable and
unstable world.

The Responsibility of the Public Relations Profession

The public relations profession must by its very nature share these responsibilities.

And it must do so of course, not merely out of a moral compulsion, a professional variant of noblesse oblige, but out of an obligation which derives from a hard-headed assessment of the long-term self-interest of industry and the society it serves.   In industrialised societies, the public relations community has already done much to persuade industry of the prudence of sensitivity to community needs and objectives.   In a world which technology has woven together as never before, that sensitivity must now reach out beyond community and nation to answer the call for social justice at the global level. As the antennae of the business community which it should be, the public relations industry has a responsibility to increase its understanding of these challenges and to influence corporate behaviour towards creative responses to them.

Years of striving for greater harmony and accord between countries have left me utterly convinced that the problem of different perceptions lies at the heart of global misunderstandings.   The picture of the world is just not the same from New York or London or Frankfurt as it is from a jute plantation in Bangladesh or the arid scrubland of a village in Mali, or the squalor of a 'favella' in one of Latin America's burgeoning cities.   It is perhaps natural that the advantaged do not readily discern what is wrong with the world; but the view as it is seen by the two-thirds of mankind that is disadvantaged is itself one of the realities of the global scene.   Even if this view is not shared by the North, there can be no fruitful dialogue and no practical response to the challenge of change, unless the perceptions of the South are understood in the North.   If they are at least acknowledged as such, it will become easier to understand why the developing world calls for a new order, and perhaps possible to respond more sympathetically to its case for change.   The challenge of change can never be met if it, simply, is not understood.

I believe that in the North generally, the political leadership today is enlight-ened to the need for real change.   It is for the greater part attuned to the imperative for social and economic justice world-wide.   It is as mindful of the winds of global economic justice that will blow throughout the '90's as was an earlier Northern leadership of the winds of political change that blew throughout the 50's and the 60's.   The Bonn Summit - last year's meeting of the directorate of the North - gave testimony to that awareness.   Let us hope that at Tokyo, next month, the perceptions are even sharper, and will lead to a loosening of the constraints that now impede decision and delay action.

But the trouble is that the major constraints derive from a failure on the part of Western societies as a whole to appreciate the changed premises of national self-interest in an interdependent world - or in some cases to even recognise that there has been a transition from the pre-war and post-war era of dominance.   Too many of us, even when we acknowledge that we live in the era of interdependence, still will not see that sustained growth in incomes and jobs in the North depends critically upon enlarging the purchasing power of the South; too easily forget that when the harvest fails in the Soviet Union and Russia buys wheat from the United States, the price of bread goes up in Jamaica; too readily ignore that when Third World countries reel under massive balance of payments deficits, their imports of manufactured goods decline, and jobs in Europe are threatened.   If not a divinity, there is at least a mutuality of interest between rich and poor, 'that rules our ends - rough hew them as we may'.

Safeguarding the Quality of Life

On our responses to these several challenges of change will depend the quality of life of billions of people.   Certainly, when we look to the challenges that arise in the areas of human failure, economic factors dominate the social aspects of change; housing, education, health, nutrition, clothing, sanitation, drinking

water, all these and much else in the social sector turn upon the prospects for a
new economic order.   For the public relations profession, specific challenges are
easy to discern in such areas as the operations of the Third World countries.   But
the broader issues I have touched upon have a vital bearing on the business
community and therefore on those who serve as its voice as well as its eyes and
ears.

Most of them have relevance for your professional work - whoever your client,
whichever your product, whatever your cause.   Quite often the influence of your
work is indirect;   sometimes, you may even be unaware of its ramifications; but it
is an implication of the success of the communications industry that our world has
become a township - a global village.   Messages you send are received by uninten-
ded audiences beyond your immediate target;   and, because there is no escaping the
consequences of community, you have to be concerned as well with the implications
of those messages even for publics beyond the reach of your signals.   What you do,
and how you do it has become a matter of consequence beyond the area of client
relationships.   It has wider national, and often international, import.   It
implies therefore wider responsibilities - and wider opportunities.   How you
discharge those responsibilities and respond to those opportunities will be a
significant element in our global response to the challenges of a changing world.
The responsibilities in particular are immense and I hope you will permit a lay-
man's excursion into some aspects of them.

One facet of public relations troubles me above all others;   and it has relevance
to a wide range of issues - economic, social and political - involved in the
challenges we face.   It is the temptation to which the public relations
profession is constantly subject - the siren song that insistently calls you - to
mould reality closer to the heart's desire - or at least to the desire of your
client for the time being;   the temptation to present a partial picture of reality
so as to elicit particular responses.   But the truth is, is it not, that the
successful public relations exercise of this nature while it may secure its
initial objectives, produces countervailing returns - for it cannot of itself
change reality.   The facts persist;   what your professional skills achieve is to
shape the perception of them by a particular public.

But, not only does reality remain, so too does its perception by other publics.
Therefore, when you shape the perception of events significantly differently from
reality and, therefore, from its perception by others you orchestrate disharmony.
To the extent that your projection is distanced from reality your very success
activates discord and renders convergence and agreement less possible - for the
several publics no longer have different judgments about agreed facts, they pass
judgment on different facts, or more precisely on facts differently perceived and
understood.   The resulting views and positions run along lines that never meet.
Within Western democracies, this potential of the practice of communications can
assume quite disturbing proportions for it can build up pressures for national
action - often with international implications - and, of course, in many cases,
this is precisely the objective.

There may have been times when public relations work of this order did not matter
too much;   when all one needed was to secure particular courses of conduct on the
part of those operating the levers of power.   But power now has limits, important
ones, and the strongly held views of others cannot be so easily discounted.   The
laws of Newtonian physics are not applicable in all their rigour to public
affairs, but we do well to remember that in our contemporary world there is often
for every action an equal and opposite reaction.   'Public relations' success
cannot be measured only in terms of responses induced from particular publics
where the issue is one that touches many publics.   The IISS Strategic Survey to
which I referred at the beginning of this talk confirmed these new realities when

it highlighted the fact that:

> "The major strategic trend of the decade was the growing pluralism and
> diversity of the international scene, the diffusion of power, and the
> inability of the two major countries to shape and control events not only
> in the unsettled regions of the Third World, but even, to some extent,
> within their own alliances".

The public relations profession may not labour in vain, but its labours can add
materially to world disharmony unless it acknowledges these new realities and takes
account of them in setting new standards of achievement in the 80's.

Perhaps one conclusion is that there is a large area of unmet need for your services.
But like lawyers before the introduction of legal aid, only the rich can afford you.
And without a similar publicly-subsidised system for public relations, your high
cost expertise remains outside the reach of those who espouse the broader public
interest. The result is that, at least in the short term, the prizes go to those
with the biggest purses, and the clash of opinions honestly held by which truth is
often divined does not take place. The case of truth goes by default – but the
winner is thereby often the loser also. As a lawyer myself, let me acknowledge that
the fault lies not only or even mainly with the professional – but with the system
in which he must function. And lest you feel that I have delivered too stern a
Phillipic rebuke, let me say that the note of mild reproof in Prince Philip's
message to the Congress was itself plainly noticeable:

> "While most people," he said, "are aware that a major revolution in
> communication techniques has been going on for a number of years, there
> are a great many thinking people who are convinced that the content of
> the message has been deteriorating. Truth, reality and exactitude are
> gradually being swamped by dogma, illusion and vagueness. Ends are
> beginning to justify means".

My final thoughts, therefore, are these: In at least certain areas of change
public relations could be a dangerous game played in the name of public interest
and private freedom. If we mould reality to our dreams, or to our separate interests,
we will eventually get trapped inside fantasy and cut off altogether from reality.
In the end, this will be harmful to the profession and to that wider public whose
real ends and concerns will ultimately assert themselves. This is, I believe, one
of the respects in which the public relations profession must adjust to the
challenges of a changing world.

Correspondingly, is it not time that the profession evolves a role for it which is
more akin to discerning and communicating public reality rather than to colouring
it. The profession, I am sure, sees itself as doing more than being in the business
of creating new wants, at pointing out differences between products that are not so
different, at securing public acceptance of policies over which it exercises no
independent moral judgment or at making the market place the seat of judgment on
the human condition? In the face of the challenges already at hand, must not public
relations begin another communication – or deepen and enlarge it where it has
already begun – a communication of the public to government, to business, to
industry, to the infinite variety of the profession's clients, a reverse flow of
messages that would inform cabinets and board-rooms and their equivalents of the
real needs and aspirations of their several publics and of the real means available
for their satisfaction in the world that is real. Certainly, in the areas of human
failure, but I venture to suggest in the areas of human progress also – such a
grass-roots upward orientation could enlarge your professional horizons in the 80's
and by among your most effective responses to the challenges of our changing times.

A discussion then followed.

Question from Nigeria.   In your assessment of social change what future do
you see for the abolition of racial discimination as practised by racist South
Africa and to some extent by some whites in the United States and even in Britain?

Ramphal.   I would like to think that the prospects are better than current
concerns suggest they might be. I believe that deep down the world abhors racism
and must abhor apartheid. Western societies have given some of their greatest
gifts to the world, through their concepts of freedom and an elevation of the
dignity of Man, but racial barriers have somehow stood in the way of
universalising them. Within recent years, I think it is true to say that
Europeans and North American policies have been moving towards that measure of
universality. But it is easy for braking effects to be applied upon the process.
Massive efforts have been made, particularly in Southern Africa in recent years,
and we are at the moment when those efforts can move upwards to higher levels or
turn downwards and backwards to retrogression. Which way we will go will depend
essentially upon the West. The future cannot be in doubt. Zimbabwe must one day
be free and so must Namibia. Apartheid must end in South Africa. The option for
all of us, but for the West in particular, is how it ends. And I think that if
that orientation replaces what are sometimes short-term considerations and the
belief that there are short-cuts or there are temporary deviations around the real
issue - then it can prevail. Certainly within the context of the Commonwealth it
must be a paramount consideration to ensure that it does and that is as true of the
deep problems of racialism within Southern Africa as what I hope are going to be
the transient problems of lingering racialism within North America and Western
Europe.

Question.   I should like your Excellency to expand on one phrase that you used
earlier in your talk this morning and that was the remark that relationships were
changing from one of status to one of contract.

Ramphal.   I thank you for the perception which you picked up that phrase
because in a sense it encapsulates much that I was trying to say. Status is and
was the essential relationship of dependency. It was the hand maiden of
colonialism. It was the essence of economic power. Just as within societies at
one stage a class system determined the economic fortunes of people so within the
world community we have been living through a period when those fortunes were
determined by status. Status in the world economic context. With of course the
developing world - which was largely the colonial world - occupying a position of
peripheral and subordinate status. My thesis is that that world is ending. That
the reality of interdependence is making it end. And that one of the imperatives
that interdependence produces is a contractual imperative. An imperative to agree
upon the character of relationships. And as we move to that phase we must surely
be moving away from relationships founded and rooted and made immobile in status
term to relationships that will be based on contract - on consensus.

Question.   You have given us individually and corporately a significant
challenge. I wonder what focus there is within your own secretariat that could -
between this Eighth World Congress and the Ninth World Congress - ensure that there
is consultation and cooperation - perhaps in a joint project with your secretariat
and perhaps the secretariat of the United Nations.

Ramphal.   It is a great tribute you pay to imply that we might, in some
measure, be able to render that assistance. Let me assure you that the will exists

to explore the creation of that machinery. Brian Urquhart was with you yesterday afternoon – he represents the embodiment of the objectives of the United Nations system. We lunched together and I said to him then what I say to you now – that the Commonwealth and the Secretariat is in the service of the international community. We are there to advance the objectives of the United Nations, indeed, if we do not advance those objectives, we cannot advance the objectives of the Commonwealth or of its member states. And so the linkages already exist in terms of our will to proceed. That, such a congress such as yours – that a profession such as yours – operating at the non-governmental level should be ready to sit down with those of us who work essentially in the sector of governments – could only augur well for the prospects of facing the challenges we are talking about. And I remain ready to attempt to explore with you how we can proceed.

Question. It has become very fashionable for government departments to appoint public relations officers for their own departments, despite there being a ministry of information. We now experience some kind of friction between public relations practitioners of independent government departments and information officers of the ministries of information. What recommendations could you make to bring about some kind of harmony between practitioners in governments and government information?

Ramphal. Of course, some of those governments you talk about are part of my constituency, so I have got to be careful how I respond to you. Let me say first of all that it would be part of my thesis that there is greater need – and I hope you share that view – that there is greater need for the best in your professionalism to inform and influence the information work of government. You surely cannot see an adversary relationship between governments and their information departments. I would like to think that in the fullness of time it is what is best in your profession that will enthuse and take over that kind of role. But, of course, it would be a role I would see in terms of enlightened responses to the kind of challenges we are talking about. Now in terms of all that, what I can say to you is that we have been examining very actively the possibilities of bringing together the information ministers of Commonwealth countries; trade ministers meet and finance ministers meet, and so on – and health ministers. The information people who very largely lie at the heart of inter-governmental relationships never meet. And perhaps in a meeting of that kind – not on the scale and not I hasten to add on the style of UNESCO – but in the context of what might be done in a practical way to develop, enlighten and progressive approaches to information on the part of government – I hope such a consultation might assist. And perhaps in that, the non-governmental organisations – at least within the Commonwealth in which the public relations profession plays a role might assist in that process of consultation.

Question. You mentioned that public relations should have more than just a sensitivity to immediate community needs but a broader atunement to social justice at the global level. Would you not say that this is too tall an order for the normal public relations practitioner?

Ramphal. I have such a high opinion of the normal public relations practitioner that I cannot put it beyond his reach, but I believe in fact you do not have a choice. I think the world has changed sufficiently to make it inevitable for you if you are to pursue your professional pursuits successfully to obtain that reach, and if perchance it may be beyond your grasp today it will assuredly be within your grasp tomorrow.

<u>Question</u>.   Our experience in Canada endorses and may possibly encourage your suggestion of cooperation between the information and public affairs communities of the Commonwealth. In our vast country of Canada, with its small population and its confederation problems, the attempt has been made successfully for the central government and provincial information departments to pool their resources and their concepts - so it is conceivable this could happen within the Commonwealth.

<u>Ramphal</u>.   You give me a clue to where I might start within the Commonwealth, in developing these approaches.

<u>Question from Denmark</u>.   I detected some wry smiles when you spoke of the high price of public relations services. I am not sure that everyone would agree with that view. But would you not agree that the reason why some people find the fees are high is that they do not see the point which you have put over so admirably this morning and do you think that something could be done to influence and inform the professional circles we are in contact with - say scientists or auditors, engineers and lawyers?

<u>Ramphal</u>.   Well of course I do not mean to imply that all public relations work is a distortion of reality. It would be absurd for me to do so. What I seek to do is to highlight and draw attention to that area of public relations work which does indubitably take on that character. And why one has now to be much more conscious of the implications of that for circles far beyond the immediate problem in terms of the price of your services. Of course, I do not expect many people to agree in this audience that they are a high price, but let us face it as we are professionals together - they <u>are</u>. I agree with you that there is need for a much greater awareness of the contribution which your profession can make to human understanding. And that some of those costs need legitimately to be incurred. The answer to the high cost of the lawyer's services was not to lower them but to recognise that they were essential if we were to secure justice, and therefore it was a cost that had to be borne by society and it was in that direction that I was reaching, a direction in which I hope you would concur.

5

Public Relations Training in Europe
(Lecture of the Foundation for Public Relations Research and Education)

Jean-Marie van Bol

Director of Inbel, Brussels

In the Beginning was Passion

All creation is born of passion and of determined will.

There were a few of us at the European Centre for Public Relations who shared this passion - namely, to give our national associations a body of common instructional material.   Exactly four years later, we met again to put this project into effect.

They say that passion is blind.   This is certainly true in the sense that passion does not worry about details but just on the essential.   And on the other hand, passion is almost clairvoyant in its imaginative perception of how to translate its goals into reality, how to breathe life into its desires.

One question had to be asked from the beginning.   Was it reasonable, at a time when social changes were on the increase, to dare to conceive of a basic programme and, having determined the time needed to draw it up, to promote its propagation?

Is it justifiable to attempt to lay down a course towards a future about which we know, firstly, that it is the job of education to prepare for it, and secondly, that at the time when our students complete their courses the problems will no longer be those with which we are familiar today?

.......Followed by stubborn hard work

Is it not simply an exercise in style, a theoretical ploy that will comfort teachers and students rather than providing realistic preparation for the demands of the immediate future?

The promoters of the project made sure that they had the answers to these questions before they undertook any work on either the text or the programme.

The scientific foundation of their research was based on the ideal programme of Lucien Matrat, who has made such a great contribution to European public relations, on CERP research studies, on the research of a number of our colleagues, and on the study entitled "Organisation of Communications in 1980" and presented to the Geneva Conference at the instigation of Cerp.

In addition to these recorded and documented works, we also bore in mind Paul Valéry's famous words about "frenzied professions, those trades whose principal instrument is the opinion that one has of oneself, and whose raw material is the opinion that others have of one".

What if, when he wrote "Monsieur Teste", the author of "Le Cimetière Marin" in fact had us in mind?

However that may be (and it is to be hoped that we have at least not lost our sense of humour which would make us hopelessly tedious), we reached a number of prefatory conclusions.

First prefatory conclusion.   There is no point in claiming any kind of professionalism if that professionalism does not cover instruction of a standard commensurate with its ambitions.

But instruction can be based only on research.   Whatever profession is being envisaged, research blossoms out in two directions – basic research, and specialised research.

Second prefatory conclusion.   In a world of change, we must work essentially in the middle term, so as not to risk losing touch with reality and preparing our students to work in the past rather than in the future.

This can only mean the drawing up of a sort of outline law, which can then be adapted to local requirements and circumstances.

Looking into the future consists less of giving shape to a dream than it does of making use of serious investigation to discover how to take the next step as happily as possible, or anyway with the minimum of damage.

Third prefatory conclusion.   We are led, not only by the general climate of our societies but also by the specific nature of our profession, to think in terms of social co-responsibility and therefore in the particular case of instruction to reserve a large role for dialogue with our students.

Fourth and last prefatory conclusion.   We are living in a material society and on a given continent, at a particular period in its history;   and we consult academic experts just as much as those in the profession.

It is only by bringing these different groups face to face at the planning stage that a project can have any hope of expecting them to contribute meaningfully later on.

Towards a European Programme

All of our efforts were oriented according to the guidelines of these four prefatory conclusions, in particular those of the Instruction and Forecasting Committee of the European Centre for Public Relations.   This body was especially well placed to listen to all opinions and to serve as liaison between the various groups involved.

The six-monthly meetings of the Instruction and Forecasting Committee, which is currently chaired very efficiently by my colleague from Barcelona, August Ferrer, have over recent years been very largely devoted to these problems.

The intervals between the meetings of the Committee have enabled its members from different countries to become familiar with reactions in their respective countries and to bring the project to fruition.   But this has of course meant that a considerable time has elapsed between the first rough outline and the final text of the "European programme" that we have today.

It is quite clear that the project would never have got off the ground had it not

been for the constant support and persevering hard work of these national
correspondents.   The programme was unanimously adopted by the General Assembly of
the European Centre for public relations when it met at Palma in 1977 and was given
its final "post-natal care" at Lisbon in 1978.   And it is to these participant-
correspondents that we owe whatever chances the programme has had, and has, of
being heard.

I therefore cannot thank them enough.

Integration of The Prefatory Conclusions

The writers of the programme continually bore in mind the integration into all
planning of the principles arrived at through the prefatory conclusions.

Where did the study of these prefatory conclusions lead us?

The link between professionalism, and both instruction and research

This meant the closest contacts in both senses.   There had to be meetings between
representatives of the university and representatives of the profession.

This in turn meant that we were unable to favour one party or the other if we were
anxious that the programme should be adopted by both of them.   Each of them had a
specific contribution to make.   Theory would be livened up by practice, and
practice informed by a more reflective attitude.

The evocation of such exchanges meant that the project would need the benefit of
top-level instructors, but that it must also take other instructors into account
if it was to respond adequately to the technical demands of training.

We also had to secure research grants, for which all the canvassing has still to be
done.

In a changing world

Our second prefatory conclusion echoed the rapidly-changing nature of our
environment.   So we could not envisage building a pyramid or even a Bailey bridge
to reach the next decade.

Our eyes firmly on the future, but with a certain degree of flexibility, we were
led to indicate directions sufficiently exactly for them to be of use, but with
sufficient room for manoeuvre that they could be adapted as and when necessary to
suit local conditions.

There were two traffic signals that warned us of crossroads, even if they did not
exactly tell us which way to go.

The first was at the intersection of standardising data-processing and polyform
creativity.

Since both directions needed to be preserved, how should the guidelines be set up
to guarantee symbiosis and not division?

It seemed to us - and for us Europeans this is all somewhat new ground - that our
thinking should have the benefit of automated systems.

It was not without significance that our students should be initiated in these new
jargons, and that they should be capable from the beginning of them of
conceptualising operational procedures.

This involves a whole series of procedures and methods which can be conveniently dealt with by computer, such as press-conference check-lists, conference preparations, press analyses, interview analyses and so on.

This lightening of the work and study loads, at least as far as memorisation and frequent repetition are concerned, allowed the inclusion of the innovative and the original, of the alternative solution in the context of training and work.

That is why, parallel to the limitations of the computer, we had to impose limitations on liberty.

Socialisation and personalism

This closed dual-system of the computer and the open system of creativity now led to another crossroads.

More questions had to be asked.

We are familiar with the socialising role of instruction as described by Durkheim in "Education and Sociology".

Education certainly tends to the more or less harmonious integration of individuals.   It is through education that the young adult achieves recognition by its peers and avoids feeling excluded.

But for about half a century, the integrating function of education has been based equally on the principles of democracy and of change.

One can immediately assess the extent to which these partially contradictory tasks give rise to problems where teams of teachers are concerned.

In the light of these two currents - the transfer of the past, and the introduction of the new - we must determine, with those demanding instruction, the share to be accorded to each of them.   And we must also establish ways of supplying them with sufficient intellectual and technical means to bring about change without calling into question the advantages to be gained.

The second traffic-signal - socialisation and personalism - has very direct implications in our particular field.   For it is obvious that the only successful people in public relations will be men and women who are sufficiently sure of them-selves to give way completely to the professional messages entrusted to them, and not allow any more of themselves to appear than is necessary for effective communication.

This task, this negotiated form of teaching, where the student becomes an inter-locutor instead of a mere auditor, means that the students must be "converted". And this is by no means the least of the difficulties when it comes to professors of public relations, who ought after all to be experts at communicating.

Negotiating the future

Our penultimate prefatory conclusion is heavy indeed with consequences. It is as difficult to ignore it altogether as it is to integrate it into theory and practice.

We feel the pressure of those who say they want to take part.   But we are often led into a certain confusion in the face of the help they provide.

Nevertheless it is certainly part of our job to help those to be heard who have neither the right nor the strength to make themselves heard.

We declare that businesses have a social responsibility. We affirm that the worker is better than and counts for more than *homo economicus*. We believe that we are privileged to pass from the world of "having" to one where "being" is more important.

But how can we really practise all this in our teaching, and in our professional lives?

Do we agree to give ear and listen to, and draw consequences from, those whom we permit to make themselves heard?

We are spokesmen for our societies and our businesses, from what we know concerning our students - just like public opinion loudspeakers, and the least popular at that.

I know very well how unsettling this step is, how disappointing, and how difficult, because to begin with sharing means losing something.

I also know that taking it should be our pride. Otherwise, how can we hope that tomorrow our students will take advantage of it, if we do not interpret it for them ourselves today?

I am not making a plea for Laxist education, for some sort of carry-all where the experiences of the teacher and the desires of the taught are submerged, but rather for a growth in vigour and in professionalism.

And this will come not from the authority of the teacher, but from the conviction that he has interacted with his students, and from negotiated contracts.

Our schools and institutions are still too crowded with students finishing their protected adolescence with no clearly defined plans, or with only a rather woolly determination to achieve a solid qualification.

I am talking here about the situation in Europe, and would not pretend that it applies everywhere else.

And now we come to our final prefatory conclusion.

Envisaging an outline law for Europe - a multicultural and multilingual continent - is a specific problems but, taking certain necessary transpositions into account, it could be applied to other continents too.

It is in this frame of mind that I accepted the flattering nomination of the "Foundation for Public Relations Research and Education". I saw in it not only the recognition of the interest that the European position could have in the material, but also the occasion to demonstrate that international cooperation is possible even when languages and cultures are different as is the case in Europe. Moreover, I consider myself a spokesman for the work of many of my colleagues, and it is in their name that I am addressing you.

The attachment of the past

Europe has a rich past. But this very richness encumbers it. Recognition of ancient historical bases for things tends to put a brake on innovation.

As far as instruction in public relations goes, we had to take into account situations and traditions that were already firmly established.

Situations like, for example, plurilingualism, or suspicions regarding profitability, or the habit of secrecy.

Traditions like the independence of the university - something that I too hold to be essential - but also with regard to its lack of experience hitherto in contact with the business world, its "splendid isolation" in some cases, its frequent desire to disassociate itself from the necessities of day-to-day - all of which have often led the university to produce graduates for whom there are no jobs.

We can see, in the exasperation caused by these tendencies, one of the causes of the explosion of 1968 - and, in the desire of the university to merge better into its environment, the choking-up effect which it continues to provoke.

Let me here also add the fact that public relations on the Continent does not enjoy a uniquely positive audience, and you will see at once that drawing up an outline law, sufficiently precise to work and sufficiently flexible to be adaptable, is no simple problem.

We had to take into account national frameworks, the different evolutions of socio-political systems, juxtapositions of languages and cultures, student expectations, professional subject-matter, and educational traditions.

There is no time here to give a complete panorama of European public relations teaching.

Let us simply remember that there are three types, unevenly distributed according to country.

The first type, associated with universities and institutions of higher education, is found particularly in Belgium, France, Spain and the Netherlands.

The second type occurs at all levels, and involves a more or less detailed introduction to public relations in the context of general education. This type occurs everywhere, and varies from excellent to mediocre.

The third type includes studies arranged by professional associations, or realised under their aegis. This is the case in Switzerland, Germany, Italy and Belgium.

And who can ignore the excellence of the teaching available at the CAM Education Foundation in London?

Yes indeed, twenty years ago one spoke of a desert with a few oases. But today it must be agreed that today it is more like a large marshalling-yard with tracks more or less clearly marked out.

The future, a cry in the dark

Until very recently the dichotomy in public relations training material has been essentially horizontal.

Above, there was university education. Below, there were the other media of instruction. And each of these assiduously neglected the areas covered by the others.

Within such a clearly defined framework, the originality of the step we took was twofold.

We had first to verticalise the demarcation line between university and other types of training.   And we then had to space out the periods of training on a time-scale.

The first step: the verticalisation of successive levels of training.

What we mean here is that, contrary to what has been the practice hitherto, there will no longer be a body of material reserved for first-level training and another for second-level, but rather a homogeneous grouping of material and practices that must be familiar to anyone wanting to work in this sector - but, according to the needs and ambitions of the particular student, in varying degrees of depth of study.

The variables no longer correspond to the spread of materials, but to the length of the road that it has been decided to follow.

Thus we believe, like a boat-builder, that a sail, a hull, a keel and a super-structure are essential in all cases to make a sailing-boat.   But the same components could go to make a weekend sailing-boat or a mighty clipper of the high seas.

Everything lies in knowing the objective for the student.   And for the teachers, in being honest about what is proposed and in being precise about what is expected for those who sign on.

A scaled programme

The European programme is presented as a scaled programme.

It is divided into three phases, just as the elements of a multiple ladder fit into one another.

The basic section embraces different branches of the human sciences.   The middle section, the sectors and techniques of communication.   And the final section, the public relations side itself.

But we believe - so well defined is the project's thinking - that every student should, in the course of his training, climb up every stage of this ladder and not miss out any of them, although still with highly individualised variations.

Another point, which is implicit but is probably worth expressing directly anyway: we believe that training in the field is not on its own sufficient within a reasonable period to equip the student of public relations with this multi-disciplined basis in theory, technique and practice that we deem necessary to his professional flowering and his correct placement in the working milieu.

The very economy of this project leads us to propose it also as a directive for permanent training.   This is part two of our step, and we shall come back to it in a moment.

But let us now have a look at the details of this basic programme.

Three poles of training, and two complementary approaches.

The first element in the ladder embraces a body of material concerning all the human sciences.

Those which we believe should be included turn about four axes: psychology, sociology, economy/law, and history.

In *psychology,* we begin with the problems of individual psychology and go on to social psychology.   Themes worth considering are obviously social behaviour and group dynamics.   This list is not exhaustive.   It might well be added to with the influence of milieu and environment on behaviour, group integration, and breaching phenomena such as motivation and class psychology.

This axis is closely bound up with the next - sociology.   In fact it is obvious that the fullest advantage cannot be taken of these specific studies unless they are examined in the light of their constant interaction.

If it is true that we create our own milieu, this milieu recreates us in a process of continual feedback.

The *sociology* axis covers social theories and systems, their history and their attempts to interpret collective experience.

Care will be taken at all times to afford a proper place and role to opinion in this sector of studies, and also to ensure that things do not get bogged down in an over-historical viewpoint.

Attention will also be paid to the sociology of organisation, to problems of work and leisure, to research methods and analysis of results.

The *economy/law* axis should allow the student to understand the economic system in which he lives, and the occupations of those with whom he is likely to come into contact.   This overview should also go into the details of business management and business law, personnel management and work laws, and accounting and statistics. Of course this approach will not mean very much if the student does not already have a more general analysis grid, in other words a general background sufficient for the location of precise events.

The last axis of the first group, *history,* must be focussed essentially on history as it is made, starting off from the image provided by the media.   This way of looking at things is extremely important at a time when the symbolic value of the school as an institution is being seriously questioned, and when the media are being spoken of as a "parallel school".

This bringing-together of ideas and facts presented as they interact politically should be complemented by two kinds of consideration.

The first will be concerned with cultural and contemporary forms of human activity, and the second with an introduction to the scientific and technological world, in which public relations practitioners are all too often ill-founded.

The second part of the ladder consists of two groups, containing various practical work, the importance of which cannot be stressed too much.

The first consists of the rights and duties or the ethics of communications, the theory and history of communications, its methods, its economy and some measure of their effects.

The second includes various techniques, beginning with advanced study of the native language and a reasonable knowledge of one or more foreign languages, seen in a communications context rather than a literary.

Everything still is based very largely on the written word, and it is here, particularly nowadays, that the shoe pinches.

Then there will be study of techniques of printing and publishing, the art of the spoken word, the handling of still and moving pictures, and the diffusion of a message.

This apprenticeship will be based very largely on practical exercises that will if possible involve real problems. The theoretical introduction acquired by the student will be minimal.

This period should also be used for instruction concerning data processing and its possible application to the areas the student is working in.

The final element of our curriculum covers public relations as such.

This involves the final polishing in the training process, and making what has been learned into something that can be used.

This teaching will allow discovery of the history and ethics of public relations, specific application of communication theory, national and international structures of the profession, departmental organisation in both the public and the private sectors, working methods, and evaluation of results in terms of costing.

The working tools of public relations, up to and including the societal overview, will be examined in turn and illustrated by real instances that have actually occurred, whether they are used or inserted into a global programme.

Indeed it is by recourse to case studies that this approach has given the best results so far.

Since public relations is an applied science, it operates within a specific environment: that is why we think it essential that a sufficient number of hours should be spent on determining just what that environment is.

There will also be explanations of the communications structure of the country in question, and of its social organisational system, including its unions, politics, economics and administration.

The same rung of the ladder will also include study of the particular problems of the public and private sectors, work relations, development of consumer protection associations, the questions being discussed of the ecology and the goals of participative democracy.

This range will have two additional complementary approaches. The first of these will be a systematic combing of reality, and the second a compendium of advice for permanent training, the whole rounded off by training periods.

It will have been seen, I hope, that this programme stems entirely from our prefatory conclusions: advanced instruction and in-depth research; a programme that is adapted and adaptable, and open to dialogue; multi-disciplinary teaching, and the door wide open to practitioners.

We do not believe that it would be worth much if it is not relayed with vigour and tenacity by the professional associations best able to adjudge the fruits of this "tree of knowledge".

Learning to learn

Our second step, if we may recall it by continuing the metaphor, consists of making active grafts on to old or irregularly developed trees.

Which means, in other words, bringing in all the permanent training systems.

Our scientific basis has been in accordance with the documents already cited, the extremely searching work of our friend Carlos Tomas entitled "The Next Ten Years in Continuing Education in Public Relations".

From this we were able to deduce the use of such a programme, and the extent of the fields which it could cover.

We were also aware of the difficulties that lay ahead of us.

To name a few of them:

-   The absence of professional recognition.   In France there is a law, but no sanctions in the event of abuse of that law.   Spain has a professional register.   Elsewhere, a yawning gulf: freedom, no doubt, but also at every crisis of credibility abuses of that freedom which it brings on.

-   The difficulty for the recognised but largely self-taught businessman to "go back to school".   A whole new kind of teaching needs to be thought up, and teachers trained for it.

It is however clear that such a programme can only be planned with the help of businessmen involved in the milieus where public relations people work.   The whole programme would involve a total of 720 credit hours accumulated in succession.

If from now on selection criteria for these "students" had to be laid down, no doubt nearly ten years' experience would be required for a consultant to be admitted to retraining, and nearly five years for a technician, because of course technology advances rather rapidly.

The new objectives

If we were able, with justification and based on studies and experience, to establish the basic programme on known data, the retraining programme will have to rely far more on the second mission of the Instruction and Forecasting Committee of the European Centre for Public Relations: the forecasting and consideration of the progress already made towards a new objective for professional work and a re-allotting of working time, training time and leisure time.   These modifications are not conjectural, but herald new structures that may produce profound changes of attitude.

Just to cite a few trains of thought, the new views on the responsibility of businesses being expressed in particular by social awareness, and the preferential development of communications systems compared with the one way information system should be taken into account.   Where and how to enter, in a new climate of openness to information for which we are partly responsible, and how to define the profession, are other avenues to be explored.

Having opened up the economic and social world to the information dimension, should we not increase our fields of action? And having established contact with a public capable, by its decisions and attitudes of influencing the life of a business, should we not obtain a systematic response, even perhaps instigate what they say and present our case to them?

This something of a new departure, public relations being more used to broadcasting messages than interpreting "the signs of the times" and causing them to hatch.   By acting in this way, public relations, far from limiting itself to the defence of a system - an accusation that has been levelled at it more than once - would contribute to a very real change in society, but more in the capacity of a negotiator than of a revolutionary therapist.

Forestalling the event, because they would have revealed the premises, public relations people would then be able to contribute to a development, rather than being content to react to crisis syndromes. And we would then be able to speak of a significant contribution to the social responsibility of a business, which would for once have taken the initiative rather than simply responded to a pressure that had become intolerable.

New teams

The state of European business requires that retraining schemes should appeal, at least partly, to "professors" outside the country where the "post-natal" training will take place.

It will be up to the Instruction and Forecasting Committee to draw up the list and to act as a central gathering-point for these complementary teachers.

It may be envisaged that this would provide the basis for a certain harmonisation between efforts in different sectors and different countries.

It will mean that this team of itinerant professors will have to be extremely flexible and adaptable, as well as have a considerable body of knowledge, in order to be able to impart the "European touch" in all the milieus in which they might be called upon to work.

On the technical side, the Europeanisation of thinking will be helped by the "Henri de Bryune" courses, which allow young technicians and executives to move about within the member countries of the European Centre for Public Relations.

This is indeed our final objective. For, as Jean Monnet says, "When an idea corresponds to the necessity of the times, it ceases to belong to the men who thought of it, and becomes stronger than those who are in control of it".

Indeed we believe that the time has come for open thinking. We must make a contribution, here and now, towards giving Europe the taste for hope and for enterprise.

The danger of the empty fortress

There is one danger awaiting us - that of creating an institutional world that is economically satisfying, but of building in the process what Bruno Bettelheim calls an "empty fortress".

On the other hand we would have good technicians, capable engineers, and wise experts working on the forward march of technical civilisation and on the other hand, teams of social therapists trying for better or for worse to come to the assistance of those handicapped by progress, by turn manipulators and manipulated.

But we will have lost the taste of things, the savour of the earth and of bread, we will be living in the way described by Thomas Molnar in a "disfigured model" subjected to democratic totaliterianism, as de-personalising as the others, and the house of man will no longer be inhabited.

We will have written everything, conceptualised everything, rationalised everything, and we will have lost in terms of being what we will have accumulated in quantity of riches.

There is no magic potion

Of course public relations cannot act against this risk as a "magic potion" to reverse the course of events.

However it may contribute to an avoidance of certain obstacles and to the preparation of a more human world.

And of course education has its place in this process.

And this is what I would like to finish with.

If the worries which I mentioned just now come about, and if it is also true that ideological discourse says roughly the contrary, referring everything to "conscious" man, "enlightened", liberated, capable of exercising his citizenship with greater awareness, then we may attempt to bring the project closer to reality.

There is a regal way to do this: communication, the tool of that social discipline of which we are the craftsmen and which is based on dialogue.

If we succeed in establishing contact between our enterprises, our organisms and our institutions, and the public who are involved with them, and if in the same movement we manage to give a voice to that public, we shall perhaps succeed in re-establishing contact between all those who are separated by mountains of wealth and valleys of deprivation.

Creating trust through dialogue

In the pubic relations teaching project, we must prepare and assist men and women for a unique responsibility: the creation of trust through dialogue.

In so far as the teaching of public relations contributes to making men heard, to allowing them to be freed from cultural, economic and social constraints, and to re-open a dialogue with others - understanding them because they listen, and listening to them because they are themselves allowed to speak - then we shall be able to say in the evening of our lives that we have lived on the side of hope, that we have lived on the side of trust.

And without that, we shall have achieved nothing.

We know full well that without scrupulous respect for our professional ethics, sooner or later our efforts are doomed to failure.

For technique is nothing.   It is the motive of those who employ the technique that everything truly depends on.

I should like to close with a bit of science.

The prisoner's dilemma

Gregory Bateson, the American researcher and husband of Margaret Mead at one point, explains in one of his books what he terms "the prisoner's dilemma".

There are two players in this game, and the object is to win in two moves.

The equipment is a board divided up into four squares, each with a series of two points.

Each throw gives the player a certain number of points, as well as automatically giving the other player a certain number too.

Two squares jointly involve a maximum gain and/or loss for one or other of the players, the more one wins, the more the other loses, and vice-versa. One square gives an equal negative score to both players, and the fourth square gives an equal positive score.

It soon becomes obvious that even if a risk is run the first time, in 80 per cent of cases the second throw ends up in the square giving the equal and negative score. Rather than risk losing or winning all, one complicitly prefers that both players should lose.

Gregory Bateson reckons that these choices are so well-established that he postulates a polyvalent key to individual relationships and even collective relationships.

If, in their personal relationships, people are definitely inclined to be resolved to lose a little - their partner losing too - and accept implicitly that these negative results pile up, some choose the square where both win five points, and in the course of the games of life, accumulate positive results.

If we remember that Gregory Bateson extrapolates this diagram to include group relations and even international exchanges, and if one also knows that in every case the choice of the square involved in two positive results is based on a sole element, trust, then we can no longer doubt the validity of what we are trying to set up.

And the author also says, about the reason for this trust won or lost, that he cannot explain its working.

And if that was precisely our function, our role and our raison d'être.......?

If, thanks to us, more men and more women, more businesses and more countries, more institutions and more continents could get "ten out of ten", then we would surely not have wasted our time, indeed we would surely have earned our living?

And that is what I wish for all of us.

6

Government Information Services
Use and Abuse

This concurrent session attracted a large audience as the subject is one of
considerable interest in most countries. In the United Kingdom the current
rumours of a purge of United Kingdom information officers and the recent election
campaign added topical interest to the session. The speakers represented the
experience from three different countries: West Germany, the United States of
America and the United Kingdom. The interest aroused by the three speakers was
such that it was a pity that there was not more time available for discussion.

The speakers were:

Karl-Gunther von Hase   General Manager, Zweites Deutsches
                               Fernsehen, Mainz Germany

Adam Raphael   Political Correspondent, "The Observer"

Greg Schneiders   Deputy Assistant to the President on
                               Communications, White House, Washington,
                               United States of America

The British in the room were presented with some fundamental questions to ponder,
about the real attitudes to democracy and free speech apparently indicated their
country's secretive governmental system. The "nudge and wink" methods so
effectively illustrated by Adam Raphael, Political Correspondent, *The Observer*,
were, he believed, rooted in the hierarchical basis of United Kindgom government
and the bureaucracy's unfaltering consistency in the face of party power changes.
That the press so willingly endorsed the system may also be a comment on the whole
communities apparent need for hierarchical certainty. Despite its pretensions, the
press in Britain is not the fourth estate, it is "Grub Street", those who wield
national power treat it accordingly. Therefore, it is not so surprising when the
select band of its representatives allowed to join the power club do not seek to
abolish the entry rules. That Raphael could not reveal even how the lobby system
works, such as who briefs whom, summed up its effectiveness.

By chance the other two speakers illustrated opposite approaches to tackling the
problem of distinguishing government propaganda from the information the public
needs. Karl-Gunther von Hase, General Manager, Zweites Deutsches Fernsehen,
pointed out how the legacy of Goebbels presented the Germans with a major
credibility problem when the Federal Republic was established in 1949. The

solution adopted was to separate the central information system from direct
political control supplemented by individual ministry spokesmen independent of
each other. This was accompanied by an overall policy of maximum disclosure. The
intimate size of Bonn, which throws journalists and officials together constantly,
may also have made this policy a virtue of necessity. Von Hase believes this
system and policy still works and backed this up by citing the agonising which
occurred when a news blackout was imposed on the Hans-Martin Schleyer kidnap. He
also, optimistically, believed this was unique and will never recurr.   The
avoidance of propaganda he illustrated by a strict 1976 court ruling which out-
lawed a campaign on the government's achievements being handled through the
Federal Information Office and established a precedent for all levels of
government.

Perhaps typically, the Americans have straight forwardly recognised that
politicians in power like to have a sophisticated propaganda machine and
preferably one paid for out of taxes.   The White House system is divided between
the well-known Press Office, currently headed by the colourful Jody Powell, and
the Office of Communication. As deputy head of the latter, Greg Schneiders
describes its function as unashamedly political; seeking to obtain public support
for the President's programmes. The White House also has had its credibility
problems in recent years but Schneiders demonstrated that the Office of
Communications had an even more crucial role in the decision making process than
ever before. With the breaking down of mass loyalties and an increasingly
"undisciplined" Congress, the US President had lost his traditional means of
implementing policy. The "appeal to the electorate" over the heads of Congress
is, perhaps, the only power left to the presidency. A sophisticated and well
funded propaganda system was essential for this.

That the system was not abused unduly, Schneider ascribed mainly to the free
access of the press to the information used by government to arrive at its
decisions, and the consequent freedom to disagree with them. He believed no other
system in the world works better.

A passing comment by Adam Raphael threw a new light on the rumours of the cuts in
UK government information officers. It has been said that Mrs Thatcher believes
ministers and officials should be more directly responsible for communicating with
the media. With the proven ability of officials to deter press enquiries or at
least undesired publication, and ministers' ability to manipulate the "off the
record" system, will this be a sizeable step backwards for open government?

7

Public Relations Education
Progress and Needs

Introduction

As chairman of this session of the 8th Public Relations World Congress, it is my pleasure to welcome all of you and to extend my personal greetings to the members of this panel and to this audience, made up of public relations colleagues from the four corners of the world.

Our subject today is "Public Relations Education - Progress and Needs". To my way of thinking, there is no subject of greater import over the long range for those of us who practice in this developing profession.

A profession that does not properly educate its future practitioners and leaders, will not have a future. Eventually, it will deteriorate, and decline in prestige and public esteem.

We have a distinguished panel to speak on the subject of public relations education today. They include: Paul Ansah of the College of Journalism and Mass Media at the University of Ghana, Legon, Ghana; Norman Hart, director of the Communication, Advertising and Marketing Education Foundation, London, England; Jolly Kaul, public relations manager of Indian Oxygen Limited, Calcutta, India, and Anne van der Meiden, professor in public relations at Utrecht State University, Utrecht, Netherlands.

The importance of public relations education is widely recognised. It turns up as a topic on the agenda at every important conference or meeting of public relations people in all parts of the world. Yet, there is very little agreement on how public relations education should be structured, or about the educational level at which it should be taught, or about the content of its syllabus, or, indeed, about whether there is any need at all for specific education in public relations.

Among public relations practitioners in the United States, there is a general consensus favouring programmes of public relations education at the bachelor's and master's degree levels in our colleges and universities. Public relations is widely taught in our higher institutions of education.

The first formal course in public relations in the United States was established 55 years ago in 1923 at New York University and the instructor was that great pioneer in our profession, Edward L Bernays. Mr Bernays recently desribed that first course as follows:

> "These earliest lectures emphasised the study of public opinion, the
> psychology of individuals and groups and how maladjustments between

them are handled. These lectures placed emphasis on how and why
people behave as they do, how to intensify favourable attitudes,
convert those on the fence and negate negative attitudes and
always in the public interest (sic). The public relations
practitioner was envisaged as an applied social scientist,
along the lines of the recent definition adopted by the Mexico
City conference of world-wide public relations organizations".

Today, courses in public relations are offered at some 400 institutions of higher
education in the United States.

A recent report prepared by Professor Albert Walker of Northern Illinois University,
under a grant from the Foundation for Public Relations Research and Education,
identifies 61 colleges and/or universities that have public relations sequences
leading to a bachelor's degree; 37 institutions that have both bachelor's and
master's degree programmes in public relations, and 13 that offer public relations
sequence or areas of concentration at the doctoral level, in addition to bachelor's
and master's degree programmes.

Additionally, many other four-year and two-year colleges offer one or two
introductory course in public relations.

In colleges with public relations programmes, there are 86 chapters of the Public
Relations Student Society of America, which was founded by PRSA some years ago.

Most of the sequences or programmes in public relations are taught in schools and
colleges of journalism, although it is estimated that more than 100 schools or
departments of business administration in various universities also offer some
education in public relations. Eighteen of the bachelor's degree programmes that
are conducted in schools of journalism in the United States have been approved -
or accredited - by the American Council on Education for Journalism, which is
officially recognised by the United States Government Department of Health,
Education and Welfare as the appropriate accrediting agency in this field.

The first programme to be accredited was at the University of Oklahoma. It won
accreditation from ACEJ in 1957. Over the succeeding ten years, public relations
sequences at six more schools were accredited by the American Council. Those were
at Boston University, the University of Georgia, Ohio State University, Ohio
University, San Jose States University and Texas University at Austin. In 1968,
the Public Relations Society of America was invited to become a member of the
American Council on Education for Journalism. Since then, PRSA has been
represented on the Council, and PRSA members have participated in the
accreditation teams that are assigned when public relations programmes are seeking
accreditation.

The American Council on Education for Journalism is composed of several academic
societies representing professors in various fields of journalism and the
administrative staffs of journalism schools. Among these are the Association for
Education in Journalism, the American Association of Schools and Departments of
Journalism, and the American Society of Journalism School Administrators.

The Council also includes representatives of organisations representing
practitioners in various fields of communications, including such organisations as
the American Newspaper Publishers Association, the National Association of
Broadcasters, the National Council of Editorial Writers and, of course, the Public
Relations Society of America.

In addition to the criteria that ACEJ applies in the accrediting of public relations programmes, there have been other efforts to standardise the various programmes of education. In 1975, for example, a special commission established by PRSA and the PR Division of the Association for Education in Journalism prepared a report entitled "A Design for Public Relations Education". The recommendations in this report have been widely recognised and followed.

Some public relations practitioners in America have objected strongly to the teaching of public relations in schools of journalism. Notable among these is Bernays, who has argued strongly over the years that public relations programmes should be taken away from schools of journalism and developed in closer alliance with studies of the social sciences. However, it should be emphasised that even in the schools of journalism, 75 per cent of the educational programme - according to the standards established by the American Council on Education for Journalism - must be devoted to general studies, including the liberal arts and the social sciences. Therefore, it is incorrect to assume that journalism school graduates do not have a rounded educational experience.

While much can be said for Mr Bernay's point of view, it is not likely that schools and colleges of journalism in the United States will relinquish their hold on public relations programmes. In many of these institutions, the enrolment of students in the public relations programmes is growing rapidly - and in some journalism schools or colleges, the number of students enrolled in public relations sequences exceeds the number enrolled in news-editorial sequences.

It would appear that public relations education is firmly established at the college and university level in America. This is not to imply, however, that there are no other educational opportunities available.

The Public Relations Society of America, in cooperation with New York University and other institutions of higher learning, has over the years conducted numerous special short courses designed to permit practitioners of all ages and levels of experience to enhance their skills. This particular programme is now being enhanced with the establishment of a formal "professional development program" by the Public Relations Society of America. Additionally PRSA chapters hold numerous workshops and seminars around our country each year.

In summation, while public relations education in the United States is well rooted in our institutions of higher education, we do not feel our system has by any means reached a state of perfection. We have a long way to go in developing more sequences or programmes that are accreditable by ACEJ. We have a long way to go in developing more and better programmes at the master's and Ph.D levels.

The dispute about where public relations should be taught probably will continue for a long time and indeed this issue may never be settled. It would be encouraging however if more public relations degree programmes were to be established in colleges of business administration or of social science, to give more competition to the prevailing dominance of the journalism schools. Even so, if this were to happen, students in such programmes in schools of business administration and social science would nevertheless have to receive some training in communications techniques and this probably would have to take place in schools of journalism. Since many universities encompass all three of these areas, this would not constitute a major problem.

With this brief introduction, I turn now to my colleagues on the panel for their views on these questions and others.

The African Point of View

Paul Ansah

College of Journalism and Mass Media, University of Ghana

Probably because of the relative newness of the subject in our part of the world and the rapidity with which public relations departments are being set up within many organisations, there is certainly a fascination for a career in public relations among young people wanting to enter into the communications field. Almost all the candidates we interview for admission to our School opt to take public relations as their elective in preference to broadcasting or photo journalism. The main reason they often give, and a very pragmatic one I think, is that prospects of employment and subsequent advancement are better. When they are questioned about what public relations means or entails, one quickly discovers that they see it as only a sophisticated version of press relations.

And their misunderstanding is based on what they see around them. They see that since it became fashionable to set up public relations departments within organisations, those employed to work there have been journalists who have entered into their new career without any further or special training. They also see that many of the practitioners confine their role to press relations, organising parties, doing protocol duties and producing a house journal. For those we admit, it does not take us long to disabuse their minds and to teach them that public relations training involves the acquisition of both skills and a body of knowledge usually in the area of the social sciences.

Even the most cynical definition of public relations as 'mass conditioning' presupposes that the practitioner should have some knowledge of human behaviour and responses. Seen properly as a management function, public relations having its basis in the social sciences hardly requires elaboration here. If we agree with Cutlip and Center that "the 1970's public relations man should be the catalyst for social programmes, not merely the specialist who publicises them", it becomes obvious that public relations training goes far beyond being trained in the art of communication.

The setting up of institutions offering courses in public relations in conjunction usually with journalism shows some awareness of the need for specialised training in the subject. However, the level at which it is taught, the content of the course, the balance between the academic and vocational aspects of the training deserve a closer look to determine where improvements can be made.

Public relations education in Africa

Since the public relations function is becoming more appreciated, it is important to take a fresh look at the question of training. A traditionalist view holds that knowledge of the theory and practice of public relations is best acquired on the job and not in the classroom. Opposed to this view is the American practice where public relations is taught in universities at both the undergraduate and graduate level. It is this latter practice which is being adopted in Africa as a departure from the British educational tradition we inherited in which journalism and other "vocational" studies are frowned upon at university level. It is not difficult to demonstrate that the traditionalist view is not in line with the proper appreciation of the public relations function. It will therefore be more rewarding to look at the content of a public relations training programme at university level, for I am persuaded, for reasons which will become clear presently, that a university is the most suitable place for public relations studies.

Within the last 20 years, schools of journalism have been established in a number of African countries, with most of them operating at the pre-university level. In some of these schools, public relations is taught as an adjunct to the basic journalism course. University-level courses in communication exist in about six countries, but of these only three institutions in Ghana and Nigeria teach public relations; the two universities in Nigeria teach the course at the undergraduate level and the one in Ghana at the graduate level.

I have had the opportunity of looking at the course content of public relations at these various levels in my capacity as external examiner, and I have no doubt in my mind that the teaching at the pre-university level is so perfunctory that those who benefit from it need further courses to get real insights into what public relations really involves. The social studies background needed to back up any proper training in public relations cannot be satisfactorily taught at that level, especially since most of the students are not of the highest calibre; the very good ones usually pursue their studies with a view to entering the university later.

Basing myself therefore on this empirical evidence, I believe that the aim should be to encourage university level courses in public relations. Even in this situation, I am convinced that the subject is better handled at the graduate rather than the under-graduate level. The undergraduate course should give the student the broad humanistic education after which he will become sufficiently mature to tackle the principles of public relations while he reinforces his knowledge in the related social science fields.

Public relations and social sciences

In many universities, the present tendency is to start professional courses at the graduate level after the student has obtained some solid background in the liberal arts and social sciences. The aim of this arrangement is to broaden the outlook of the professional by first plunging him into the social environment. This development can be applied to the study of public relations with considerable benefit both with a view to improving the quality of personnel and building up a body of knowledge that will facilitate giving to public relations the status of a recognised profession.

Before we go into the details of what can be contained in a syllabus for a public relations course, it is pertinent to recall that in addition to the ability to communicate, the public relations practitioner should have some solid knowledge of human behaviour since his work basically involves persuading the various publics to develop and maintain favourable attitudes towards his organisation. For this reason, a multi-disciplinary social science approach to the study of public relations commends itself.

In this connection, subjects which readily come to mind include communication theory, cultural anthropology, social psychology, public opinion, survey research methods; I am taking it for granted that other basic subjects such as economics, history and politics would have been covered earlier. Social psychology, for example, will give the student insights into individual and group behaviour, motivation, persuasion and gratification. Such knowledge will be most useful when he has to decide on the contents of a house journal, for example, or when he has to advise on rewards and punishments. Similarly, communication theory will enable him to know how to send messages, taking into consideration the media habits of his intended audience, the channels to be used, the choice of a credible source and the responses he should anticipate from his audience.

If it is essential for a public relations practitioner to be able to gauge public attitudes and opinions, it is important for him to acquire the basic skills in survey research so that he knows, for example, what sample will be sufficiently representative of his population or what margin of error he should tolerate in specific cases. It is also important for him to know that the opinion of a vocal minority cannot be considered as "public opinion" any more than the opinion of an uninformed majority hence the necessity for courses on how to determine public opinion. I am not suggesting that the public relations practitioner should be a statistician, but he must have sufficient skills to be able to undertake basic surveys methodically and to understand or interpret more sophisticated studies done by specialised consultancies.

It is this social science dimension that distinguishes proper public relations from mere publicity. The public relations professional need not be an accomplished behavioural scientist, but he needs to have sufficient acquaintance with human behaviour to be able to deal with the internal publics, especially the employees, and his training should therefore include such studies. Even in terms of evaluating his own performance, he needs certain skills which only an initiation into social science research methods can give him.

Public relations studies at the university

I know that reservations have been expressed in certain quarters about the desirability of having such a comprehensive, polyvalent public relations course taught in a school of journalism and communication. While this reservation is understandable because of the fear that traditional journalism schools are more likely to put the emphasis on communication skills rather than on the social science courses, much depends on the level of the school and its philosophy. In many schools of journalism, communication is studied not only as a writing skill, but as social behaviour. Moreover, it is possible to find in communication schools or within a social studies faculty in a university opportunities for teaching all the needed social science subjects within a single course structure. In this case, the course labelled "public relations" will deal with the basic principles or the general framework, while the other courses will provide the background or foundation.

The point needs to be emphasised that journalism and communication schools have evolved to the point where teaching is not confined to reporting, editing and writing. In addition to these, courses are provided in media management, mass media and society, the interface between mass communication and interpersonal communication, techniques of persuasion, research methods for evaluating media performance, among others. All these courses provide knowledge that is extremely useful for the study of public relations. In addition to these courses related directed to communication studies, a school of journalism based at a university can easily arrange to call on the services of people from other departments to provide other relevant courses such as marketing and social psychology. All that is needed is to design a course taking into account all the relevant disciplines required to produce a public relations practitioner who will be a social catalyst rather than a mere publicist.

In such a setting, public relations will be an elective subject which will be only one in a whole range of courses providing the necessary breath and depth of knowledge in all the relevant disciplines needed to make a solid, versatile well-rounded public relations practitioner. A vocational course limited to the bare principles of public relations with a sprinkling of case studies, in my view, is not adequate training for the almost Protean role that the practice by its very nature entails.

The university level course I am proposing is the ideal that should be aimed at. I do not think it can be achieved within the next decade, and therefore it will be necessary to maintain the lower level courses. In any case, even at these levels, it is important to incorporate the relevant social studies courses in the programme. This is the dimension that seems to be lacking in the various lower level courses that I am aware of. This also appears to me to be what should be emphasised in refresher courses for those practitioners whose training placed more emphasis on communication skills than social science inputs.

Combining theoretical studies and practice

But the raw body of knowledge and skills that a person acquires in the classroom and all the case studies discussed in class cannot make him a good practitioner. Working in a real atmosphere and having to grapple with management that is not properly educated about the importance of public relations, or facing budgetary problems or even finding oneself accused of encroaching on the territories of personnel in other departments such as marketing, personnel and industrial relations are things that one cannot learn in a classroom. It is therefore imperative that during the course of training, there should be greater cooperation between public relations teachers and practitioners. Arrangements should be made to enable students to do regular internship with practitioners. In this way, the students accumulate experience and the teachers obtain feedback from the potential employers about the quality of training being offered. Practitioners should also be invited to give guest lectures to the students.

This cooperation and maintenance of regular contact between teachers and practitioners in public relations is important for a number of reasons. For one thing, the academics have access to journals and have plenty of time to keep up with developments in the field. They can therefore put their working colleagues in touch with these new developments and also undertake research of benefit to the public relations community. For another, the practitioners can reciprocate such academic inputs by giving their academic colleagues the benefit of their practical experience. All this will result in enhancing the quality of training and increasing the body of knowledge about public relations.

Furthermore, such cooperation will predispose educational institutions favourably towards organising refresher seminars for practitioners who may not have had the benefit of systematic training in their career. It will also remove the concealed suspicion that tends to exist between practitioners and those considered to be abstract minded theoreticians in a number of professions. In the end, it is the profession itself which will benefit from such mutual contact. I am suggesting, therefore that since more is being found out about human behaviour everyday through systematic research, there should be continuing education in the field to acquaint people with the latest findings.

A combination of theoretical studies and practicals will also help remove the artificial distinction that people tend to make between 'academic' degrees and 'practical' diplomas. There is no reason why an academic degree should not have some practical content, and there is no reason why a diploma should not have solid academic basis. The distinction appears to me to be artificial and the analogy false. It is like comparing a university trained mechanical engineer with an auto mechanic trained in a polytechnic. The difference is only related to the level of sophistication and I believe we should aim at sophistication. I think I have sufficiently demonstrated the need for dovetailing the two aspects of training in public relations to produce an efficient and versatile practitioner who can initiate fresh thinking about management problems rather than one whose capacities do not go beyond publicity and press contacts.

Conclusion.

Though the importance of public relations is being realised at the management levels of financial and industrial establishments, voluntary associations, government organisations and educational institutions, the proper appreciation of the profession will be long in coming if the education of practitioners is not accelerated. As long as this problem is not seriously tackled, the practitioners, especially in areas where public relations is not well developed, will continue to act as press relations people and ordinary publicists. They will thus fail to make an impact on management and continue to maintain the lowly status to which most of them are relegated.

It should be remembered in this connection that many organisations have set up public relations departments as a sort of managerial cosmetic without being really convinced of its importance; they have done it because it has become fashionable to do what everybody else is doing. The only way to convince management of the profession's importance is for the practitioner to initiate thinking of policies and to present to management proposals that will help the organisation to secure the full benefits of effective public relations. The practitioner can do this only if he has got the necessary knowledge about human behaviour and the skills to translate these into a sensible agenda for action. This way he will earn the appropriate status and force management to take notice of him. This is the most effective way to accord the profession the important place that it deserves in modern society.

A Basic International Qualification?

Norman A. Hart

Director, Communication Advertising and Marketing Foundation

It must be rare for two authoritative articles on public relations education to appear in one issue of any publication, as happened with the April issue of *IPRA Review*. The broad perspective and sound common sense contained in these two pieces must surely have set people thinking about achieving some tangible action. And it is to action that I am addressing myself in this small contribution on the subject. The justification for my doing so is that, with students in 40 countries, the CAM Foundation has a close familiarity with the disparate needs of students and practitioners world-wide. This leads me to attempt to outline the basis of an international qualification which would be equally relevant in any country.

Let me start by extracting three short quotations from the Carroll Bateman article.

1.   'The number of qualified people in public relations is incapable of meeting the demand for competent practitioners.'

2.   'Many courses are taught by instructors who themselves are not fully qualified in the theory and practice of public relations.'

3.   'If public relations practice is to move further in the direction of professionalism, the educational process must be strengthened and standardised.'

Turning now to the Edward Bernays paper, it is difficult not to commend his apt analogy of 'surgical instrument manufacturers helping to accredit schools for medical surgery', as a way of demonstrating the position of journalism in relation to public relations. He may have made the point before, but until practitioners and educators pay some regard to it, it must continue to be repeated. He will not be unaware of the fact that in most (if not all) countries in the world, PR is still an abbreviation of Press Relations. The particular extract, however, that I wish to refer to is in his recommendation No 2 that an IPRA committee should develop ideal public relations programmes....' This I will deal with as a fourth point for comment, but with some specific suggestions for action.

The United Kingdom Scene

Since much of what has been written deals with the situation in the United States it is maybe worthwhile outlining briefly what happens in the United Kingdom. The first and major difference is that there is no university course in public relations whatsoever, nor anything remotely approaching it. Neither is there any advanced full-time education in any other type of educational establishment. And yet we have what has been described by one American commentator, as one of the most

52

advanced *qualifications* in the world in the form of the CAM Diploma.

Briefly, the Diploma scheme is for young people already in public relations. There are a number of part-time courses which lead to a Certificate level, usually gained after two years' study and a Diploma which commonly requires a further year's work.   The Certificate calls for passes in six related 'learning' subjects:

Public Relations: Communications: Media: Research and Behavioural Studies: Marketing: Advertising.

At Diploma level, examined and taught largely by case studies, students are required to demonstrate their ability to use their knowledge to resolve business problems. They are examined in three specific areas: Public Relations for Commercial Organisations: Public Relations for Non-Commercial Organisations: Public Relations Management.

These educational programmes have naturally been developed in conjunction with the Institute of Public Relations and the Public Relations Consultants Association for whom we act as the national examining body.

The International Scene

The range of courses, programmes and qualifications is so wide as to defy simple categorisation. The variety is in breadth and depth as well as in skills and concepts. The level of courses also created problems as evidenced by one particular Business School course leading to an MBA where the Research Fellow in Public Relations had as his 'relevant' qualification the CAM Certificate subject in Public Relations - hardly an advanced qualification, though perhaps completely adequate for that particular country. This factor reinforces the need for an internationally acceptable qualification, but also indicates that it will probably have to be at a relatively unsophisticated level at least initially.

In earlier studies, existing courses have been categorised as 'university, inter-mediate and practical'. I would prefer to regard courses as being fundamentally 'academic or vocational' which avoids confusing teaching establishments with subject matter, and does not give any implied level of achievement, eg that a 'practical' course is of necessity inferior to that of a university, which itself could surely be practical or indeed intermediate.

Academic studies then would be those which concerned themselves, very properly, with concepts and theories whilst vocational studies would concentrate on application to the job, or 'practice'. Both streams have an important contribution to make to the profession, and could well be regarded as parallel studies leading to an ultimate 'terminal qualification' which would be a long-term international goal, but initially should remain the responsibility of each national professional body which would set standards appropriate to its own local requirements.

One further word on the international scene and that is in regard to quantity. Studies conducted so far have tended to look at courses from a content or qualitative point of view. An examination of data however indicates that quantitatively,public relations education hardly exists at all in world terms. Little wonder that practitioners seem to be regarded in many places as a bunch of fixers when you consider the student population to be probably below one per cent of the total number of people in public relations.

Demand for Qualified People

Taking the first point from the Bateman article. I would support strongly the contention that well experienced, let alone qualified people in public relations

are so few as to make education and training our main task in the next decade.   I
have introduced the word training deliberately since, for real progress, I believe
there must be a parallel programme of short intensive courses for people who are
already engaged in public relations practice, but who have not had the opportunity
of acquiring expertise across the whole range of activities now expected of them.

The provision of skilled and qualified people will involve an initial expense which
must come from public relations practitioners themselves, but this investment must
surely pay off handsomely in the long run.

Instructors are not Fully Qualified

The plain fact of the matter is that world-wide the full-time educators do not
have either the theoretical knowledge or practical experience to teach students
adequately.   This deficiency will be with us for many years, and we must therefore
design our programmes accordingly.   Measures such as visiting lecturers,
correspondence courses, seminars, a wide range of text-books, case studies,
occasional papers....must all be used until a really sound educational base has
been established.

Standardised Education

The proposition of standardised education must evoke an immediate antagonism since
people will question how there can possibly be one system which is equally relevant
to New York on the one hand, and the reaches of the upper Amazon on the other?
This reaction is understandable, but it is no more valid than to compare the public
relations needs of the Amazon with those of Sao Paulo, and somehow the Brazilians
have to cope with this.   For those who know the UK environment, there would be
similar difficulties if one were to move what has been termed the 'gin and tonic
brigade' from London into the Outer Hebrides off the north of Scotland!

Surely a properly qualified professional is able to adapt to any environment:
given that there are intrinsic differences in culture and affluence, the principles
involved are surely likely to be the same.   The possibility of standardisation has
already been demonstrated by the common courses and qualifications laid down by CAM
for students all over the world.   Internationally, after the UK our largest blocks
of students come from Nigeria and then Singapore - two entirely different cultures.

A Plan of Action

Let there be set up a small committee or working party charged with the task of
putting in motion a basic or even elementary qualification in public relations,
which is both taught and examined internationally.   Such a scheme has already been
initiated by the International Advertising Association and shows every likelihood
of succeeding.

Let the common syllabus be vocationally based so as to provide the fastest
possible direct contribution to professional practice in the countries concerned.
Indeed, the initial syllabus outline has already been provided by Carroll Bateman
in what he describes as the Public Relations Core Studies.   To put some further
interpretation onto this, I would suggest that a first international certificate
in public relations might have as its syllabus the following:

Draft Syllabus
AIM: To provide students with an awareness of the many different publics with
which an organisation is concerned and a knowledge of the professional context in
which people working full-time in public relations operate. Also to provide an
understanding of all means of communication by which these publics can be reached.

Public Relations as a Management Function (3)

The service nature of public relations, the PRO as a channel of two-way information and communication.

Ethics of Public Relations (2)

Codes of Professional Practice and the reasons behind each clause. Protection afforded to members. Professional Bodies.

Laws affecting Public Relations Practice (2)

Operational PR (7)

Problem analysis, programme planning, costing and budgetary control, case presentation to client or management, programme execution, assessment of results, appraisal, objectives, targets, methods, recommendations, budget, progress report.

PR Practice in Organisational Frameworks (4)

Staff: Consultancies: Central Government press and information officers: local government public relations. Counselling: counselling/services: services only: personal and product publicity.

Types of Media (5)

Description, characteristics, advantages/disadvantages, costs (capital and running), major 'publics'/audiences.

(a) Basic Media.

     i.   Person-to-person (public speaking: TV/radio techniques.
     ii. Printed work (editorial, advertising, direct mail, print).
     iii. Two-dimensional/graphics (photography, film slides, charts).
     iv. Audio/tape (tape recordings, discs, CCTV, VTR, EVR).
     v.   Three-dimensional (models, displays, signs).

(b) Composite Media.

     ie. Press conferences, formal meetings, special events, facility visits, exhibitions, export promotions, conferences, sales presentations, sponsored sport, artistic or educational activities.

Timing and Handling of Material (5)

News and features.
Demands of all types of media.
Public relations material – what is required, how it is used.
Proof-reading, sub-editing, and preparing for press.

Professional Attitudes (2)

Freedom of the press – including radio and TV.
Society and the journalist – in all media.
The journalist and public relations – in all media.

NB: Numbers in parenthesis indicate the suggested number of lecture units.

Teaching would be the responsibility of the national institutes, but the examination would have to be the responsibility of IPRA, but this could be delegated to an examining body such as CAM. Students would be charged a registration fee which would be so fixed as to make the whole scheme self-supporting after an initial start-up period. Examination papers could be in any language and the facility would exist for questions to be re-phrased from a basic format to suit local conditions.

Situation in the Developing Countries

J. M. Kaul

Public Relations Manager, Indian Oxygen Limited, Calcutta

The situation in the developing countries differs in a number of respects from
that in the advanced countries. This, I believe, calls for certain special traits
in the public relations practitioners in the developing countries and public
relations education in these countries therefore needs to be so oriented as to keep
in mind the need for developing these traits. This does not mean that the
fundamental principles and the basic techniques of public relations have to be
redefined for the developing countries. But it does mean that besides teaching the
basic principles and the various techniques and tools of public relations, a special
effort has to be made to understand the specific features of the environment in
these countries. Public relations practice in the developing countries will require
an ability to adjust to the needs of that specific environment.

In my paper I shall draw upon my experience in India and discuss the problems of
public relations education as they have emerged in that country. Since these
problems are not very dissimilar to those faced by developing countries generally,
it should be possible to draw some conclusions from the Indian experience which
would be more or less valid for most of the countries of the developing world.

Thereafter, I shall also make some general observations on public relations
education with specific reference to the Bateman-Cutlip Report. I shall also
express some views on the question of an international qualification on public
relations which appears to be exercising the minds of many who are concerned with
public relations education.

The Indian Environment

The purpose of public relations education must obviously be to prepare
professionals to handle the jobs they will be given and since an essential part of
the job is to help the organisation for which he works to adjust itself to the
environment, he is expected to have a very thorough understanding of the nature of
that environment. Even more important, since the environment itself is in a state
of flux he should be able to see the emerging trends and the direction in which
things are moving. In other words, he should be able to make a fairly accurate
guess of the shape of the environment a few years hence and not only to see it as
it is today.

Some of the important features of the Indian environment - and many of these,
though not all, are common to most of the developing countries - are:

a) About 70 per cent of the population is dependant on agriculture. And
    even agriculture is in the main carried on by primitive and age-old methods

of cultivation resulting in a low level of productivity. However, there are a few pockets where modern techniques of cultivation are followed and productivity is high.

b) Organised industry absorbs hardly 2 to 3 per cent of the population. Small-scale and cottage industry and retail trade absorb the rest of the urban population. Productivity in this unorganised sector is also naturally low.

c) Population has been growing at a very high rate, nearly 2.5 per cent per annum in the last decade.

d) As a natural consequence, living standards are low and more than 50 per cent of the population is living below the poverty line which in India means a per capita income level of less than 200 dollars per annum.

e) Nearly 70 per cent of the population is completely illiterate. And of the remaining 30 per cent who are literate, the percentage of those who have been through Secondary schools would be hardly 10 per cent.

f) There are many languages, many cultures and ethnic groups. Although politically a sense of nationhood has undoubtedly developed and economically the country comprises a single market, culturally instead of a common composite culture emerging, there are at least 15 or 16 distinct cultural groups with their own language, their own way of living. Linguistic and cultural differences are not disappearing but growing sharper.

g) India is a land of contrasts. Side by side with primitive methods of agriculture, there are pockets where the yield of wheat for instance is as high as in the United States if not even higher. India has a highly developed Steel and Heavy Engineering industry, sophisticated petro-chemical complexes and refineries, one of the largest railway systems in the world and is exporting turnkey projects and technological know-how in certain fields to countries abroad, including some of the developed countries. India in fact, ranks 7th among the industrialised nations of the world. There is a developed infra-structure of technical training institutes, scientific establishments and laboratories. India has the third largest number of trained scientists in the world.

h) Add to this the fact that although a free market economy the public or government sector controls all the strategic sectors of industry and that industry and commerce are subject to a plethora of controls and regulations and the complexities of the tasks confronting public relations practitioners in India become apparent.

To be able to work successfully in this kind of an environment, public relations practitioners need to have certain qualities and personality traits without which it would not be possible for them to cope successfully with the problems constantly being thrown up by the society around them. One of the most important requirements is that they must have a scientific outlook and a modern mind. In the developing countries a constant battle is raging between tradition and modernity. The process of industrialisation, the frequent contacts with the developed countries, the inflow of modern technology and the need for modernisation of agriculture itself to provide sustenance to a burgeoning population, all act as agents of change driving these countries in the direction of modernity. But the shackles binding them to the past are too powerful to be snapped easily. Moreover, growing awareness of the effects of excessive industrialisation such as environmental pollution, break up of family ties, emergence of new values - many of which are repugnant to cherished values - tends to produce a backlash which often leads even highly educated intellectuals to question the need for industrialisation and modernisation. Obviously the developing countries cannot afford to follow mechanically the example of the advanced industrial countries. Science and technology imported from the Western world must be judiciously blended with what is best in the local culture and adapted to indigenous requirements. The public relations practitioner has an important role to play in influencing opinion leaders and decision makers in their countries to take a balanced view.

Considering that the developing countries are engaged in a desperate struggle to take their country forward despite serious obstacles such as a lack of financial, capital and even trained human resources, the public relations practitioner to be able to operate successfully should have something more than just a commercial outlook. He should be able to identify himself and his organisation with the national goals and objectives. Thus a sense of dedication and something of a missionary zeal is required of him. He must have breadth of vision and to be able to look a little beyond the constraint and irritations of the immediate surroundings.

While an ability to use the latest tools and techniques of public relations is necessary, the skills required to operate in as complicated an environment as exists in these countries have to be of a very high order indeed. Communication with vast masses of people who cannot read or write, who are almost inaccessible in remote rural or hilly areas on the one hand and with the emerging elite on the other, makes it necessary to develop creative abilities. Communications even to the literate masses who are so diverse in background in culture cannot be carried on by routine methods. A constant process of experimentation, learning and research are called for.

It is evident that the task of preparing and educating public relations men and women in a country such as ours is not easy. The first generation of public relations professionals in India acquired their skills on the job. Having come into the profession either via journalism or via advertising they learnt by trial and error, by experimentation and of course also from books on public relations published in the United States or the United Kingdom. Using their own knowledge of the environment, they tried to adapt the principles and techniques of public relation as practised abroad to local conditions and requirements. Formalised training and education in public relations had not yet started.

In the last decade or so, and especially in the last four or five years, the position has begun to change. A conscious attempt is being made to impart training to new entrants to the profession or to those aspiring to join its ranks. Simultaneously, senior practitioners are trying to improve their skills and to make themselves more effective by learning from one another's experience as also from available public relation literature from abroad and trying to generalise and conceptualise on the experience gained by each one of them.

The types of educational activities that are going on in India may be divided into the following categories:

1.   Seminars, Workshops, Discussion Groups.

Under the Public Relations Society of India, there are nine Chapters and the Chapters generally hold one tea meeting every month and two to three seminars/ workshops a year. At these meetings/seminars/workshop sessions sometimes experts from outside the profession are invited and on other occasions public relations practitioners themselves present papers and hold discussions on various problems.

2.   Short-term Training Courses.

Short-term training courses for junior level public relations practitioners are organised by the various Chapters of the PRSI from time to time. The faculty consists of senior public relations practitioners and people from different management disciplines as well as professors from academic institutions. Some of these short-term courses are held in collaboration with local management associations or other management institutes.

3.   Long-term Courses.

Long-term courses are organised for public relations practitioners by some of the Chapters. In many cases, senior practitioners from the various Chapters of the PRSI provide the faculty while various colleges and institutes make all the organisational arrangements. In Bombay, an eight month diploma course is being run by Bhavan's College and Xavier's College. The diploma course consists of evening lectures four days a week, special assignments once a week on subjects covered in the syllabus, visits to establishments such as newspaper offices, printers, block-makers, the television centres, public relations departments of various organisations etc. Workshops on selected subjects where specialisation is needed, are also organised as part of the course. A terminal examination is held midway during the course and a final examination at the end of the course. Successful students who wish to get an opportunity for practical training are assigned to public relation departments of large corporations for short periods.

Some colleges which are conducting courses on journalism or in advertising and marketing or in business management, also cover public relations as part of the syllabus and here too public relations practitioners are invited to act as the faculty. This is the case, for instance, in the Department or Journalism, Calcutta University, Institute of Social Welfare and Business Management, affiliated to Calcutta University and the Indian Institute of Management, Calcutta.

4.   Degree Courses.

The Madras University has a degree course in public relations. A number of colleges affiliated to Madras University, such as the Government Art College, Stella Maris College, Nandanam College and Islamia College, run these courses. An average of about 20 students are enrolling in each of these colleges every year. A Post-Graduate diploma course in certain subjects related to public relations has also been started by the Madras University recently.

The Osmania University in Hyderabad is running a degree course as well as a Masters' course in Journalism and Communications. As part of the syllabus of these courses they have papers on public relations and its various aspects. The journalism course in Osmania University started in 1954 and up to date about 750 students have graduated in the field. The Head of the Department of Journalism of this University is the President of the Andhra Pradesh Chapter of the Public Relations Society of India.

5.   Institute of Mass Communications, Government of India.

Apart from this, there is an Institute of Mass Communication run by the Government of India. Courses on various aspects of mass communications are held in which not only Indian students but also students from many Asian and African countries participate. Most of the courses are being run to prepare Information Officers for the Government of India and various Asian and African Governments.

Under the auspices of the Institute of Mass Communications, public relations courses have also been organised for public relations practitioners in the public or Government sector.

Syllabus

Based on the experience of the courses being conducted in various parts of India, the National Council of the Public Relations Society of India has prepared a standard syllabus for a short-term as well as an advanced long-term course. Most of the courses now being conducted are based on this syllabus that has been prepared by PRSI. (See Appendix).

Case Histories

Appreciating the importance of case histories in any educational programme and having regard to the fact that case histories based on a totally different environment would not be suitable for training programmes in India, an effort is being made to prepare a number of case histories involving use of public relation techniques in different situations and different management disciplines. The PRSI instituted a research fellowship in the Institute of Management, Ahmedabad, which is one of the leading management institutes in India, for the preparation of such case histories. The result of this research is expted to be published in book form jointly sponsored by the Indian Institute of Management Ahmedabad and the Public Relations Society of India.

Problems

A common complaint of public relations practitioners in India is that they are not being given the status that they deserve and public relations inputs are not being used in management decision making. On behalf of management on the other hand, it is often stated that they are not getting the right type of public relations men and hence they do not feel they would benefit by taking their advice. Owing to the limited career opportunities in public relations and the failure on the part of top management in most organisations to give public relations the recognition it deserves the calibre of the people who are currently seeking admission into public relations is not always of a very high order. Thus a vicious circle has been created. Management feels that the right type of public relations people are not available. And the right young people aspiring for a career in business and industry prefer other management disciplines such as finance or marketing or personnel rather than public relations because of the higher rewards they offer.

This vicious circle can only be broken by a determined effort to educate people in public relations and to ensure that those thus trained are able to make a contribution to management decision making.

Another problem is that there is a serious lack of educators. Almost the entire burden of imparting education in public relations is being borne by what I referred to as the first generation of public relations practitioners who have been trained on the job and who while being well qualified from the point of view of their extensive experience have, however, limitations in certain spheres such as teaching, methods of carrying on research in public relations etc.

Another problem being faced is that so far the major institutes of management have failed to accept public relations as a management discipline in its own right. Public relations is either ignored altogether or covered very inadequately as part of the marketing syllabus.

Finally, there is the need for carrying on original research on various issues of importance in so far as public relations in India is concerned. But obviously such research has to be sponsored either by business houses or the universities or the management institutes - none of whom has yet come forward in this matter. The research fellowship at the Institute of Management, Ahmedabad sponsored by the PRSI with funds raised from different business houses of which a major contribution was made by the House of Tata, has been the sole exception in this area so far.

Bateman-Cutlip Report

The Bateman-Cutlip Report has been a very valuable contribution on the subject of public relations education and I am in agreement with their basic assumptions. Public Relations courses being organised in India, with the exception of the Madras and Osmania University degree courses, are confined to the smallest of the three concentric circles referred to in the Bateman-Cutlip Report. It is necessary, however, that a course on public relations in the developing countries should cover areas such as the economics of growth, various political systems functioning in the developing countries, the dynamics of social development, the culture and the history of various nationalities and also that part of the legislative framework which is relevant to public relations activities. While some attempt has been made to cover briefly some of these subjects in the syllabus recommended by the PRSI in India, obviously a much more detailed treatment is required if a young graduate is to shoulder the responsibilities of public relations in a complicated situation such as that which exists in India.

What the Bateman-Cutlip Report has stated in regard to the public relations educator is very true in the case of the educator in India. As mentioned above, public relations educators in India come entirely from the rank of public relations practitioners who have their strong as well as their weak points. Arrangements should perhaps be made in collaboration with some universities and institutes of management to develop training programmes for equipping educators in public relations. Without this, public relations education at the under-graduate level is bound to be of a poor quality.

The remarks on public relations research made in the Bateman-Cutlip Report are also very relevant to India. The need for original research by public relations educators and public relations practitioners is even greater in a country like India where we have still a long way to go in conceptualising our experience. There are also a large number of virgin areas crying out for basic research such as, for example, how the decision making process operates in India, how organised media affect the conduct of the rural masses, the kind of social background that our political leaders have and the extent to which it affects their decisions on industry etc.

An International public relations qualification

In the light of what has been stated above, some views can be expressed on an international public relations qualification. In view of the wide difference in the problems, the techniques to be used, the qualifications and personality traits that public relations practitioners need to have in the developing countries, an international public relations qualification would only make sense if the syllabus and the examinations are made flexible enough to cover the experience and the requirements of the developing countries. In other words, while there is some merit in the suggestion that there should be an international public relations qualification, the mode of awarding the International Public Relations diploma would have to be devised in such a manner that it would have relevance to different types of countries. Thus for the developing countries if the syllabus is divided into a number of papers and if eight papers are to be taken up to qualify, only three should cover general principles, history of public relations, tools and techniques and cases of the use of public relations in the advanced countries. Two papers should deal with the situation in the developing countries, the economic, political and social environment in these countries and the kind of techniques being used in them. The remaining three papers should deal with the specific environment of the country to which the student belongs and where he intends to practise. It should cover the legislation and the history of that country, the socio-economic environment and cases based on experience of public relations in that country.

Would it be possible to organise courses, develop a syllabus and conduct examinations in this manner from one centre or would it represent too complex an exercise? If indeed the administration of such a diversified syllabus and examination is impossible to execute centrally then perhaps it might be better to conduct the examination nationally with the help of some international guidelines.

Syllabus for Training Course
Advanced and Short Term
Approved by the National Council of
the Public Relations Society of India

Introduction

1. Existing Practices

Training programmes and courses on public relations are being run by various
Chapters of the PRSI from time to time either on their own or in collaboration
with different institutions. However, so far there has been no standardised
courses and each Chapter has devised its own training programme. Seminars on
various topics have also been organised by almost all the Chapters. These are
generally in the nature of one or two day meetings and are confined to some single
topic. Some of these seminars have also been organised in collaboration with other
organisations such as local Management Associations or the All India Management
Association.

Apart from this an undergraduate course on public relations has been started by
the Madras University and some of the affiliated colleges are preparing students
for this course.

Lectures on public relations are included in the MBA Course of the Calcutta
University but only as part of the Marketing syllabus. The Indian Institute of
Management, Calcutta has also, on certain occasions, invited members of the PRSI
for occasional lectures on public relations but again as part of the marketing
courses run by them.

The Government run Institute of Mass Communication in New Delhi runs courses on
mass communications which are intended to train information officers and other
personnel working in the Government controlled organisations and mass media such as
Door Darshan and All India Radio.

The Osmania University has a course on Journalism which covers a lot of ground that
could form part of a public relations course. The Department of Journalism of the
Calcutta University has also provision for a paper on Advertising and Public
Relations.

The Institute of Communication Studies which is part of the Bharatiya Vidya Bhavan,
a private educational trust, also runs courses on public relations and
Communications.

2. Nature of this syllabus

A study co-sponsored by the Public Relations Division of the Association for
Education in Journalism and the Public Relations Society of America which
presented a report known as the Bateman-Cutlip Report has expressed the view that
the curriculum for the education of the student preparing for admission to the
practice of public relations may be pictured as a series of three concentric
circles.

The smallest, central circle would enclose those subjects specifically concerned
with public relations practice. The second circle, somewhat larger, would

encompass related subjects in the general field of communications. The third and largest circle would represent the general liberal arts and humanities background expected of all students.

For the present, the PRSI has set before itself a limited objective. This is to have a standardised syllabus for two types of courses: 1) a short-term course for junior practitioners, new entrants and students aspiring for a public relations career and   2) a more advanced course for middle level practitioners. This course will deal with only those subjects specifically concerned with public relations practice. In other words, it will be confined to the smallest of the three concentric circles.

Advanced Training Course

1.   Principles, scope and function of public relations

        Introduction

Explanation of the public relations concept
Definition
Public Relations in the Indian setting : present status and future scope
Public Relations as a modern management tool : the scope of public relations in almost every area of management functioning.

2.   Historical perspective

Beginnings of public relations in the 19th Century
The First World War and use of public relations by the US Government
Early 20th Century - the American scene
Mid-20th Century - US, Europe, Asia
Factors that gave rise to the development of public relations
The public relations international scene today
Stages in the development of public relations in India
Early 20th Century till the Second World War
Second World War till the early half of the Sixties
From mid-Sixties to the present day : the rise of professionalism in public
  relations
History of PRSI
Review of the bi-annual public relations conference.

3.   The environment

Industrial revolution and its aftermath
The global outlook - crises, conflicts and conciliation
The Indian Scene:
-       Demographic features
-       Emergence of political institutions, parties
-       The sociological pattern
-       The industrial policy resolution and its various modifications
-       The Indian economy - basic features
-       The political pattern - parties and groups
-       The cultural pattern
-       Influence of religion and tradition

Ecology : pressure groups and the citizen.

4.   Human behaviour

Patterns of human behaviour

Some recent thinking - transactional analysis
Attitude improvement
Credibility and acceptance
Public opinion, its importance in public relations:

-         Formation of attitudes
-         Power structure in society - opinion moulders
-         Contemporary and future agents of change

5.   The various publics of public relations

        The employee public:

-         Developing good relations
-         Importance of attitude formation
-         Surveys and evaluation of attitudes
-         Employee communication
-         Participation and motivation.

        The investing public :

-         The shareholder
-         The financial institutions
-         The stock exchange and stockholder associations
-         Personal contacts, reports, plant visits
-         The Annual General Meeting.

        Special Publics :

        The Government :

-         Federal and local
-         Legislative process and the Legislators
-         Parliamentary Committee
-         Bureaucracy
-         Moulding public opinion
-         Case studies

        Youth and the educational institutions :

-         Parent/teacher groups
-         Grants : Scholarships.

        Labour Unions :

-         Role of political parties
-         Legislative constraints
-         Case studies

        Dealers and customers :

-         Product publicity and reputation
-         Opinion surveys
-         Marketing considerations
-         Rise of consumerism
-         Case studies.

The Community

- Importance of the immediate neighbourhood
- Developing community relations programmes
- Case Studies

6.   The Counselling role of public relations

Monitoring of the environment
Interpreting changes in the environment and changes in the public attitudes
In the light of these changes advising Management of action needed
Role of the staffman
Role of the outside consultant.

7.   The Communication role of public relations

The nature of communication
Questions of semantics
Barriers to communcation
The formal structure of communication
Communication downwards, upwards and lateral.

8.   Media

   a)   Press

      A two-way operation
      Basis of press relations
      Providing information service, issuing news and information
      Press releases, writing a press release
      Press conference
      Press interviews
      Factory visits
      Letters to editors, editorials, special articles
      Feature stories, supplements, assessing press activity
      Relationships of public relations man and credibility.

   b)   The printed word

      The principles of good writing
      Style and design - layout and artwork
      Typography
      Logo and trademark
      "Face of the firm"

      Blocks, printer and printing methods, paper, house journals,
      company brochures, bulletins, direct mail etc.

   c)   Photography

      Photographs and communication
      Quality of photography
      Uses of photographs
      Special events
      Photographs for news stories
      Photographs for publications, photograohic libraries, securing
       best results.

   d)   Advertising

    i) Prestige advertising and institutional campaigns

       Theory of advertising : Elements of advertising

       Advertising for special events (plant openings, special achievements etc), editorial features

       Use of supplements.

    ii) Factual advertising : credible advertising

       Unfairness in advertising : criteria for determining unfairness.

    iii) Selection of an advertising agency

       Agency working

       Briefing

       Review of proposals, media selection

       Budgets and scheduling

       Checking and billing

       Pre-testing and evaluation after campaign.

e)   <u>Exhibition and Fairs</u>

    Local, national and international fairs
    Criteria for participation
    Planning and designing of exhibits
    Design of pavilion
    Information at fairs
    Publicity for fairs
    Dealing with enquiries
    Staffing
    Follow up etc.

f)   <u>Audiovisual</u>

    i) Radio/TV
      Sponsored programmes
      Scope, planning and production coverage of company news through Radio
      Contacts and techniques.

    ii) Film :

      Documentaries for special screening and for circuit screening
      Planning, production and screening
      Covering special events as news through film circuit.

    iii) Other Audio-visual media :

      Slide/sound presentation for special audience
      Filmstrips etc.

g)   <u>The Spoken Word</u>

    Word of mouth communication
    Public speaking
    Training
    The techniques and uses of the public address system

Voice of the firm, telephone manners
Speech kit.

9.   Other Tools and Techniques

Sponsored programmes
Social Service projects
Rural development
Donations and scholarships
Fund raising for charities
Other public relations projects.

10.   Planning and Implementing a public relations Campaign

The need for research
Research methodology and market studies, sources, references,
documentation etc
Setting up public relations objectives, development of plan of action
and time schedules
Selection of media, evaluation and setting up budgets
Identify target audiences
Implementation of the campaign
Evaluating results.

11.   Specialised public relations

a)   Financial public relations

Targets :

Shareholders
Stock Exchanges
Brokers
Banking and other financial institutions
Security analysis
Financial press, insurance companies
Other miscellaneous groups.

Tools   :

Trade Journals
Direct Mail
Annual reports and interim reports
Corporate advertising
Annual General Meeting
Chairman's speech
Plant visits
Exhibitions at annual general meetings
Welcome letters
Also discuss public issue/public relations responsibility
Evaluation of results.

b)   Public relations within the Organisation

Employee as spokesman :

Importance and advantages
Educating the employee on company and industry
Attitude improvement programmes
Coordination with public relations department
House journals

        Managing Director's annual letter
        Bulletins
        Abstract service
        Special events
        Service awards, annual day, sports, scholarships, marriage awards etc.
        Developing managers as industry speakers
        Encourage employees to participate in community welfare programme

f)   Public relations for Government Legislators

        Government officials
        Ministers
        MP's
        MLAs
        Delegations
        Representation
        Lobbying
        Direct Mailings
        Involving key men in company events
        Plant visits
        Public relations man and Government liaison officer coordination
        Use of audio-visuals.

12.   Public relations for the Public Sector

Objectives and profile of the Public Sector in India - its growth and development

Role of Public Sector in India

Range of Public Sector operations and their performance

Yardsticks of performance - financial and social objectives

Role of corporate communication in the Public Sector

Expert Committee Report on public relations for Public Sector undertakings.

13.   Organisation, Budgeting etc.

Place of public relations in the organisational structure
Relationship with other functions and departments
Public relations department - a service unit
Reporting to top management
The public relations budget - a plan of action
Budgetary control.

14.   Research and Evaluation

The Evaluation Task

        The need for research and a research outlook
        Types of Research:
            Pre-testing
            Post-testing
            Measuring results.

Re-identification of policy, plan, publics

Evaluation and feedback :
A continuing process.

Case Studies.

15. Public Relations and Special Groups

Trade Associations
Chambers of Commerce
Professional Societies
Hospitals and Welfare Agencies
Religious organisations
Political parties
Defence services
Public utilities
Multinationals, UN and foreign government agencies.

16. Public relations as a Profession

Professional requirements
Professional education
Licensing and a Code of Ethics
Role of professional organisations

Syllabus for a short course on public relations

1. What is public relations?

An attempt at defining the concept
History and origin.

2. The Environment

An over view of current social, economic and political climate in India
The place of public relations therein.

3. The Role and status of public relations in management

A study of the current management scene and managerial concepts
Structure of organisations
What management expects from public relations
What public relations expects from management
The role of the staff man
The role of the outside consultant.

4. The public relations process

Research and fact finding
Evaluation and feedback
Development and implementation of public relations plans and programmes

Evaluation and reporting to management.

5.   <u>Public relations and its various publics</u>

Employee

Shareholder

Customer, dealer, etc.

6.   <u>The tools of public relations</u>

An outline and assessment of the various mediums of communication available

Mass media

Press relations

Press conference.

7.   <u>The role and significance of communication</u>

Word of mouth versus the printed word

What makes communication effective

The need to give greater status to internal and external communication processes.

8.   <u>Public relations for the Public Sector</u>

Objectives and profile of the Public Sector in India – its growth and development

Role of Public Sector in India

Range of Public Sector operations and their performance

Yardsticks of performance – financial and social objectives

Role of corporate communication in the Public Sector

Expert Committee Report on public relations for Public Sector undertakings.

9.   <u>Public relations for special groups</u>

Educational and social institutions

Government

Multinational companies

Professional organisations.

10.   <u>Public relations as a profession</u>

Professional requirements

Professional Societies

A Code of Ethics.

Experience in the Netherlands

Professor Dr. Anne van der Meiden
State University, Utrecht, The Netherlands

1.   Public relations programmes in the Netherlands

I must apologise for the fact that I start this speech with a portrait of the state of public relations education in the Netherlands. A Dutchman might be well known as a traveller, but he always prefers to start from home and to return as soon as possible.

An Education Commission of the Netherlands Public Relations Society started ten years ago to plan public relations education at different levels and in a comprehensive way the commission was very ambitious but was not forced to create an education plan from scratch.

For many years we had already had short- and long-term courses for practitioners in public relations and for those who wanted to go into public relations. These courses (see the Explanation of the Schedule) were and are still organised by private institutes, but the Netherlands Public Relations Society is responsible for the final examination under supervision of the Government. We enjoy the fast growing appreciation of this Diploma very much. It means, for young practitioners, an important step-up in their public relations career.

The commission was however confronted with three other levels (partly corresponding to the Bateman-Cutlip Report, 1975, which were not filled in at that moment).

1.   The full-time education at College-level (Middle-class executives).
2.   The University-level (public relations advisers level).
3.   The post-Academic level (top-executives, advisers).

Let me explain the Dutch Education System at these levels. The college level is separate from the university level. We have Higher Vocational Education Schools for our journalists, policemen, technicians, teachers, social workers, analysts, experts in tourism, librarians, etc. They offer three or four year courses after twelfth degree High-School.

Our University programmes are, generally speaking divided into two parts: The "candidate" level (three years) and the "doctoraal" level (three years). These levels do not exactly correspond to the Bachelors and Masters degrees. After your "doctoraal" examination you become a "doctorandus". The Doctors degree can only be obtained after writing a thesis, either immediately after your "doctoraal" examination or long afterwards, in any discipline you like.

Education at post-academic level (continuing education) is organised in a brand-new

Law. Universities can set up courses, but only in cooperation with professional organisation. The programmes are State-aided.

What was the commission able to achieve in ten years?

a)   In the first place, a department of communications was started in August 1978 in one of the Schools for Higher Vocational Education mentioned above. It was the School for Higher Economic and Business Administration. There were a few starting-points for this programme which are interesting enough to be mentioned in our discussions here.

We first concluded that young people cannot decide to go into public relations at the age of 18-20, but they can decide to study the broader field of communications. The image of the profession is too vague. When they choose this study, they first choose an educational programme and secondly a field of work. So we decided to offer them a broader campus and cooperated with the Dutch Advertising Organisation and the Association of Practitioners in the field of Public Information. These three fields of interest were melted together in one programme, set up for three and a half years, based on a wide and varied background of liberal arts and sciences (economics, languages, sociology, social psychology, law, social development, statistics, etc). In this programme two periods of three months for practice are included. We called it a "department of communication". Public relations is not an optional subject in this programme. The students are trained equally in public relations advertising, and public information.

Now I would like to introduce two terms to mark the contradictory developments in public relations educations we are confronted with: I call them *centripetal* and *centrifugal Forces*.

Centripetal: three fields or practice: advertising, public relations and public information have found *one* basis for education: the study of communications in a wider sense.

Centrifugal: we realised that young people should be "Multi-applicable" in society and therefore we rejected the idea of specialisations and "pure" skills courses. The next starting point was: how do you recognise young people capable of filling an executive post in public relations? Here again we concluded that you can better recognise one's suitability for an education-programme than for a job. The programme provides the best possibilities for young people with highly classified contactual facilities and an open mentality to analyse communicational situations, with interest in sociology and psychology, management and planning, and with a nearly "generalistic" way of thinking.

b)   The second goal the commission realised, was a chair for the theory of public relations at the State University in Utrecht, one year ago (April, 1978).

At university-level we met the same centripetal and centrifugal forces. Let me explain this very shortly:

It was clear from the beginning, that there was a need for a minor programme, an optional subject, in the "doctoraal" phase of the study. Students from different faculties apply for a 500-hours course in public relations. Why? To become public relations executives or public relation managers? No, in the first place to be a doctor, a lawyer, a minister or an economist with better understanding of their "environments". Some of them, with a background in social sciences ask for a double optional subject, 1000 hours, and decide to look for a job in the field of public relations or public information.

What was our starting-point in Utrecht? First: to give them a basic introduction into the theory of mass communications. That is the first phase. The second phase is a theoretical introduction in public relations, the third: a six-week orientation in the field of practice and the last phase is literature-study in combination with a final essay. Students on this level like to "recognise" communication-problems, to be confronted with practical and theoretical solutions (case-studies), with analytic and strategic models of public relations policy and last but not least with research-problems.

I realised from the beginning that a pure, "centripetal" programme would not be successful. I had to start in the broader field of communications first, then to pass the public relations-field and finally to end again in the wider scene. In other words: I used the shaped model.

The main reason to use this model is, that graduates from varied disciplines should be trained to identify the function of public relations in our rapid changing world. When I say public relations, I mean the management - supporting function to analyse the position of the organisation in the environmental field and to provide the techniques and methods which might support mutual understanding.

c)   The third success of the commission was the organisation of Post-Academic Courses. The new law on continuing education for practitioners in the Netherlands enables us to offer a programme of 30 evenings for graduates working in public relations and public information jobs. The law provided this possibility for non-graduated higher classified public relations managers to join the courses. The interest in these courses is very encouraging and recently our Government subsidised this work, so that we could appoint a coordinator for the organisational work. Three universities and a lot of professional organisations are brought together in one executive commission for Post Academic Education in Public Relations and Public Information.

For far these are the results of the ambitious commission. We may conclude that there is now a possibility to study public relations in one way or another for people at all levels, but this is not entirely true. The "missing link" to the top of public relations management is still a full "doctoraal" study at university level. This ideal can only be reached if we succeed in setting up a programme with "ingredients" from mass communications, business administration, cultural sociology, economics, law, management philosophy, etc. We are very lucky that we are not complete!

2.   International developments: trends and qualifications.

Congress papers taught me that there are very interesting international developments in our discipline. The Board of this congress formulated some questions. In order to be sure that I do not speak for myself alone, I organised a meeting with Post Academic Graduates in public relations and educators in public relations courses. It is impossible to sum up now all the interesting answers they gave me. Some of these answers I have already mentioned. In the first place there is the problem of the senior people, transferring to public relations as a second or a third career. I think the possibilities of training for these people depends on their background, training, age, professional level and the kind of job they want to go into. As far as I can see we must organise special evening-courses for them, with an introductory character. Another possibility is "invading" with public relations education programmes the re-educational training programmes, offered by the corporation or organisation they want to enter.

And now the problem is the international qualification of public relations. If I may say so, it is not very clear to me or the people I consulted at home, what exactly is meant by the term "international qualifications". Do we mean the

qualifications for the job? Or of the man or the woman? Or of the curriculum and
the different disciplines to be taught, expressed in teaching-hours, books or
examination-requirements? Is it a qualification expressed in a diploma with
international status, or is it a qualification for a course of training programme
awarded by an international jury and guaranteed by an international certificate or
is it a qualification for the practitioner who meets the requirements, formulated
in an international check-list with which his or her ability, mentality, skills
and vision can be measured? I think an international qualification for the
different courses at a lower level as a guarantee for quality seems to be
interesting, but we must not forget that the national character of the courses
prohibits international ""measuring" to an important extent. Maybe the upgrading
of our profession is served best by this qualification, but there still remains a
difficult question: Who qualifies the qualifiers? Where do we get our criteria
from to judge?

Let me make three proposals for further discussion.

First: Let IPRA set up a committee with the task of:

(a) "gathering" study-curricula from all over the world, (b) analysing the
content of these curricula and the "weight" of the programmes expressed in hours,
tasks, etc (c) defining the "civil effect" of the diplomas and the ways of
examining, literature-study, etc. In other words: bring the educators together,
at least one time before 1982. I do not mean to propose one programme for every
country, but simply an inventarisation!

Second: Let IPRA set up a committee with the task of analysing the educational
problems in public relations in developing countries. What can be done for these
countries? It might be possible to exchange educators, paid by UNESCO or local
Funds for Foreign Aid. Let developing countries tell this IPRA-committee what
they need.

Third: Let IPRA set up a committee with the task of analysing the possibility of
an "International Public Relations Education Programme" at University level
(Masters or Doctors), given by 5-10 universities all over the world, supported by
the national Public Relations Societies. It might be possible to give a three-
months programme every year by another university and that a small team of
educators in basic theoretical problems travel around. This corps of teachers
must be added by practitioners who can present cases and by "local" educators and
practitioners. Only in this way might we succeed to upgrade the educational level
in public relations and to strengthen the international understanding of public
relations.

APPENDIX

Explanation Schedule

1.   a) orientation courses   :   1 afternoon
      b) practical courses   :   6 afternoons
      c) professional training pgrammes   :   26, 28 or 30 afternoons and/
          or evenings.
          Different examinations by the Dutch Association for public relations
          and public information, under inspection of the Government.

2.   Vocational education and training on college level, 3½ years after High

School, taken up, together with advertising and public information in a department of communication of so called higher economic and administrative education-schools.
Main topics in the schools, besides communications are: economics, languages, sociology, social psychology, law, etc.

3.   University of Utrecht: 500 or 1000 hours education (theory of public relations research) for post-graduate students of all disciplines, as optional subject in their doctoral study.

4.   Post - Academic: Two years course (30 evenings) for graduates who work in the fields of public relations and public information.
Universities: Utrecht, Leiden and Wageningen. Theory and practice: research project.
Accessible for non-graduates who work on a high level in the public relations profession.
Character: "Continuing education".

5.   Special courses: Introductory courses for managers etc., varying from one afternoon to several days.

Summary

Summary

Public relations is not an international science with exact standards which mean the same thing and can be measured the same way in every country of the world. Thus it is unlike any branch of science or medicine or engineering or other professional activities based on internationally recognised formulae.

Public relations relates to the local environment in which it is being practised, and although there are many fundamental principles, public relations education must usually be national. Occasionally there can be groupings for countries with common languages or historic and cultural links, or which fit within the same framework of economic development. It must, however, be recognised that even within some countries there are variations of language, culture, religion, and economic growth. There will, therefore, be some cases where public relations education needs to be on a sub-national basis since public relation practice is also on a sub-national basis.

Against this background, it is acknowledged that the introduction and development of public relations education grows and flourishes far more successfully when encouraged by the traditional academic system and the appropriate Government agencies.

The development of an education programme by a local public relations association or society working in isolation, is likely to fail, or at best become so introspective that it atrophies.

If it is accepted that education is the fundamental key to professional stature then it is vital to create an international definition of education in public relations. This definition will need to cover four elements; the recognition and development of basic aptitudes; teaching; examination and practical experience. An education process which embraces all four provides the basis for professional stature, and is geared to the internationally accepted concepts of bachelor degree status.

In the same way that there are internationally accepted standards of degree status throughout the world, there will need to be equally acceptable standards of national public relations qualifications. However, there probably cannot be a universal absolute international qualification.

The majority of public relations practitioners throughout the world recognise that education is a necessity but for many it is an unfulfilled need, particularly those who take up public relations as the second major career in their adult life.

Examination of both full and part time public relations education throughout the world, shows that the routes are mainly divided between the journalistic, social science and communication and business management faculties of colleges and universities. This creates a controversial situation because educators are hungry for students (their standing and salary are often geared to the size of the student body) and are, therefore, competitive. There is, therefore, a tendency for educational establishments to either solicit students to attend their establishment, or obtain a qualification through private study in countries other than the one in which the establishment is based. It some times leads to a situation where public relations is in danger of becoming a socially popular or status qualification without necessarily being geared to career opportunities or basic aptitude.

Public relations education should grow from straight forward training in communication techniques, and then draw in a skilled understanding of social awareness and responsibilities together with academic and practical knowledge of human behaviour and psychology. To achieve this it should ideally be linked to a university or college base which provides the simplest method of linking together the necessary multi-discipline aspects that are required to create a public relations course.

Whilst it is accepted that those teaching the social sciences and psychological aspects of the course are well qualified, there is considerable doubt at an international level concerning the abilities of those who are teaching public relations itself, whether it be on a full or part time basis.

If education is to be geared to the creation of public relations as a profession, then there needs to be a greater national study of the economic climate in which public relations operates. The majority of countries throughout the world carry out long term forecasting of their national needs for engineers, scientists, doctors, lawyers, accountants, etc. This forecasting is done either by a Government Department or by the appropriate professional body itself.

A result of the forecasting of the future manpower need is the creation of a complete education and training system to satisfy that need. This kind of discipline needs to be carried out by the public relations profession in most countries. Failure to do so will result in either a considerable short-fall in trained people, or alternatively, as has been suggested earlier, the creation of a public relations education system which satisfies personal or political vanity, rather than economic need.

The possibility of creating an international public relations qualification or examination was considered and rejected for the present, but it is felt that there can be a supplementary international qualification sponsored by IPRA on the creation and operation of international public relations programmes. This would be a supplementary qualification to a national public relations qualification.

It was further felt that in the short term there were three priorities for IPRA.

The first would be to create an international panel to check on national education and examination bodies, so that IPRA can approve national qualifications and thus grant accreditation so that such qualifications would be accepted not only by national public relations organisation, but by national education systems.

The second programme of action would be for IPRA to create an approved list of lecturers and tutors who can, through travelling lectureships, contribute to public relations education in countries other than their own. Since there is a particular need for such travelling educators for the Third World countries, discussion should also be held with UNESCO and other international agencies to examine the working and funding of such a scheme.

The third area which could be a prelude to the first two, would be for IPRA to sponsor an international conference forum for those throughout the world concerned with full time public relations education, and those from national bodies who are playing a vital role in encouraging and monitoring such education to meet to exchange views and ideas.

8

New Concepts in Internal Communications

Introduction

This session was chaired by MICHAEL MARSHALL, MP, Parliamentary Under-Secretary of State at the Department of Industry.

There were three speakers. MISS JULIA CLEVERDON, Director of Publicity at the Industrial Society, considered the subject both in theory and practice, with some emphasis on the role of the trade unions. BURKHARD JAHN, Director of the Public Relations and Information Department of the Germany Chemical Industry Employers' Association, approached the topic from a primarily managerial point of view. PROFESSOR ANDRZEJ KOZMINSKI, from the University of Warsaw, examined aspects of communication within enterprise in the socialist economy.

MISS JULIA CLEVERDON

Internal communications are of key importance to British industry today. They can be considered in three connections - as an aid to motivation, as a means of involving people more closely in large organisation, and as an element in the growing role of the trade unions.

The outside world believes that Britain is on a downward path. The Industrial Society takes quite a different view, seeing Britain ahead of the world - in the range and variety of its problems concerning the economy! With the establishment of the Welfare State, Britain is the first country to achieve the maxim 'Unto each according to his need'. It is consequently also the first country to experience the difficulty of trying to implement the other part of the maxim 'From each according to his ability'.

The old motives do not seem to work any more. People are no longer wage-slaves, driven to work by economic necessity. As Alex Jarratt, Chairman of Reed International, has said: 'It is exciting to be managing in a world where in just five years we have abolished both the stick and the carrot by law, but we still expect to get work from people'. In this situation we have to develop new concepts of communication, which will ensure that a rational understanding of the necessity of productivity and profitability in the national economy takes the place of a sense of personal financial need.

As industrial and other organisations become larger all over the world, it is increasingly difficult to give people a sense of personal involvement in the aims and achievements of their particular enterprise. It is no longer useful to spend thousands of pounds on house journals telling people that they are not mere cogs in a wheel – they can see a hundred other cogs sitting around them. The solution seems to be to concentrate on breaking down large work-forces into smaller, self-aware teams, with a leader through whom communication is possible. An important element in this is the avoidance of decision-making in remote headquarter offices with which workers feel little sense of contact. Involvement in decisions, and under-standing of the reasons for them, need to be passed as far down the organisational hierarchy as possible.

Within the growth in the power of the trade unions, it is vital to develop new and effective methods of communicating and consulting with them. There is a considerable misunderstanding of the control and influence exercised by trade union leaders in a free society. Unions are represented not by the traditional broadly-based pyramid, but by a pyramid upside-down. This means that setting up machinery to influence or persuade trade union officials or shop stewards is fundamentally a waste of time. Such people can certainly represent the views of their members (with whom the real power rests), but they cannot be positive carriers of a management message to the workers without themselves becoming identified with management.

As a two-sided, practical body, equally concerned with both managers and managed, the Industrial Society is much engaged in trying to provide answers to the problems indicated above. Where unions exist in an enterprise, it is important to recognise them and then communicate the various procedures and agreements in accordance with which the two sides will together do business. Trade union representatives must somehow be involved in the business and meetings with them should form a regular part of management activities – they should never be allowed to become something which only happens when 'negotiations' are needed. Real business problems should be on the agenda for such regular meetings; and discussion should be steered away from trivia like 'cold tea and toilets'. Participants need, for example, to be trained in the understanding of financial and economic information about the enter-prise, as well as in technical and staff questions.

Communication does not stop at the representative meetings; it needs to extend through supervisors to all employees. It is not a question of putting the unions out of business – but of putting management back into it. Apart from fostering contact between management, trade unions and employees, industrial leaders should encourage the unions themselves to hold meetings which develop their potential as positive contributors to the common purpose. Union meetings at parking lots are useless. But union meetings in proper conditions, with the active encouragement of management and with authoritative briefing about the problems to be discussed, can really contribute to the harmony, efficiency and prosperity which are so vitally needed in British industry and commerce today. Communication is really all about the understanding of a common purpose which aims at the creation of wealth in the widest sense of that word.

MISS CLEVERDON ended her talk by suggesting a slogan based on the initials of the title 'Public Relations World Congress'. The letters might be taken to stand for 'Participation', 'Representatives', 'We', and 'Common Purpose'.

BURKHARD JAHN

In the last few years, German enterprises have experienced legal institutional
changes which go further than changes occurring in other countries. They are the
result of laws introducing 'co-determination'- a phenomenon described in Great
Britain by the term 'industrial democracy'. Since 1951, the supervisory boards of
companies in the German coal, iron and steel industries have had to include equal
numbers of elected representatives of the workers and the owners. The relevant
legislation was the result of British initiatives for strengthening trade unions
and controlling vital industries in post-war Germany. In 1952 came the 'Works
Constitution Act' which was remodelled twenty years later. This provides for a
works council — a body of elected employees' representatives — in all German
enterprises with more than five people on the payroll. The same act gave employees
in all joint stock companies the right to elect one third of the supervisory board
members.

In 1976, a new co-determination act was introduced. This required equal representation of owners and employees on the supervisory boards of all companies in the
Federal Republic operating either as joint stock or limited liability companies,
and employing more than 2,000 people. Two or three of the workers' representatives
have to be external unionists, although owners have a small majority since the
chairman of the supervisory board has two votes.

Workers in Germany thus have legal rights far more advanced than their counter-
parts in other countries. Out of a population of 60 millions, 25 million are
engaged in active work. 21 million of them are employed workers and only 3 million
of these are not covered by co-determination legislation. 18 million — the vast
majority — can elect their representatives to various controlling bodies, right up
to the highest levels. This kind of industrial democracy operates on lines very
similar to those of ordinary politics. Since 1976 industrial election campaigns
have been frequent and have made substantial demands on companies in terms of
both time and money.

But there have never been any objections to co-determination from German employers.
They believe that it has contributed much to the social stability of the country.
However they do feel that institutional change has now reached a point where it
could not be taken further without amending the constitution and without in-
fringement of the principle of private ownership on which the Germany conception of
democracy is based. The unions would undoubtedly like to go further, but there
would be no parliamentary majority for anything more than parity co-determination.

German experience shows that, if industrial democracy is organised with a sense of
social responsibility, it will not conflict with the basic principles of information
theory and business organisation. Business enterprise remains achievement-
orientated. Internal communications reflect this orientation and it seems that
most employees favour the dissemination of information closely related to the jobs
they do.

Thanks to technological developments, the information media have been able to
create an almost perfect communication network. The difficulty is that the individual's ability to absorb all the information presented to him, both at work and
in his leisure time, tends not to keep pace with the technical advances. It is thus
very important to ensure that information is handled and circulated in the most
effective way.

The approach to information differs quite markedly among different categories of
employee. For example, blue-collar workers give higher priority to oral than to
written information. They want to be addressed in 'their language' and want infor-

mation about their immediate working conditions; other groups, like white-collar
workers, salaried employees and managerial staff, want more written information,
particularly when the content is factual. Germany industry therefore adapts its
methods and means of internal communications to a variety of target groups; and
the internal communication network is correspondingly complex.

Living in an open society means recognising and accepting the existence of
different interests. A free flow of information is vital in harmonising such
differences. For private enterprise, this means that its own internal information
services have to compete with those of other organisations such as the trade unions.

MR JAHN ended by noting that the German chemical industry might perhaps be more
progressive than others because it was traditionally an industry of innovation.
Experience in the Federal Republic of Germany generally might seem more advanced
than elsewhere. But in the long run, developments in other countries would go in
the same direction and the challenge would have to be taken up.

PROFESSOR ANDRZEJ KOZMINSKI

As a social scientist, PROFESSOR KOZMINSKI recorded two impressions on arriving at
the 8th Public Relations World Congress. Delegates meeting him tended either to
express disbelief in the existence of internal communications in Eastern Europe or
to suggest that his attendance at the congress would be helpful to him in widening
his experience of a subject with which he was likely to be relatively unfamiliar.
In fact, communications were an international feature of enterprise; they were a
basic function of management and could not be separated from it. Other
contributions to the success of an enterprise - management by objectives and the
like - were used very similarly in both socialist and market economies. But in
socialist economies social and political influences exerted a stronger effect.

PROFESSOR KOZMINSKI went on to explain that in the socialist economy the character
of the planning process is highly centralised. Social, political, economic and
technical objectives are all embraced within the activities of the Central
Planning Board which determines goals and the assignment of resources. There is a
strong hierarchical or vertical element in the system which makes the exchange of
information between the various levels of great practical importance. For example,
determination of wages stems from assessments made in the higher echelons.

The managerial decision-making process is subject to a variety of influences.
These include the Party (which has a constitutional right to intervene in
management), trade unions, local government (which has important rights in
connection with such matters as working hours and conditions), and the workers'
self-management council (which has to approve the overall production plan for the
enterprise). All these factors make the planning process both slow and difficult
but they do ensure a regular flow of information in many directions. The senior
manager in a given enterprise *can* take his own decision against these other
influences - but if he tries to do so too often the system will break down.

On the other hand, the manager is not isolated. There is much solidarity within
socialist enterprise. Managers have no interest in paying workers less. They are
anxious to produce and to ensure that a profit is made. But there is a tendency
towards over-employment because of the absence of certain pressures which would be
felt in a capitalist economy.

Inevitably, the management team is keenly conscious of circumstances outside the
enterprise. It is, indeed, involved in a kind of game with its environment, and
internal communications are a significant factor in its success or failure. The
environment itself is complex: The ministries which form part of it sometimes
have overlapping functions and this means that different messages to each may be
required so as to achieve a single objective. Furthermore, enterprises are
regularly visited by Commissions of Control, each of which needs to speak different
'languages' to different categories of worker.

The number of meetings, and the strong emphasis on personal contracts, may seem
excessive to an observer from a market economy. But it should be remembered that,
even in an increasingly industrial society, the rural cultural heritage of Eastern
Europe remains very strong. This depended essentially on informal, face-to-face
communication which might not always achieve absolute accuracy of understanding
but satisfied the need for personal exchange. In following this tradition, the
socialist economy may be less precise than its western counterpart, but the system
of communication certainly has closer connections with the historic roots of the
community.

Discussion

Several questions were put to PROFESSOR KOZMINSKI and the other speakers. One of
them related to the effect which the provision of information had on the
integration of a worker within the enterprise. Another of the speakers on the
panel, MR JAHN had said that a survey on this subject had been undertaken in the
Germany chemical industry: one of its findings was that a foreman or supervisor
was often not sufficiently informed in time to be useful. PROFESSOR KOZMINSKI
added that similar research was being done in Poland, where experience showed that
the foreman was a key factor. The structure of industry was so top heavy that in
1978 the status of the foreman declined. Measures were now being taken to correct
this situation. Specialist training in communications and in the general understanding of business was being given. The foreman's crucial role in the production
process had been recognised by giving him a certain discretion to grant bonus
allowances for improved productivity on his own authority.

Another question to the panel of speakers suggested that this might be the last
year of truly private enterprise: it seemed likely that there would be a
modification of aims in individual undertakings in the interest of the nation as a
whole. PROFESSOR KOZMINSKI commented that he thought that the efficiency of an
enterprise would soon be more important than it was now: industry *ought* to function
under a play of pressures reflecting the national interest. In his view, free
enterprise had to be equated with the satisfaction of egoistic needs and interests.
The importance of developing systems of self-management was now being recognised
all over the world. In Europe, instances of this were to be found in Germany,
Poland, Yugoslavia and elsewhere.

9

Public Relations and the
Transnational Consumer

Introduction

Speaking first was DR SANJAYA LALL, an Oxford economist with special knowledge of Transnational Corporations (TNCs) and developing countries, and their relationships. He gave a broad survey of the importance of TNCs and the criticisms levelled against them. He pointed out that it was not only goods that were in question, but also services, news and even entertainment. However, he came to the optimistic conclusion about the future that the problems will eventually be solved. He cited particularly drugs, which can be dealt with by the World Health Organisation (WHO).

Then ANNA FRANSEN, Vice-President of the International Organisation of Consumers' Unions and director of the Netherlands Consumers Union, put the case for consumer organisation, pointing out that they were weakest where they were most needed, in the developing countries. She made a strong plea for governments to prevent the export of goods which were not up to the safety and other standards required at home.

Finally, chartered engineer DR DAVID SHARP, general secretary of the Society of Chemical Industry, presented the case for manufacturing TNCs, but he declared that they should shed their sensitivity and demonstrate that they are open to constructive criticism.

Social Issues and Transnationals

Dr Sanjaya Lall

Senior Research Officer, Institute of Economics and Statistics,
Oxford University

The transnational corporation (TNC) is the most powerful single entity in the world economic scene today. The largest TNCs dwarf most Third World countries in size of production and income. They have the most effective and widespread international communication networks that span our globe. Their investment decisions can affect the future of many countries seriously, so seriously that the heads of the large corporations are received in foreign countries with more intentness of purpose (if not more pomp) than most heads of state.

Of course, it is not only their ability to invest and produce that is important. To a great extent the TNCs are also among the leading influences that shape our future. They dominate the high-technology industries which are searching the frontiers of science to produce new products and apply new techniques. They also dominate the high-marketing industries which provide the brand-named and power-fully promoted goods which consumers buy, but only in the affluent countries but, increasingly, in the poorest and remotest areas of the world. Thus, they influence - if not determine - what will be demanded tomorrow and how those needs will be fulfilled.

If the industrial transnationals are important to our economic life, there are now appearing other kinds of service transnationals, which are following the outward surge of the large producers, that are also of significance. One has only to look briefly around the City of London to see how transnational the financial world has become. Even the poor developing countries have set up banking networks overseas; the rich countries have seen their financial institutions grow into massive, almost uncontrollable empires. Then there are transnational insurers, hotels, publishers, consultants, builders, advertisers, restaurateurs and entertainers. Surely there is no need to spell out the enormous growth of the international communications industry.

It is hardly surprising that many countries, developed and developing, worry about the impact that such a concentration of power - economic, political and social - in entities beyond national control can have [1]. National governments seek to control the activities of transnationals by various fiscal, administrative and other ways; trade unions seek the same by calling for greater accountability; international bodies seek to institute international measures by recommending codes

---

(1)   For a more extensive discussion see S. Lall and P. Streeten,
        Foreign Investment, Transnationals and Developing Countries,
        London: Macmillan, 1971.

of conduct.   Several such codes are being prepared, some by associations of transnationals themselves, testifying to the felt need for some sort of regulatory
action beyond the normal legal and administrative procedures.

The protection of consumer interests is one important element of transnational
regulation. In the following discussion, I shall endeavour to sketch why it is
felt that consumer interests need to be protected, how transnationals should
respond to these interests, and how the communication/media industry can help in
furthering them. I will confine myself to the issues as they relate to the
developing countries.

Why should transnational companies raise special concern about consumer welfare in
the Third World?

A quick review of the literature [2] reveals two broad sets of issues which bother
the developing countries.   The first is the marketing and promotional practices
of the manufacturing firms which specialise in mass-produced consumer goods.   The
second is the socio-cultural influence of the service transnationals that control
the dissemination of information, news and entertainment.

The marketing and promotion practices of the consumer goods transnationals drew
three sets of criticisms.   First, at the most general level it is argued that
they subvert traditional patterns of life, consumption, religion and personal
relations.   Thus, the transnationals act as spearheads of the forces that import
alien influences into existing social forms, and present them in a glossy,
attractive package which is generally difficult to resist. While some modernising
influences are admittedly beneficial for progress, some others, which rock the
foundations of stable and old cultures, are painful and disruptive.

Second, closely related to the first, is a more specific criticism that the alien
form of consumption which is powerfully promoted by the transnationals is also one
which caters to the need of a narrow élite, which creates new and unnecessary wants
in societies where even the basic human needs of food, clothing and shelter are not
met, and which even diverts consumption from more health-giving to less nourishing
commodities.   There is clearly a great deal of truth in these arguments.   The
transnationals, by their very nature large scale producers of heavily promoted
products, base their success on a mixture of 'new' models and persuasive
advertising.   Since their main markets are in the rich countries, they generally
transfer the same products and techniques which they employ there to the poor
countries.   However, what is an item of mass consumption in the rich countries is
usually a luxury in the poor.   The transnationals are necessarily confined in their
activity to meeting and moulding the demands of the rich.

Since most consumption-goods industries can remain dynamic and profitable only by
introducing new products to fulfil old needs, or by creating new needs and then
the products to fulfil them, it is easy to see the point of the criticism that
transnationals specialise in meeting 'unnecessary' wants rather than basic needs.
Surely there is something grotesque in the contrasts in consumption and life styles
which we see in the poor countries, especially in the large cities where extreme
wealth and squalor both congregate with enormous waste and ostentation by the one
and near starvation by the other. It is not, however, clear whether the transnationals are really to blame. Given the existence of extreme inequalities of
income, the rich would be just as ostentatious and frivolous in the absence of

---

(2)   See R.J. Barnet and R. Müller, *Global Reach: The Power of the Multinational*
      Corporations, New York: Simon and Schuster, 1974, and K. Kumar, "A Working
      paper on the Social and Cultural Impacts of Transnational Enterprises'.
      Honolulu: The East-West Centre, 1978 (mimeo).

transnationals: Their consumption would simply take more 'traditional' forms.
Still, there is something to be said for 'traditional' luxury consumption in the
form of keeping retinues of servants as compared to 'modern' consumption in the
form of electronic gadgets and holidays in Europe.

However, transnationals not only give a modern content to the spending propensities
of the rich, they also sometimes divert the poor from necessary to harmful
consumption.   Thus, while a well-fed man can happily drink Coke and a well-off
mother safely provide sufficient baby food to her child under required sanitary
conditions, the messages that induce such consumption can cause damage to the poor
and the simple.   When poor workers cut down on basic nourishment to buy the
glamour of bottled aerated drinks, and when mothers stop breast feeding to provide
insufficient and unhygienic baby foods that promise her a smiling, healthy baby,
the innocent promotional message assumes a horrible dimension unknown in rich
countries [3].   The baby-food scandal is now sufficiently well known, so the
arguments need not be rehearsed here. The dangers of perverting tastes are obvious,
and the evidence is incontrovertible.

The third sort of criticism of manufacturing transnationals is related to the point
just made, but is even more cutting. Some firms deliberately distort information
about their products in order to sell more, even when correct information is
crucial to the direct well-being of the consumer. The prime example of this is the
pharmaceutical industry, where several studies have shown that transnationals
observe much laxer standards in advertising in poor countries than at home[4].
Thus, the indications for which drugs may be taken are much broader, and the
counter-indications far fewer and less specific. Such practices, while not
strictly illegal in that they conform to the laws of the country concerned, are
certainly unsocial and cynical. A number of instances of harm caused by over-
consumption or mis-consumption of drugs which were avoidable had correct
information been provided, have been recorded. The 'Smon' case in Japan, in which
millions of dollars of compensation are now being awarded against the drug
companies, is a recent case in point.

For these three sets of reasons, we can argue with some conviction that the
national consumer needs protection from the transnational manufacturer. As far as
the destruction of traditional cultures is concerned, unfortunately it is difficult
to think of solutions that do not involve drastic and inadvisable measures like
cutting off all socio-economic contacts with the developed world. As far as the
other problems are concerned, however, there are measures which national
governments, the transnational corporations and the media industry can undertake.
Unnecessary, luxury consumption can be prevented by the government by licensing and
tax measures.   Misleading advertising can be controlled by all the groups
concerned, even (or especially) in the absence of consumer groups, and wrong
advertising likely to cause harm should be banned by the government and strictly
regulated by the enterprises concerned.

---

(3)   See R.L. Ledogar, *Hungry for Profits,* New York: IDOC/North America,
       1975, and C. Medawar, *Insult or Injury?*, London: Social Audit, 1979,
       on the practices of U.S. and U.K. transnationals in the food and drug
       industries.

(4)   See Ledogar and Medawar, IDOC/North America. and M. Silverman, The Drugging
       of the Americas, Berkeley: University of California Press, 1976. It also
       seems that pharmaceutical multinationals sell drugs in developing countries
       which have been withdrawn from use in developed ones as being too dangerous.
       See S Lall and S Bibile. (1977). The Political Economy of Controlling Trans-
       nationals: The Pharmaceutical Industry in Sri Lanka. World Development.

Beyond this, of course, it would be foolish to ask transnationals to redress social and economic inequalities or to preserve traditional values. All these are subject to forces beyond the control of individual private enterprises, and critics often go too far in placing the blame for all social ills on the transnationals.

The media transnationals are criticised on grounds similar to those presented above. The news agencies, in particular, have been strongly attacked in several Third World meetings for distorting and filtering their product in a way that, at best, is unsympathetic to the conditions and aspirations of the poor countries and, at worst, is inimical to their development[5]. The fact that violent passions were aroused at the last UNESCO meeting on the subject testifies to how widely and strongly this view is held, and contested, by the poor and rich countries. It is probably correct that the interpretation and presentation of 'objective' events is as important as the content of the views, and it is likely that Western journalists approach events in poor countries with values learnt and blinkers placed in their own cultures. Furthermore, the news 'value' of certain events (disasters, scandals) is much greater, especially for unknown foreign countries, than of more mundane but also more important aspects of their socio-economic progress. Thus, the initial process of filtration and interpretation is repeated in the head offices of the international media, and the ultimate result may well be one which is neither sympathetic nor objective.

Similarly, the operations of international advertising and entertainment companies can be seen as imposing alien values, cultures and needs on the developing countries. Some studies have even found[6] that the imported messages place the local inhabitants lower on the social scale to the foreigners (who construct the messages), and so incude feelings of inferiority and inadequacy. In a sense, the media companies reinforce in their own sphere the dominance that the rich countries exercise over the poor in economic and political fields.

The influence of such transnationals is very difficult to regulate officially without undertaking strict censorship measures, which are undesirable for other reasons and probably impractical in any case (as the Third World news-system experiment has proved). The only agents who can undertake change are the companies themselves, most importantly by granting autonomy to their affiliates in developing countries and employing nationals at the higher levels. They can also undertake specific educational programmes to counter inbuilt prejudices and dogmas. And, finally, Third World countries should foster their own media enterprises to challenge the dominance of Western firms.

In this brief survey I have only touched upon the vast array of important social issues raised by the operations of transnational companies. I hope that I have elucidated at least some of the major concerns felt by developing countries, which have led them to ask for stricter Codes of Conduct and countervailing measures in the Third World to reassert their cultural and social autonomy. I do not see easy solutions to these problems, and the measures I have suggested are tame when compared with the processes that are under way. Still, one always keeps hoping that better understanding rather than more communication is by itself a step towards a solution.

---

(5)   See J. Somavia, 'The Transnational Power Structure and International Information'. *Development Dialogue*. (1976).

(6)   See K. Kumar. *Development Dialogue*. (1976). for references.

The Consumer's Point of View

Anna Fransen

Vice-President, International Organisation of Consumer Unions,
Netherlands

What is consumer interest? The answer is surprisingly simple: to be in a position to buy what you need and to make a selection from a variety of products of good quality at fair prices. This does not happen automatically. In this country Adam Smith discovered the invisible hand which was responsible for all consumers getting their share by competition on the market. We all know that markets are not always so competitive and that - even when the mechanism of competition is working - it does not solve the problems of poverty, ignorance and cultural lags. That is the reason why societies - generally represented by their governments - have turned to measures for supplementing and correcting the production capacity of the market economy.

Nowadays in almost all countries the consumption of goods and services by private households is served through two channels: the market economy and government-financed or public services. Within the market economy everybody pays for himself. We pay by taxes for the production of public services and individual taxation is not directly related to individual consumption.

In most western countries the part of the national income that is spent on public services is growing. I do not intend to go into details, but would like to pick out one main point: societies want to safeguard the satisfaction of certain needs for all consumers, without regard to their personal income or other individual possibilities. It is a cultural phenomenon, the proportions of which are typical for this century and - with exceptions - typical for rich countries.

Both sectors, the private as well as the public sector, should do their utmost to serve the consumer interest, and for walking on their toes both need stimuli and regular checking. As I am addressing now an audience that largely comes from private companies, I would like to focus your attention on the market economy.

Needless to say you will agree with me that from a consumer's point of view competition is far from perfect, not only the market economy has its imperfections but the labour and the money markets as well. Adaptation to new developments is late sometimes. Shortages and surpluses are not dealt with in an economical way. Adequate information about products is often lacking. Many goods and services are so complicated that most consumers are hardly able to evaluate them in a proper way. Moreover many products have side-effects, which cannot be foreseen. But although the weaknesses of the market economy are liable to criticism - and consumer organisation are very much inclined to do so - the market economy remains a most important system to ensure a high standard of living. That is why it is important to safeguard its good and to stop or correct its bad sides, to minimise its weaknesses, to keep it like a train on the rails in the right direction.

With apologies to others I would like to ask your special attention for two types
of guardian angels (maybe you will prefer the word watchdogs) who consider it
their duty to correct and counter-balance the imperfections of the market economy.
They are the national governments and national consumer organisations which both
have their own international ties.   National governments belong to UNO, the
Council of Europe, the EEC or other international organisations. Consumer
organisations work together internationally in IOCU (the International
Organisations of Consumers Unions) and in BEUC (the Bureau Européen des Unions de
Unions de Consommateurs). I have been invited here to speak to you on their
behalf.

What is my background and what do consumer organisations do? It is their task to
work in the interests of the individual consumer as well as consumers as a group,
and although their activities may differ, they usually supply consumers with
information about the market and products offered, both goods and services. This
is often done by comparative testing, because this method supplies the consumer
with relevant facts and practical help to enable him to make his choice. And
investigating products and markets, and helping consumers with information and
advice, in hearing their complaints and solving their problems, all phenomena and
abuses of the market become clearly visible.

That is why consumer oganisation do not confine themselves to testing and
supplying information. They also use their influence to put pressure on
governments for the benefit of consumers. Safety regulations, standards for
quality, guarantees, credit and competition policy are safeguards of substantial
parts of the general consumer interests. The growing interlacing of the world
caused consumer organisations not only to approach national governmnets, but also
to work together and to address international governmental bodies. Up to now this
has been most advanced with the EEC.

There is also international cooperation between consumer organisations with regard
to other aspects. We do a lot of joint testing. Joint investigation of
internationally known holiday-resorts has taken place. There is a regular exchange
of information about dangerous products, about consumer laws and their enforcement.
There are joint projects in the field of consumer education. Cooperation systems
between western countries are flourishing- for instance in Europe, and there are
ever growing links between consumer bodies in western and third-world countries.
All these international links have made very clear:

- that the consumer's position in third-world countries is mostly
  more awkward than in the western hemisphere, not only because
  he is poorer, but mainly because abuses of the market are more
  substantial and corrective agents (governments and consumer
  organisations) are weaker.

- that the possibilities of transnational corporations facilitate
  them to escape the consequences of activities undertaken by
  governments or consumer organisations to regulate market-
  consumer interests in any country, rich or poor.

These two facts form the basis of the demand for a Code for Consumer Protection,
arising from the Commission on Transnational Corporations of the UN.

Within IOCU we highly favour the introduction of such a code and I would like to
ask your attention for the following three points:

1.   Although all over the world specific objects and degrees of seriousness
may differ, consumer problems are very much alike. A general framework for a set

of rules is relevant for all consumers and all countries, but it is relatively more useful to poorer consumers and less developed countries.

In the world of consumer organisations there is a general concept for the outlines of such a framework. Its specification may differ from one country to another, but my personal opinion is that much differentiation, originating form tradition and habit, is not always necessary. In the long run more uniformity in the specifications will work to the advantage of both consumers and business, at least within large areas with some internal conformity, as for instance the EEC.

2.   Such a framework should include a set of rules for the behaviour of trade and industry and for governmental consumer legislation. Among other items, both should support and promote fair consumer information. The enforcement of rules is not less important than the rules themselves. In developing countries the enforcement of legislation is often a big problem. Transnational corporations, originating from developed countries with more reliable enforcement systems, meet lots of opportunities to avoid the effects of existing legislation in developing countries. A voluntary agreement not to make use of these opportunities, would be a very remarkable result of this conference.

3.   Consumer interest and consumer problems are universal. National legislation and circumstances can be specific. Transnational firms have a special opportunity of taking advantage of national differences to the disadvantage of the consumer. An international set of rules should therefore give special attention to transnational corporations and international trade.

I would like to refer to some examples that have arisen from our work as consumer organisations.

-       An international investigation by IOCU showed that a well-known American producer of pharmaceuticals exported a drug that he was only allowed to sell within strict limitations in the United States to at least 21 countries all over the world, mostly without any warning against the very severe risks;

-       A comparative test of motor helmets in the Netherlands proved that the checking system for the enforcement of safety regulations was less effective than in the UK. At the same time large numbers of British helmets, having failed the test in their home country, were exported to Holland;

-       British, Belgian, Dutch and German consumer organisations often cooperate in comparative testing of household appliances sold in their countries. The same happens with regard to motorcars. We often find - hidden under the same brands and types - differences in quality, safety and warranty showing quite clearly that lower standards in one of the countries attract imports of faulty goods from the other three, if higher standards and/or better enforcement are applied in those countries;

-       In most western countries there is some system of government policy with respect to consumer prices or at least food prices. In spite of the fact that these systems differ, there is a general rule that reasons should be stated for a rise in prices. It goes without reasoning that transnational firms have special opportunities to manipulate with transfer prices;

- Transnational corporations are often very large firms who
  act in several markets. These two characteristics give
  plenty of opportunities for monopolistic practices; sometimes this is supported by patents as is the case for
  example with pharmaceutical products. Several consumer
  organisations, among them BEUC, studied prices of drugs
  in a number of countries. These studies showed very
  clearly that high prices in some markets are possible -
  and very profitable for the manufacturers - by artificial
  international market segmentation;

- The transfer of defective products over borders, the
  making of profits by unfair pricing, these abuses of the
  market are outrivalled by activities like selling milk
  powder to Asian or African mothers in poor countries as
  a substitute for natural baby food. When I heard for the
  first time that companies were advertising this I personally
  thought that it was an accidental stupidity caused by lack
  of knowledge of cultural and hygienic conditions in
  tropical countries. But from my contacts with Asian
  consumer organisations I got to know that this special
  activity is no exception, that there are lots of similar
  campaigns and that the consequences are sometimes awful
  and often serious. The promotion of products which are
  suitable for the American or European way of life in
  countries where there is neither the prosperity nor the
  culture to digest them without damage, is easier for
  transnational corporations because they can rely on their
  widely known brand-names.

Summary

Transnational corporations have more possibilities:

- to restrain competition
- to avoid price and tax regulations
- to profit from national differences in product or safety
  standards
- to distort national consumption patterns.

It has been proved over and over again that transnational companies not only have
the opportunities, but also make use of them to their own advantage, often to the
disadvantage of consumers, mostly in the lower-income brackets or countries.

As countervailing power, national governments should also think "transnational"
and should be more willing to accept international agreements, international
standards and even international enforcement systems. In particular there must
come an end to the existing habit in most western countries, that production for
home-consumption (especially food) has to adhere to meticulous standards, but that
at the same time there are no rules for the export of any misfits, however
unsuitable for use, unsafe or dangerous.

Consumer organisations, too, should think and act more transnationally than they
actually do, but I had better tell that to another audience.

Transnational corporations, individually and together, should reconsider their
practices and try to put limits on undesirable effects by mutual agreements,
careful screening and responsible behaviour.

The Transnational Company

Dr David Sharp

General Secretary, Society of Chemical Industry

1.   The transnational companies – that is to say, companies operating in more
than one country and usually major industrial companies – may be divided very
roughly into three broad types:

    (i)   those companies that consciously promote their name or brand image;

    (ii)   those companies whose international activities are generally known,
certainly to the discerning customer, but who tend to trade and
promote companies or brand names more closely associated with their
country of operations rather than promote their international name
and brand image;

    (iii)   those international holding companies who do not seek to promote
the name of the holding company and whose ownership of companies is
not well known.

Examples of the first category include most of the major oil companies, such as
Shell and BP, many chemical companies including ICI and Hoechst, and at least one
major automobile company, Ford.

The second category – those companies who do not seem much to promote their
international image, but who are nevertheless well known as international
companies include Unilever in the food and detergent areas and, in the automobile
industry, General Motors. Whilst many consumers will know that, say, Birdseye and
Walls are subsidiaries of Unilever, both Birdseye and Walls trade very much as
independent companies and promote their own brand image. Similarly, it is
generally known that General Motors Companies include Opel in Germany and Vauxhall
in Great Britain, but the cars are sold as Opels or Vauxhalls – not as GM.

Perhaps the best example of the third category is British American Tobacco or BAT.
BAT have diversified into all sorts of areas but is not well known as a transnational company. Their retail stores include Gimballs in the US and Sachs of
Fifth Avenue as well as department stores in West Germany. The Group also owns
Wiggins Teape in paper and Yardleys in cosmetics, as well as, of course, as its
tobacco interests. In cosmetics, BAT manufacture in 38 countries and sell in 143,
but who links Yardleys with Benson and Hedges?

2.   The advantages of promoting a well known international name are obvious.
It is hoped that the consuming public – and we are all consumers – will employ
lateral thinking – if the company has made its name in one country it will carry
it with it into another; similarly if a reputation has been made in one field and
the company moves into another, it is hoped that the established reputation in one

field will "rub off" on another.

Similarly, if a new enterprise is to be set up in a new country, particularly in the Third World, confidence would be built up if the company is known and seen to have the resources of a major international behind it.

3.   But this promotion of the single brand name and of the wide ranging trans-national major company does have disadvantages. The consumer knows that he or she is dealing with one major company and would expect that some standard of service throughout – and may not get it. Often faults will be ascribed to the major company that are not its concern strictly speaking at all. For example a petrol station selling say, BP, will be expected to show a certain standard of service which it may be difficult, if not impossible, for BP to influence if it does not own the petrol station concerned. But in what we have come to call "consumerism" by which we mean dealing with organised consumers, the large well recognised multi-national company may be in a more vulnerable position than the large national company or, *a fortiori,* the small national company.

Looked at from the stand point of the organised consumer, the transnational company has the reputation of being concerned with its own transnational affairs rather than with the well being of the country in which it is operating. The very size and efficiency of good transnational companies give rise to that mixture of admiration, envy, distrust, and antagonism that we all know so well. It evokes the "us and them" approach.

4.   Before going further into this, let us first of all consider how trans-national companies operate. In this, of course, they differ not only from each other but also from time to time. No large companies have a static organisational structure – there is a continually evolving one. Changes may be found to be beneficial and are persisted with; other changes may prove not to be and so are altered or discontinued.

By no means all transnational companies are large but by definition all such companies sell in a variety of countries; to a greater or lesser extent they may manufacture in other countries and they may assemble manufactured parts in another country. Frequently there is a mixture of all three. The motor car industry is an obvious example of this. It is reasonably well known that Ford manufacture their Granadas in Western Germany and import them ready assembled into this country. Vauxhall assemble a number of cars here from parts made in the Opel factories in Western Germany. Oil companies may well export some of their products and may well establish local refineries. In chemicals, ICI, as is well known, operates in this country through a number of product divisions. It has, however, a number of companies in other countries which serve both as a marketing organisation for all ICI divisions – a national selling company – and as the local manufacturing unit. Such ICI companies have been established in all Western European countries and in the main manufacturing countries round the world. In Western Europe ICI has an organisation known as ICI Europa, which has a general coordinating role, responsibility for the national selling companies and also for the manufacture of a number of products throughout Western Europe. ICI Europa is, therefore, partly a coordinating and partly an operating unit. ICI and Bayer really make a matrix organisation work. Both companies have some directors with a vertical responsibility for a range of products together with a horizontal responsibility for a particular geographical area.

This pattern of horizontal selling organisations in other countries for a range of products is a fairly common one, although where manufacturing is also carried out arrangements need to be made under the matrix so that, where appropriate, international product considerations are taken into account by the territorial organisation.

5.   British and Anglo-Dutch transnational companies give a substantial degree
of freedom or autonomy to their subsidiaries in other countries. As regards
Unilever, in 1973 Sir Ernest Woodroofe, at that time Chairman, in a publication
entitled "The Social Role of Multi-national Enterprises", said:

"Clearly, decisions taken at headquarters should be kept to essentials and local
management should be given wide independence within guidelines laid down by the
centre. These guidelines will be the international policies of the company such
as the kind of products the company wants to make and sell, marketing strategies
for international products in contrast to purely local products, the objectives
for yield on capital employed, the policy on local borrowing. In the case of
Unilever, these policies have wide tolerances within which national managements
can operate. To aim to give to local management as much independence as is
feasible is not just a sop to national sensitivities. If the majority of the
local management are nationals, as they should be, then it is sheer commercial
commonsense to reserve to the centre decisions on major investment and on top
appointments, and the authority to insist on certain standards of competence and
integrity of management and on the quality of its products".

It will be noted that Sir Ernest refers specifically to reserving for the centre
decisions on major investment and on top appointments. These two areas would be
quoted by all major transnational companies. Rather than "major investment" ICI
suggested that finance and the capital programme should be controlled from headquarters, but also group strategy. This is echoed by Sir Ernest Woodroofe who
refers to the imposition of international standards of operation by which he said
he did not simply mean standards conceived by headquarters, but by the input from
all countries of operation. In the case of ICI the senior executive would often,
but not always, be a national of the country concerned.

6.   One area that is controlled from the centre is what might be called
financial probity. One person in a senior company who had better remain nameless
talked about the "export of morals". Just as the Colonial powers with their
missionary zeal prohibited such indigenous religious customs as the burning of
widows or female circumcision, so the transnational companies have imposed their
own standards of probity on their subsidiaries. The payment of backsheesh and the
establishment of "slush funds" is definitely out. It will be noted that certain
transnational companies whose names are household words have withdrawn from
operation in a number of countries, not necessarily confined to the Third World
countries, on what may reasonably be believed to be these grounds.

7.   Turning now to how the transnational companies deal with what we have
come to call "consumerism" by which is meant the coordinated action of consumers,
the persons to whom I have spoken have drawn a sharp distinction between the
consumer as the customer and the consumer movement. As a person in one large
company remarked the average consumer votes with his or her feet and that the
organised consumer unit really speaks for a small fraction of consumers with
(my words not hers) "bees in their bonnets". Someone in another major transnational company said that consumerism is usually a single facet of the argument
on which attention is particularly focussed. Perhaps the organised consumer
movement may be divided into the following categories:

    (i)   Campaigns for honest value - against undue packaging, presentation,
           advertising and promotion.

    (ii)   The environmental lobby, and, closely linked with it -

    (iii) the conservation lobby and -

(iv)   the health and safety lobby.

(v)   Objective tests and value for money assessments carried out by consumer associations.

(iv)   Legal protection of the consumer; labelling; responsibility for supply of faulty goods; and related matters.

These various aspects of the consumer movement have one thing in common - they all tend to put the manufacturer, including the large transnational company, on the defensive.

8.   Dealing very briefly with (i) I remember Sir Ernest Woodroofe telling me many years ago now that when Unilever was up against considerable pressure to reduce costs of promotion of washing powders and the like it was enjoined to produce a product which became known as "Square Deal Surf". This was to be packed in plain packages to cut out all frills. Having done this the then President of the Board of Trade said to Sir Ernest: "Now you will promote this properly won't you?!" Which I think encapsulates the whole problem.

The environmental lobby, and I use this term with no disrespect; I like to describe myself as a member of it anyway - has had signal successes. The multinational companies are having to operate within widely differing philosophies in different countries in this important respect. At risk of over simplification of a complex problem I would suggest that the approach and attitude is markedly different in the United Kingdom from the Continental European Countries, and the USA in the following respects:

The Continental legal system is based on the code Napoleon - it is dirigiste. Thus in the important matter of discharge of effluent into water courses or of toxic substances into the air, the immediate Continental reaction is that all cases should be treated alike - that limits should be laid down for controlling the discharge of all noxious substances into the environment. This approach has found its echo in the USA although the legal system in the USA is based on that of Great Britain. This seems to have arisen because of the traditional hostility between big business and Government in the United States. This has led in the United States to a very serious situation. On 12th March 1979 Monte Throdahl, Group Vice-President of the Monsanto Corporation, speaking to a meeting of the Society of Chemical Industry in London, commented that American legislation concerned with pollution increasingly uses the word "nil", which to a chemist has no meaning. As analytical techniques develop so it is possible to detect smaller and smaller amounts of substances. Whereas detecting parts per million was difficult some years ago, now parts per billion or parts per trillion - are now relatively common place. Therefore a chemist never says "nil" but "less than a certain amount as determined by an approved method of analysis". Unfortunately, the dialogue between Science, Industry and Government in the USA has broken down to such an extent that this approach does not seem to be possible whereas it is standard practice in the United Kingdom. We are very fortunate indeed in the United Kingdom that we have had an Alkali Act for over 100 years which enshrines those famous words: "Best practicable means". The Alkali Act has led to collaboration between the Government Department concerned, the alkali inspectorate and industry. The environmental lobby tends to have criticised this approach recently, claiming that the inspectorate was too lenient. Be that as it may, it has worked extremely well and the same approach has found its way into the Health and Safety at Work Act in which the phrase used is: "So far as is reasonably practicable".

Similarly in dealing with toxic matter discharged into the environment, the UK approach is to determine what should be allowed or not allowed by the total effect on the environment concerned and that standards should be set for the *environment* rather than for the discharges to it.

In British eyes it is nonsense to insist that an effluent discharged into a small inland stream should have the same standard set as one discharged into a large tidal estuary. The environmental conditions over a windswept island such as Great Britain differ very markedly from those of a continental land mass and yet the EEC harmonisers would wish to harmonise legislation so that all discharges are treated equally. This is arrant nonsense and I am glad to say that the UK Government has fought a very spirited battle, so far successfully, in the EEC against this dirigiste approach. Similarly the requirements for exhaust emissions from motor vehicles in California, where there is a problem of temperature inversion and strong sunlight, differ very markedly from those of Great Britain or for that matter most parts of Continental Europe. It is, however, in the field of energy requirements that the shoe is beginning to pinch. Speaking to the Republic of Ireland's Section of the Society of Chemical Industry on 30th March 1979 the President, Mr P I Walters, who happens also to be a Managing Director of BP, said that "let us also suppose that rational anticipation unblocks the policies, particularly in the USA, which prevent internal energy prices from rising to world levels and which prevent on social or political grounds the more rapid development of resources such as US coal, nuclear world wide, or oil and gas in the Third World Countries". For "social or political grounds" read: "the effects of the consumer and environmental lobbies". There is certainly an increasing, necessary and welcome tendency for energy policies to be considered on a transnational scale and this involves the transnational companies in the energy business very much indeed. The fear is, as was expressed by Mr Walters, that the very understandable concern by the consumer, environmental, and conservation lobbies may so delay necessary action to deal with a developing shortage situation that there will be an energy crisis which we shall have brought on ourselves, despite clear indications of its happening. It must be conceded that the conservationists have a very strong case, but it must also be accepted, again to quote Mr Walters, that modern industrial society has come to expect a growth economy and too rapid a move away from such an economy could lead to large scale unrest. The transnational companies have a task to persuade Government and supra Governmental organisations of these hard facts and this will call for much delicate diplomacy at the highest level. Apart from this the facts need to be put before the informed public so that public opinion can be established on a rational rather than emotive basis. Independent learned societies, such as that of which the present author is General Secretary - The Society of Chemical Industry - can and do much in this area.

9.   Independent testing carried out by consumer associations is a very sensitive area. These associations have the benefit of publicity. For strange masochistic reasons the United Kingdom, particularly, glories in knocking its own industry. (Think back for example to the publicity that surrounded the failure of the turbines in the Queen Elizabeth the II when she was new. Surely no other country would have denigrated itself to that extent). A major problem is that the consumer testing associations, with the best will in the world, can rarely have the expertise and the means available to carry out proper objective tests. As a senior person in Marks and Spencer said to me, for example: "We know far more about textiles and textile testing than any consumer association will ever know". This is undoubtedly true, but it is very difficult to get across since there is always the danger of the "big brother knows best" charge. The other side of the coin is that large organisations seem very reluctant to change their ways and to meet reasoned constructive criticism. Many of us might think for example that the Metro and bus and tram systems in continental cities are far better organised than in London. But try to persuade London Transport of this! The answer surely is for the large transnational firms to be receptive and to be seen to be receptive of sensible constructive criticism and to deal with it in a responsible way. For large

transnational companies to be successful they must be receptive of constructive criticisms.

10.   Finally, on the matter of consumer protection legislation, labelling and the rest, the major transnational companies are in the forefront in most cases of ensuring that legislation of this kind is sensible and is followed. The role of the national and international standards organisations is important here. One has seen it applied to petrol – it is easy to forget that only comparatively recently has petrol been purchasable on declared octane rating. One will, it is to be hoped, see this principle applied increasingly in other areas such as toys and electrical goods manufacture and imports to name only two. In many such areas the interests of the consumer and of the major transnational companies are completely at one in ensuring that good quality safe goods are not priced out of the market by inferior and dangerous imports.

11.   The subject we have been considering is a vast one with many ramifications, but to endeavour to sum up: The transnational companies are so established that their operating companies in different countries react to local requirements in this area. At present the companies have to react on a transnational basis to organised consumer representation only in a relatively small number of areas, but it seems likely that in increasingly response at transnational level will become necessary.

DISCUSSION

Summarising what the speakers had said, the main points made by the chairman, Harry Shepherd, were as follows:

Dr Lall said that when foreign culture patterns were imposed on a country, the good was driven out by the bad; that advertising creates new and unnecessary wants, diverts consumption from good traditional foods to less nourishing commodities.

Anna Fransen pointed out the weakness of Third World countries and said that the Third World was more exposed to possible bad practice by transnational corporations than developed countries. There was need for a code.

Dr Sharp described how the transnationals organise themselves and appealed for a sense of responsibility.

S Pandit, Phillips (India) Limited, India, said he has worked for 23 years for a multi-national and asked Dr Lall and Miss Fransen whether he had lived for 23 years 'in sin'. He said he did not have a bad conscience. He had played a significant part in persuading his company to merge its corporate objectives with national ones. And he had been brought up with ethical standards. His question was: 1. how is it the exclusive province of multi-nationals to misbehave? Nationals do so, too. If multi-nationals are forbidden certain activies, nationals can behave even worse, without the example of multi-nationals. Who is to decide what the traditional pattern of life is? It is constantly being changed by voters and politicians. 2. There is wasteful consumption not dedicated to needs but to glamour. But who is to judge? Can this be attributed only to multi-nationals?

Dr Lall expressed his sympathy with the speaker. Charges against transnational corporations were inevitable. But the questioner was at cross-purposes. No-one was trying to defend national companies, but any misbehaviour of TNCs was more worrying.

Miss Fransen said she spoke only of consumer organisations, whose purpose is to criticise and monitor bad practices. The scale of TNCs misbehaviour was worse than national companies.

Dr Sharp said that TNCs were the victims of their own communications success and expected Third World countries to absorb in one generation what it has taken the West centuries.

Jan D M Kock, Director, Public Relations, Naarden International, The Netherlands, said that producers and consumers are an entity, with one dependent on the other. Yet consumer oganisations isolate themselves, meeting producers as opponents. Regarding producer/consumer relations, there is no need to create a communications platform to remove suspicions of each other's intentions. The objective should be to restore amity between producer and consumer, and to convince consumer organisations that the producers' main interest is to serve the consumer.

The chairman pointed out that consumers and producers meet in the market place.

Miss Fransen said that in fact the entity has two sides, two platforms. Consumer organisations and producers do play a public role in society. Consumer organisations are still somewhat antagonistic, because they are new and still finding their feet. They could change in the future, but differences in roles will continue.

Dr Sharp believed that the consumer movement, to have teeth, must be a bit belligerent. They have drawn attention to details that otherwise could have escaped notice.

Miss Fransen pointed out that consumer oganisations criticise Government and public services as well as industry. In Third World countries, consumer organisations are not well enough advanced. There often are bigger problems and less possibility to do anything. National merchants may also be cheating customers in ways which would not be tolerated in the West. This should correct itself, and industry has admitted that well-behaved companies are better off when there is adequate regulation.

Peter L Walker, BOC International Limited, London, said that TNCs were carefully regulated in countries where they operated. He questioned whether a code of consumer protection would have most value if it applied to everyone, since the most effective regulating agency is the national government.

Dr Lall said he was not a great believer in codes and did not think they would have much impact. National governments can exert the most force.

Miss Fransen deplored the fact that goods which do not comply with national rules can be exported. While all national governments had legal systems, the Third World have the least satisfactory ones.

Dr Sharp agreed with Peter Walker. Regarding, for example, unsafe electrical goods, it was difficult to apply standard where measurement was not possible. The UN Draft Code does not touch on questions of switch production from one country to another, which can have a drastic effect on the country concerned.

The Chairman said that TNCs are accused of exploitation if they charge high prices and of dumping if they charge low prices.

He then invited the speakers to make one point each they considered to be of paramount importance.

Dr Sharp said that TNCs should demonstrate that they are open to constructive criticism and welcome the setting up of international standards, particularly in drugs.

Miss Fransen said all national governments should make rules of protection for consumers. Goods not up to reasonable standards should be forbidden to be exported. Governments may protect home markets, but they do not care about the consumer abroad.

Dr Lall said he was optimistic about future relations between TNCs and the consumer in developing countries. There are difficulties from some industries, but in many cases the problems will be solved. This was particularly true in the case of drugs, where the World Health Organisation (WHO) can play a decisive part.

10

Computerised News
Implications for Public Relations

Introduction

The fifth concurrent session on the 24th May at Salters Hall, demonstrated the
challenges and opportunities facing public relations practitioners with the growth
of computerised news technology.

With the assistance of live demonstrations of computerised "hardware" the speakers,
Roy Bright and David Steinberg, covered two major areas in detail.

Mr Bright, Head of the Post Office's Prestel International Operations,
demonstrated the Prestel system - which brings information on topics ranging from
news and sport to business and financial data to the screen of a modified
television receiver at the push of a button. The receiver, being linked to its
computer by an ordinary telephone line, can be installed in home or office. Its
information is thus, as Mr Bright showed, at the disposal of the public as well as
business and financial users.

Mr Bright gave practical demonstrations of how information is put into the system
and how viewers select it.

Mr Steinberg, President of PR Newswire in New York, outlined the changes which
computers are bringing to newspaper newsroom operations and stressed that, like it
or not, sooner rather than later, "public relations must become 'computer
compatible' with the press".

The practical demonstration simulated the flow of public relations copy from the
originating office, through a computerised newswire to editorial offices.
Equipment for the demonstration provided by International Management and
Operations Systems (IMOS) of London consisted of two Delta VDU's (View Data Units),
machines fitted with a television-like screen on which the text comes up as the
operator taps it out on the typewriter-like keyboard below. Push buttons on the
keyboard make it possible to correct, edit or rearrange the text as desired.

The reporter or public relations consultant can thus write and edit his story,
correct spelling, change, insert, or delete words or whole paragraphs as he
wishes.

Equipped with a lightweight portable version, Mr Steinberg said, a reporter on
assignment at a football stadium for example, can connect direct to his office
computer using any nearby telephone.

At the Salters Hall demonstration, the text of the message was fed into a PDP8
mini-computer in the IMOS head office whence it was transmitted back by an

ordinary telephone line, to a high-speed printer in the hall.

The PDP8 is the heart of the widely-used Newsmaster System, developed by the Associated Press and now working in more than 40 news operations around the world.

Equipment for the Prestel demonstration was provided by the Post Office.

The Chairman of the session was Alfred Geiringer, Chairman and Managing Director of Universal News Services in London, the editorial headquarters of Universal News International (UNI), an association of national business newswires (including PR Newswire) over which public relation material is transmitted worldwide. The convenor of the session was Mrs Nesta Hollis, Executive Director of the Hollis Press and Public Relations Annual and publisher of the Hollis PR Weekly.

After Mr Geiringer's welcome, and the speeches and demonstrations, the session was thrown open for questions, which ranged freely over aspects of both systems.

Prestel

Roy Bright

Head of Prestel International Organisations, British Post Office

The British Post Office developed viewdata, as it was then known, in the early
1970s and more recently has registered the name 'Prestel' as the trade mark for its
Public Service in this country. From the beginning the prime objective was to
produce a system which could be marketed to the public at large, rather than the
more traditional computer activities which have been aimed at the specialist or
professional users. Thus our 'Prestel' service offers two major improvements on
conventional computer-based operations.

>   Ease of use
>   Low cost

Following a feasibility study it was decided that the development of the service
would need to involve the active participation of three key parties, namely the
Post Office, the television manufacturing industry and a wide variety of
organisations interested in disseminating information to the residential and
business communities in the United Kingdom; this latter category is often
referred to as the Information Industry. In order to achieve the meaningful
developments of such a tri-partite system it was essential that an experimental
operation be created and this was duly introduced in January 1976 as the 'Pilot
Trial'. Initially, Post Office acting as a catalyst, devoted considerable effort
to demonstrating an experimental system to a wide variety of business interests and
shortly after the response became spontaneous, thus by the end of that year some 80
companies had become Information Providers to the Pilot Trial. At the same time
television industry were devoting research and development effort to the creation
of suitably circuitry which could enable the television receiver to offer viewdata
facilities.

In September 1978 a Market Trial was commenced which has involved the creation of a
User Sample drawn from both business and residential sectors numbering in excess of
1000 participants able to access a database of over 120,000 frames of information.
In March 1979 a limited Public Service operating in London only was introduced
prior to an expansion to serve other cities in the United Kingdom to take place in
the last quarter of 1979.

These Public Service arrangements entail the establishment of a series of Prestel
computer centres serving their local communities but all linked to a central
educating centre, Up-Date Centre, which acts as the central point for editing new
frames, amendments of existing frames, etc.

A simple example of the ease of use of the system typically involves the user in
operating a hand-held keypad which in addition to the television controls contains

a set of twelve buttons, ten numeric and two control buttons marked with a star and a square. One of the features of the Prestel receiver is that it is equipped during manufacture with an automatic dialler which the user initiates by pressing the Prestel button on the keypad. Thus this automatic dialler process is monitored by the normal telephone signals such as dialling tone, being relayed over the television loudspeaker. The computer responds by interrogating the terminal identifier which again is built into the receiver and is unique to each terminal. Having satisfied itself that this is a registered user it sends a Welcome Page to the user inviting further interrogations. The user is then able to make selections from an index structure based on a ten branch tree design and each successive level focuses the enquiry on to more detailed information such as News, Sport, Business material, each in turn broken down into many sub-topics.

The first three levels of the index tree are devoted to such headings but from the fourth level onwards the Information Providers take responsibility for any subsequent indexing as well as the information pages they are supplying. This is indicated by the identity shown in the top left hand corner of every page which refers to the name of the company responsible for providing that page. The Information Providers are able to supply such material on-line to the database from Prestel editing terminals located on their own premises which use the same techniques as dialling the computer centre as described above, but in addition following a further security check are allowed access to the pages which they are entitled to enter or modify. Where appropriate this enables Information Providers to up-date information several times a day if required. Currently 160 organisations are acting as Information Providers supplying material ranging alphabetically from Accident Prevention to Yoga and encompassing up to 1000 separate topics.

Mention was made earlier of low cost. The cost elements for a typical user consist of a modified television receiver, which at today's prices could amount to £1000, but in the next two or three years to drop to nearer a 20 per cent mark-up on the price of a normal television set. Usage charges include the price of a normal local telephone call plus a Prestel charge based on the duration of the connection time to the computer. A third charge determined by the owners of the pages (the Information Providers) could range from 0.5p to a maximum of 50p, though in practice the majority of pages in the system currently are priced at around 1 or 2p while a large number of them are offered free of charge. The Information Providers are themselves charged by the Post Office on the basis of an annual subscription plus an annual rental for each frame which they use in displaying their information.

Unlike Prestel, the teletext services operated by the BBC and IBA (known as Ceefax and Oracle respectively) do not incur the user in any charges other than the additional cost of the receiver. An important decision made in the mid 1970s was that the special circuitry necessary to translate the in-coming signals into alphanumeric text should have common standards with Prestel, enabling the customer to receive all three services if he wished. Whereas Prestel can offer a technically unlimited range of information the teletext services are restricted to approximately a few hundred pages per channel, due to the technical constraints created by transmitting the information via the air waves. This results in the teletext information being concentrated on only the most popular topics such as News headlines, Weather forecasts and major events, whereas Prestel can offer all this plus a range and depth of material far beyond the scope of a limited database. In practice all three parties regard their activities as complementary, rather than competitive.

Another important distinction between teletext and Prestel is the availability of interactive facilities in the Prestel service. This results from the use of normal

telephone lines by means of which the user is able to 'talk back' to the computer
as well as receive information sent out from the Central point. Ultimately it is
planned that Prestel will offer interactive services including messages and
calculations. Already the present service offers a facility known as the Customer
Response Frame, which enables any Information Provider who wishes to include in
his material a pre-formatted message which allows the user to key-in numeric
information if they do not have a full alphnumeric keyboard at their disposal. A
number of organisations are using this facility to encourage users to answer
questionnaires, indicate preferences and even place orders. An interesting feature
of the ordering process is that the Information Provider may include an invitation
for the user to quote credit card identity, resulting in the Information Provider
being able to act on and complete the transaction by quoting the users credit card
identity.

There are a number of interesting features designed into Prestel software, one is
the ability for Information Providers to instruct the system to restrict access to
their pages to nominated users only. This Closed User Group facility can be
employed either to restrict access to confidential information belonging to a
company to its own employees, or alternatively to enable an organisation to
restrict information access to its clients.

Turning briefly to international developments a number of overseas tele-
communication authorities have entered into contracts with the British Post Office
in order to acquire the computer software and know-how so that they may set up
their own viewdata systems; these include West Germany, Holland, Switzerland and
further afield, Hong Kong. In addition the British Post Office has licenced
Insac - a British Company - to use Prestel know-how in developing the USA market.

This international interest and commitment demonstrates the importance attached to
viewdata worldwide and should ensure a growing number of countries will be able to
offer similar services to their business and residential communities in the next
few years.

Computerised News Handling

David Steinberg

President, PR Newswire, New York

In the thousands of years since the first scribe chiseled his first word on a clay tablet, there have been only three innovations in printing and communicating the written word significant enough to alter the course of history. The first came 500 years ago with the introduction of moveable type. The second arrived 100 years ago as familiar telegraph and telephone poles began parading across the countryside. The third, barely ten years old, is the application of computer technology and tele-communications to the editorial operations of the world's press and publishing industry.

Since you are very much a part of this vital industry, it is certain that your own professional activities (as well as what you read in the press) will be affected by the technology now sweeping press communications and publishing throughout the world.

I am not here to confound you with the arcane scientific jargon of the engineers or dazzle you with the speed and versatility of the latest technology. It is my privilege to help to acquaint you with what these wonders do in practical, everyday terms and how they are likely to change your press relations activities, your relationships with your clients and management and even how you will write your news releases.

Like it or not, public relations must become "computer compatible" with the press.

Before you presume we will be exploring the future, let me assure you we are examining the present and the recent past. For example, today in the United States there are more computers in use at newspapers (approximately 2,000) than there are daily newspapers (just under 1,800). Every major wire service in the world is automated totally or to an ever-increasing degree. Ten years ago there was not a single electronic editing terminal to be seen in a newsroom - today the number of CRT/VDTs in daily newspapers in the United States is approaching 20,000. In fact, the manufacturers and salesmen of such equipment are beginning to face a saturated market and are wondering what they will do for an encore.

What accounts for this rapid proliferation of such expensive and sophisticated hardware?

Quite simply, apart from the necessary speed and production efficiency which it engenders, the computer brings order to chaos in the newsroom. As modern communications techniques shrink the globe, the torrent of information flooding editorial offices has all but drowned the staff. Electronic processing makes the floodtide manageable. Editors conveniently and quickly know what stories they have on hand and can determine and find what they wish to use in the next edition.

The computer makes possible immediate high-speed receipt and transmission of news and vast, compact and instantaneously retrievable storage. Its swift, silent efficiency reduces confusion, scales mountains of paper and even prevents waste-baskets from overflowing – since electronic copy can be wiped from existence with a single keystroke. In fact, some systems do not require an editor to strike a key. If a story is ignored by editors for a set numbers of hours, it is automatically destroyed to make room for later ones – and you had better hope your news release isn't one of the earlier pieces.

The most visible sign of automation in the newsroom is the ubiquitous CRT (VDT-VDU) – the primary input device for original copy. Seated before its TV-like screen, a reporter can write and edit his story and correct his spelling and typographical errors. He can change, insert, delete or move individual characters, words, phrases, lines, sentences, paragraphs and even larger blocks of copy. He can "search" through his text electronically to find, change, kill or replace certain words or phrases. He may make wholesale revisions or combine his story with another.

Correspondents in distant bureaux also may write, edit and enter their reports into the system from their CRTs, which usually are linked to the home office computer by private wire facilities. A reporter on assignment at a soccer stadium now may carry a light-weight portable CRT (with memory to hold up to 15,000 words) and connect directly to his home office computer using any nearby telephone.

News and other information also may be placed in the system through other devices such as paper tape readers and optical scanners, which read certain typewriter faces and convert them into electronic pulses for CRT editing and processing. In some instances, stories may be fed into the computer by Telex and TWX.

In addition to staff-generated copy – and often much greater in quantity – are the news files a newspaper receives each day from the various domestic and international wire services, syndicates and other general or specialised news and feature services to which it subscribes. At today's automated newspaper, virtually all of this additional information is received over high-speed wires, transmitting directly into the newspaper's own editorial computer. It is not unusual for a major daily to receive hundreds of stories every day – more than 100,000 words – from all sources, including the public relations community.

Now that the mountains of urgent news have been reduced to a staggering number of bits and bytes in the mysterious memory of the computer, how do the editors know what they have to work with? Which items are most critical and which may be handled later?

First, there is the monitor printer, which slavishly prints a continuous index of everything entered into the system from any source. A single line tells the editor where each item came from, who wrote it, how long it is, when it was entered and when it may be published – but supplies only five or six words with which to identify the subject. An abstract printer provides all the same information but adds perhaps the first 30 words of the item. It is from these indexes that editors make their selections. Each editor looks at his own departmental directory – sports, politics, financial, world news, etc.

In addition to monitoring input on index teleprinters, the editor may call up any of these directories on his own CRT – which now proves to be much more than an exotic typewriter. In a flash he can retrieve on his screen, in full, any story in which he has interest. He can perform any amount of editing or ask a staff member to take it back for a rewrite on his screen. Of course, the editor also may kill the entire item even faster than he called it up - again with a single keystroke!

When a story passes the editor's review, he may forward it electronically to the copy desk for final spelling, grammar, style and other changes. Headlines may be composed on special VDT screens, which display the headline in requested type size and column widths. There also are special CRTs engineered to layout full pages with all editorial content and advertising in position.

The final step in computerized editing is a simple keyboard command which whisks the copy off the editor's screen at 1200, 4800 or even 9600, or more, words per minute, into automatic typesetting equipment (often another computer) - which justifies margins to proper column widths, hyphenates words and checks itself for errors.

It is in this last step that automation of a newswire differs markedly from a newspaper. The last command from an editor's CRT at a wire service is "send", or "transmit". Immediately the words on his screen are off on a journey that may take them across the street by wire or around the world by satellite to subscriber newspapers, broadcasting stations or other wire services. At some media the news may still clack out slowly on aging teletype machines, at others on high-speed teleprinters. At many they will zip with lightning speed straight into the subscriber's own editorial computer.

Using his CRT keyboard, the editor at a wire service controls not only the routing and destination of each piece of copy, but also can assign priorities to the items, change the order of stories queued up for tranmission, break in with a bulletin or a flash, order a repeat, place stories on hold or slug them for later transmission.

We have come full circle. We now are back at the computerised newspaper, where the flood of time-critical information has not diminished. It may, in fact, have grown exponentially. But it has become quietly and conveniently controllable in the vast and versatile memory of the computer - eminently accessible and readily usable down to the very last moments before the presses roll out the next edition or the next news programme goes on the air.

The crucial question for public relations in all this wizardry is: How will your news releases enter the complex circle of computerized news handling?

Increasingly, the press places greater emphasis and reliance on computer-compatible electronic copy - ready for prompt recall, review, revision, typesetting or transmission. The demand for electronic delivery has resulted in formulation of international text and transmission "standards". Copy sent and formatted to these specifications of the American Newspaper Publishers Association and the International Press Telecommunications Council is accessible to editors at computerised news media because their computers know precisely what to look for to receive, categorise and store copy and create the fateful indexes and abstracts that will guide these editors in their decisions.

How will you make certain that your news will appear in these magical and decisive directories?

In some instances, the old methods will still work - in others, only the new will be acceptable. It is unlikely that any editor would refuse a good tip or worthy story only because it was hand-delivered or even hand-written. But, if your release must compete with all the other news of the day, it had best be there fast and in the most convenient form.

There may be opportunity for you to deliver to some media computers individually by Telex or by telephone dial-up from your own word processing or computer system (which, I believe, many of you will have a lot sooner than you think). But you will be hard pressed, indeed, to deliver simultaneously to all relevant media, near and far, with the precise speed and format they require. Nor is it realistic to believe that newspapers and other media will provide the expensive computer access ports and additional storage space that would be required for hundreds of corporations, government agencies, public relations agencies and other press release sources.

Not surprisingly, I suggest that PR Newswire, Universal News Services of London and our associated wires around the world remain your best electronic route to editors and their computerised newsrooms. As press communications services, it is our obligation, on your behalf as well as our own, to keep abreast of, and equipped for, the dynamic changes in our industry.

This year marks PR Newswire's 25th anniversary of pioneering the electronic distribution of press releases. We are celebrating our first quarter century by totally automating our wire and editorial operations under a unique license from the Associated Press to use the software developed by AP to computerise the world's largest news agency. AP's research and development is likewise the basis for the IMOS equipment on display here today.

In my opening I suggested that technological changes sweeping news operations will affect you - even to how you write your press releases. Think a moment about those all-powerful directories or the 30-word abstracts which editors rely upon to make their decisions. It quickly becomes clear that the first rule of good journalistic writing has acquired new significance - the news of your release had better be in the lead, where it belongs - regardless of whose ego must be massaged or what the legal counsel prefers.

I am certain the press always will respond to a good news or feature release, whether it is delivered by semaphore or smoke signal. But I take leave of you now with a bit of practical advice: While the computer may be the newest member of the editorial staff, you had better get its attention if you hope to attract the editor's.

DISCUSSION

Question.   Would you comment on the interest of consumers and providers of
Prestel information? Are there a lot of companies and newspaper groups for
instance who want to get into this service?

Bright.   There are two ends to your question, the providers and the users. The
end users I glossed over because, as I mentioned, our trials have only just got
into their stride, and the public service has only opened in March. So it is
early days. We recognise, if only because of the cost of terminals and the like,
that the early population of users will tend to be concentrated in the business
sector. I should explain that the terminals we have, tend to come in all shapes
and sizes, so the cost of the terminal can vary according to choice. The likely
reaction of residential users is that when the set prices come down we will see
the real take-off. I think that is the first hurdle to overcome. The cost of
information.......O.K, if you are selective you can keep your choice down to the
low priced information, but having said that you can only get the information if
you have a set able to receive it. That is the first hurdle for the average user.
Business users do not have the same concern and indeed they look upon these sets
as low-cost terminals already, because they are paying high prices for VDU's and
the like. In terms of information, well, we have no experience to go on. This is
a very novel situation so we are speculating, as indeed are the providers. We know
for example that in the early days games and that sort of thing are very popular,
largely because of the novelty perhaps. Whether it will remain so, it is too
early to say.

Question.   Can you get pictures on Prestel?

Bright.   No. We can not put up still photographs for example. That is the
next generation we are working on. At this moment the nearest you can get to
pictures are very simple graphics and stylised pictures, using of course all
seven colours but nevertheless a rather crude caricature of a picture as such.
But it is very good for graphs and various other tabulations, because colour helps
make it more easily coped with by the average eye.

Question.   Can you connect a printer to Prestel equipment?

Bright.   The ability to take word copy is already developed but we are up
against the barrier of cost. We have done this and it will print out that page as
fast as it is delivered to the screen, with the graphics. Technically the answer
is yes, it can be done. At the moment the printers we are using cost around
£1,000, so we think it is a bit high for the general popularity we are aiming for.

Question.   Does it have to be a true television set, or can a commercial CRT
pick up the Prestel signal?

Bright.   I have to answer by saying that the commercial CRT would itself have
to have Prestel compatability. For example, Prestel comes 40 characters across the
line, whereas teletypes and most VDUs tend to go for 80 character width. Some form
of conversion is needed. In terms of the actual transmission codes we are using
across the telephone lines, we have adopted international alphabet standards, so up

to a point the problem is solved. In fact one of the American activities of INSAC is the acquisition of a number of commercial VDUs which have been slightly modified to turn them into Prestel sets or to double as Prestel terminals. So, with a little thought and forward planning the answer is yes.

Question.   What about photos, talking about computerised news wire transmission?

Steinberg.   Well, there is photo transmission now using laser transmission, which is high speed and very good quality. However, that is an extremely expensive system. I do not know how soon that might be available as a commercial service to public relations people. Wire services themselves, however, have satellite and laser transmission. As it becomes necessary, I think that we or somebody will be in it so that you will be able to transmit photos. It may indeed be the wire services themselves who will carry photos at a fee for you. As far as getting the photos into the computers, that too is possible by digitalising the photographs. That is what comes back from space; the photos that you see from space shots are really computer digitalised information sent back and reconstructed into a photo.

Question.   Are you using cable television set-ups for Prestel now instead of telephone?

Bright.   No. We have very little cable television in this country, compared to North America anyway. There are, as you will know I am sure, in North America some cable television experiments taking place. I suppose Cube is the one that has had the most exposure, but it does not use our sort of technology. It does overcome one of the limitations of broadcast teletext which, I mentioned earlier, has the capability for only 100 frames. Cable television - full band width - can get you into tens of thousands of frames, provided it is bi-directional, of course.

Question.   For those of us from North America who may be involved in cable television, can cable television companies purchase any of the Prestel software?

Bright.   I have had one or two enquiries but they have never materialised into any significant interest. Not so much because they do not like the system, but because there are quite a few imponderables, such as bi-directional versus uni-directional. The Cube system does a sort of poll, a census type of approach for those families that are equipped with two-way facility. If you look at what it is actually doing, it is conveying a series of yes-no responses to a question, and does not act in the way that Prestel acts. But this is not to say that the line communication technology of cable television could not be harnessed to a computer with Prestel type technology. No one's attempted to do it yet.

Question.   Obviously you are a commercial organisation, Mr Steinberg, and you are interested in transmitting as many stories as possible from your customers. Nevertheless, can you tell us how critical you are with your customers' stories before transmitting them to newspapers? Do you edit them?

Steinberg.   We reserve the right to refuse copy. Just because we are commercial, we need the press to communicate that information. We take the

attitude that the press really is our customer. While they do not pay us and the
public relations profession does, if we are unable to satisfy the press we are
going to be out of business. All copy that we handle is read by people, highly
qualified newsmen, who have long experience and will read for errors of grammar,
fact, style, libel, news style. If something will simply embarrass us or, we
think, raise questions for the editors, we will refuse to carry it.

We are very much concerned about protecting the wire for the other people who use
it, and that it be well regarded by the receiving papers. The fact is, we have
been in business for 25 years, serve over 300 news media around the United States,
have over 13,000 miles of circuits, and UNS here in the United Kingdom is equally
respected for what it does. This is virtually the same thing, with perhaps even a
few more services than PRN offers in the States.

Later, as part of his response to another question, Steinberg added:

I would also throw in one other thing related to whether we turn copy down or not,
and how the wire is viewed by the press. We call it PR releases that we carry, but
we carry some very sensitive and urgent information. I can give you a perfect
example, because it was a public relations man who became involved. About two
months ago we got a 'phone call on our desk: "This is TWA. We want to give you an
item to get out on the wire right away". He started to read it and what he was
announcing was: "TWA announces that its Flight No. such-and-such from Kansas City
to St Louis is now 30 minutes out of St Louis and being hijacked". So we sent that
out immediately. Subsequently throughout the day we got 'phone calls from TWA,
because it is part of the public relations function to get it out. We advised the
press that TWA had contacted the FBI, that the FBI had arrived at the airport, that
a separate landing strip was being designated for the flight. Any information that
TWA had on that hijacking was carried over the wire.

Question.   I take it that because of the very style that the material will take
on the printer in the newspaper, those first 30 words being quite critical, the
process of writing the story will become a very critical thing.

Steinberg.   I said at the outset that computerisation will affect also how you
write press releases, and in the demonstration we showed you the directory lines
and the abstract printer. That is what the editor makes his decision on and the
best advice I can give public relations is: think about that. If you want to get
the editor's attention you have to get the computer's attention first. It does not
matter whose ego is being massaged or what the legal counsel thinks and says, if
the news is not in the lead, where it belongs, then the editors may very well
ignore it because it just will not look interesting. So that's crucial.

Question.   On Prestel, private firms can use the system for storing information ,
can you give us an example of the price for using the system that way?

Bright.   The tariff for closed user groups in other words. Essentially it
goes as a full rate. I have not really dealt with how much we charge for using the
system for open information from an information provider's point of view. Perhaps
I could rectify that by saying there are two factors in the costing equation. One
is the annual subscription and the other is a charge based on the number of frames
that the provider wishes to rent from us. That varies with length of contracts,
from, at its most expensive, £4,000 annual subscription plus £4 per frame,
annually, down to £2,400 and £2.40 per frame for a five year term. It varies

according to the length of the contract. As far as closed user groups are concerned, I do not think we have finalised the actual tariffs. The last I heard they were still being negotiated. Eventually there will be an additional charge for this added facility. Remember, you are of course no longer generating random calls. You are restricting the population of users to those who you, as provider, nominate. There is a balance to be struck there.

Question. Mr Steinberg, can you give us an idea of how many public relations companies in the States use your service?

Steinberg. Public relations agencies alone I would have to estimate for you 600 to 1,000, I do not know. I think probably around 1,000. I would guess that our customer base is approximately 50 per cent public relations agencies. It must be more than that with corporations and others. There is not a major public relations agency in the United States that does not use us.

11

Communicating Man's
Shrinking Natural Resources

Introduction
_____

The session was chaired by Professor E Braun, Head of the Technology Policy Unit at
the University of Aston in Birmingham.

The panel of speakers comprised:

Sarah Horack	:	Yankelovich, Skelly and White.
Dr J C McVeigh	:	Vice Chairman, World Solar Energy Conference, 1981.
Philippe Carvallo	:	Press Officer, Chambre Syndicale.
Charles Cook	:	Energy Correspondent, The Guardian.

In opening the session Professor Braun complimented the organisers on tackling a
subject as difficult and pertinent as that of communicating effectively the
problems associated with man's diminishing natural resources. The subject was one
of key importance to everyone in society in facing 'Challenges of a Changing
World', and it was disappointing that in competition with other concurrent
sessions so few attending the Congress could attend this session of equal
importance to anybody involved in public relations.

Papers were presented by Sarah Horack, Dr McVeigh and Charles Cook.

Corporate Priorities and the Energy Problem

Sarah Horack

Yankelovitch, Skelly and White

Energy problems are not simple problems to deal with or to communicate with others about. It is hard for those who specialise in communicating to find their way through technical mazes to messages that will be efficacious among a wide variety of audiences, each of which encompasses different points of view and can play different roles in resolving or exacerbating energy problems. A solid research base is needed so we may know how energy problems are perceived in various quarters, and how various groups are likely to respond to these problems. Using such a research base, we will be better able to tailor and target our messages.

Energy problems compete with other issues and demands for attention and problem-solving resources in the context of social, economic, and political developments. The nature of "The Energy Problem" changes from country to country and in the perceptions of various groups within a country. People's perceptions and priorities are not always clearly defined or consistent. And finally, events bring change, as the Three Mile Island incident shows, and the content itself may change in critical ways over time. We must know about such differences in perceptions and understand the policy making process if we are to communicate effectively and take a constructive part in solving problems.

Having put forward the need for research, I would like to share with you some findings from work we, at Inbucon and Yankelovich, Skelly and White, are now engaged in called Corporate Priorities. Corporate Priorities analyses the context I have been speaking of - we refer to it as the public policy making process. From this analytical vantage point we can anticipate the ways in which about 25 demands or issues are likely to impact on different industries and companies. Energy issues have been followed in this way for eight years now in the United States. Within the last few weeks, we have completed a similar pilot project in the United Kingdom, making it possible to begin drawing some cross-national comparisons.

Research which is to be used to guide communications about energy problems should be directed to two "needs to know".

First: Perceptions which define the problem.

What is the perceived nature of the energy problem and what differences are present in the way different groups of actors in the public policy process define the problem?

Second: The process of achieving resolution of such problems.

What patterns exist in the kinds and sequence of inputs various groups make to the emergence of solutions? Do issues develop according to characteristic life-cycles?

To answer these questions requires understanding of how the public policy process works and how different actors in the drama relate to each other. Understanding the public policy process in this way allows us to offer some interpretations of likely future outcomes and to assess the impact of alternate responses.

I have sketched a conceptual outline of the information needs which should be met by research if an effective communications response is to be made to a problem such as energy. Now I would like to illustrate how each of these needs can be met in terms of the energy problem based on some current <u>Corporate Priorities</u> data.

First, let us think about defining the problem, noting how different groups think about energy and how the variable nature of the problem affects the choice of response.

In the United States the public defines the crisis in terms of high prices, and feels that talk about energy shortages is exaggerated. As a result, people are reluctant to make price or convenience sacrifices to solve the problem. The public continues to lay most of the blame for the country's energy problems on the oil companies and Arab oil producers. Nearly two out of three people single out the oil companies among industries and institutions considered most to blame for the energy crisis. Energy companies are believed to be deliberately holding back on technological breakthroughs with new energy sources and to be among the worst polluters of air and water.

Oil companies are thought to have too much influence in government and oilmen are felt to be unethical, making excess profits in dubious ways. Only ten per cent say the oil companies are being genuinely helpful in trying to solve the country's energy problems. In the end, more people worry about the power of the oil companies (56 per cent) than about the possibility of either short or long-term energy supply shortages (40 per cent).

At the same time, the public is <u>increasingly</u> reluctant to expand the use of coal and nuclear power, while placing supreme faith in technology, especially solar energy, as an eventual solution.

In contrast, leaders in the United States in government, unions, the media, activist pressure groups and the financial community, have a view of the energy crisis which is radically different from the public's perception. Leaders define the problem in terms of inadequate supplies and wasteful consumption patterns for which the government and the public (not the oil companies) are primarily to blame. Leaders look to increased conservation, greater use of coal and more nuclear power plants as key components of the energy problem's eventual solution. Like the public, key leaders also have confidence in solar energy.

A more dramatic contrast in defining the energy problem can hardly be imagined; what a challenge to public relations specialists? In fact, knowing the full complexity of these perceptions helped greatly in devising with one <u>Corporate Priorities</u> sponsor an effective communications strategy. The company related to the way the public was experiencing the energy problem - that is as a price problem - and did not try to convince them that the problem had a different nature. The object was to show that this oil company was providing good value for money spent, primarily through auxiliary services and expert advice, with many of these "extras" directed at achieving greater fuel economy, pollution reduction and so forth. As a result, this company has been able to distinguish itself in a positive way from the negative aura surrounding the poor image of oil companies generally.

Turning now to our United Kingdom study, we can show a different sort of contrast in the definition of energy problems in the two countries.

Energy problems are conceived very differently by the general public in the United Kingdom and the United States. These differences can be summarised under three headings:

(1)   The public in the United Kingdom regards energy shortages by the end of the century as a real and serious threat. In the United States, as we have seen, the public is still inclined to feel the crisis is phoney and/or an eventuality engineered by the oil companies to increase prices and profits.

(2)   Leaders in both countries regard increased use of coal and nuclear energy as essential to a comprehensive energy policy, with United States leaders adding conservation as even more important than nuclear. However, the general public in Britain is more acceptable of nuclear energy development than is the public in the United States, even as measured before the Three Mile Island accident.

(3)   Oil companies in Britain are thought to have performed well in meeting the country's energy needs. Furthermore, the British general public finds oil companies credible in what they say about energy problems and solutions. In contrast, the United States public is deeply cynical and suspicious of oil companies.

Alongside these clear contrasts in public attitudes in Britain and the United States lie some interesting similarities in attitudes. In both countries people tend to reject the notion that sacrifices to deal with energy problems, in the form of high prices or inconvenience, should be borne by the public at large. One apparent reason for this resistance to sacrifice is the faith displayed by the public in both countries in new energy technologies. Solar energy is expected to play a major role in solving energy problems by surprisingly large numbers, 57 per cent in the United Kingdom and 77 per cent in the United States, provided its potential is developed fully.

Finally, in both countries, coal does <u>not</u> figure prominently in the public's thinking about energy resources, a clear contrast with leadership views on both sides of the Atlantic.

From this comparison of how energy problems are defined in the two countries, it seems that the long-term problems of secure supplies and wise use could be addressed much more directly in the United Kingdom. The United Kingdom energy situation is objectively different and the climate of opinion about business is also very different; these differences indicate that communication strategies must also be different.

Now let us turn to the <u>process</u> of resolving problems; knowing what powers and policy preferences the various participants possess provides realistic targets for communications. Trying to prompt an actor after he has read his last line or casting a chorus dancer in the part of tragic heroine is clearly to be avoided. Here I will draw primarily on our United States data because our first studies in the United Kingdom do not yet provide sufficient scope for analysis.

In one quick example, I want to emphasise the different kinds of inputs groups can make and the necessity of being able, as communicators, to weigh the relative impact of such simultaneous messages. In the United States, the general public give majority support to the principle of resource conservation in general and energy saving in particular. Pressure groups have formed and are actively working to promote this view among other leaders and policy makers. However, when faced with the trade-offs conserving energy would inevitably require, the public rejects bearing extra costs or inconvenience. Only two people in ten would support restricted use of cars or fuel rationing to achieve conservation and only one in ten thinks price decontrol or special fuel taxes are supportable.

What does all this mean? First, it means we cannot take pro-conservation sentiments at face value. Second, it means that new forms of government intervention may be required to impose measures involving unpopular trade-offs. Third, it means that this issue may be approaching a changing point we can anticipate with knowledge of the life-cycle we think characterises it. At present, real uncertainty exists about the range, the criteria for choosing and the methods for implementing alternative solutions. Tinkering with market mechanisms may take over from the push to reach substantive resolutions of energy problems - as has occurred with the problem of health care in the United States. Alternatively, we may see public resistance to trade-offs combining with industry's fear of the uncertainty caused by willy-nilly government intervention. Such a conjunction could provide necessary impetus for the emergence of a new sense of priorities, for example, more coal use and safety in nuclear development; followed by an orderly effort to reach goals which will change the trade-off arithmetic. If the second prospect seems more inviting than the first, then perhaps ways can be found to intervene in the policy making process so as to increase the changes of achieving the more orderly and substantively directed solution. Knowing what the alternative lines of development are in advance of such a changing point is bound to enhance our efforts to intervene effectively.

In another example of how important it is to understand the policy process in designing effective communication strategies, we can look at how we might respond to oil company divestiture as a potential policy response to the United States energy problems. On one hand, the public supports horizontal and vertical divestiture. On the other, they do not feel convinced that such measures would either lower energy prices or increase energy supplies. The pattern we see here is one in which the public's general disfavour of the oil industry is displayed very powerfully. However, we have determined that Congress neither favours nor expects divestiture action, regardless of public hostility to the oil companies. Clearly, it would be a mistake for an oil company to attempt to rebut divestiture directly. No matter how grim the consequences of divestiture might seem, its low level of support among the groups found critical to invoking such a policy and the negative character of public opinion regarding oil companies dictate silence.

However, sometimes it is useful to address leaders directly on an issue, as our previous example about new priorities showed for the United States. The more receptive climate of opinion found in the United Kingdom when business speaks out indicates that this may be even more appropriate now here. But how to proceed? Based on our experience with Corporate Priorities sponsors in the United States, we can offer these suggestions:

Address government before the options are set, avoiding defensive posturing.

Be prepared to contribute solid new information and be sure it is well grounded in political realities.

Take the role of a constructive participant, looking to common end goals and being ready to accept some degree of public association with the outcome achieved.

It is not clear yet how appropriate these approaches will be in the United Kingdom, but companies have applied them with good effect in the United States.

Finally, let us look into the future, to see another way research of the sort I have been advocating can assist in shaping communication strategies. In the United

States, looking just at the view of key leaders, we see non-oil solutions to energy problems emerging into the foreground.

This view seems to say some fairly clear things about what kind of messages will be accepted receptively by leaders. There are two chief features of this emergent re-ordering of priorities: first, government efforts to spur development of new exploitation technologies and alternative energy resources (primarily relating to coal and nuclear power) are favoured by nine out of ten leaders; and second, measures emphasising conservation, with relatively painless reductions in profligate use highest on the agenda, receive support from roughly the same high proportion of leaders. Oil-related strategies, notably incentives for more domestic production and freeing up market prices, are seen by far fewer as the crest of the wave of the future. For the oil industry, the two-headed issue now seems to be one of allocation – of a shortage-bound resource and of the financial and technical returns on the exploitation of this resource.

In the United Kingdom, our ability to look toward the future is being developed. The issue of lead in petrol is one we will follow closely because it has the potential to re-introduce the public's high level of concern and pollution into decision-making on energy use. We will also be interested to see how attitudes mature on the question of maximising economic and political returns on the fruits of the North Sea windfall. Some United Kingdom leaders, we have found, regard Britain's energy policies as closely linked with the country's role in the EEC. Also, we will look for any sense of closure on longer-term energy questions which North Sea oil is regarded as placing in a time frame where orderly solutions are possible. Within this frame, I want to add, responses which are well grounded in the manner I have been advocating, are likely to be constructive and well received.

To close, I want to emphasise again that energy problems are not just technical problems or problems belonging to one industry. Research is called for into the political, social and economic context of decision-making on energy issues if inputs into the decision process are to be effective. Defining the perceived nature of energy problems and understanding the patterns of interaction through which resolutions are achieved are all important if responses to problems such as the supply and use of energy are to be addressed successfully with the complex context we know such problems have. With such research, public relations specialists can guide their clients on this complex area to good effect – as we have demonstrated with the <u>Corporate Priorities</u> project in the United States of America.

The Alternative Technology

Dr J. Cleland McVeigh

Head of Department of Mechanical Production Engineering
Brighton Polytechnic

Alternative Technology (AT) is difficult to define as it is much more than the conventional mechanical technology of windmills or solar panels. During the 1960s it became fashionable to be concerned about population growth, the depletion of natural resources and pollution. Two parallel movements could be identified. One group attempted to establish a counter-culture; within small communities young people mainly in their early twenties attained various degrees of self-sufficiency in work, food and energy. Members of the different groups had a wide diversity of aims and objectives with a common theme of dissatisfaction with industrial society. Politically they tended to be broadly left-wing in their outlook. The second group were older and more established in traditional professions. Their views were often influenced by the writings of the late Dr E F Schumacher, summed up in this extract[1].

"Not many years ago we were told that we had never had it so good; as time moved on we would have it better still. And the same would hold for all the world's people, particularly those who, for one reason or another, had been left behind in mankind's onward march into the Age of Plenty. If there was one thing on which everybody was expected to agree it was this: that at long last the problem of production had been solved. Modern science and technology had done it; western civilisation had done it; and the unique and dazzling achievements of this civilisation were now destined to spread across the globe in a very short time.

The very idea that 'the problem of production' has been solved by the achievements of modern science and technology is based on a most astonishing oversight, namely, that the whole edifice of modern industry is built on non-renewable energy resources.

In short, the poor countries, which assuredly need development to regain some kind of economic health, have to evolve a life-style for which America or for that matter Japan or any other 'advanced' country cannot serve as a model, and the so-called advanced countries have the even more difficult task of achieving some basis of existence which is compatible with peace and permanence.........it is not only the problem of resources that has, suddenly and somewhat belatedly, moved into the centre of discussion; there is also the problem of pollution and of ecological breakdown. In addition, we do not need to look far afield to realise that modern industrial society is involved in some kind of human crisis which manifests itself in inflation, various types of unrest, rising crime rates, drug addiction, and so on. All this suggests that there is something wrong at the root of things - as indeed a Christian would be inclined to think. What is being called into question, so it seems, is not our *technical* competence but our value system and the very aims and objects we are pursuing".

Schumacher founded the Intermediate Technology Development Group in 1965 with a group of engineers, economists, scientists and others from industry and the professions "to provide practical and effective self-help techniques for developing countries". The Group concentrates on practical tests and demonstrations through field projects, programmes and consultancies, using technologies "appropriate" for the developing countries, e.g. labour intensive, capital saving, using local materials and simple enough to be used and maintained by the people themselves.

In 1970, Robin Clarke[2] outlined a "Third Alternative" that would combine a "new" science and a "new" technology which would integrate objective knowledge with subjective experience, reflect our real dependency on the natural world and incorporate the canons of the new eco-socialist morality; and a new array of tools and techniques that would:

".......operate on low amounts of energy; not irreversibly disperse non-renewable resources; use local and easily accessible materials; re-cycle materials locally; not produce waste products at a greater rate than they could be absorbed by the natural cycling processes; ....fit in with existing culture patterns; satisfy those who operate it;"

The term "soft technology" also appeared at this time, perhaps influenced by some of the detergent advertisements which were then current. In 1972 Harper and MacKillop[2] organised a London meeting called "Alternative Technologies" and from that point the AT movement started to spread a communications network.

Alternative Technology can be seen to be an approach to all types of environmental problem. It combines the scientific method of problem solving with the alternative social values of cooperation (rather than confrontation), decentral-isation, small-scale systems and non-violence. It seeks after knowledge to live in harmony with people from all nations and with Nature, rather than trying to master Nature. In the AT approach, conventional wisdom and analysis are always questioned. There is no blind obedience or faith in established political or spiritual beliefs. The philosophy can be seen to be sceptical with authority, rather than having faith in it. It is a political approach to the problems, both in defining what the problems are and in putting the answers into practice.

The environmental movement, of which AT is a part, is critical of the direction in which our technological society is moving. As Davis[3] puts it:

"those of us who look for another way are calling for a different change in outlook to that which is required for a high growth vote".

It does not intend to do away with science, but is sometimes critical of many of its applications to society and of the establishment figures who run it.

Conflicting or Converging Viewpoints?

The nuclear industry has always attracted considerable criticism in the AT literature and the two leading establishment figures in the United Kingdom, Sir John Hill and Dr Walter Marshall are often singled out for special attention. For example, the February/March 1979 issue of "Undercurrents" prints their photographs with the caption, "Hill and Marshall - can they be retrained for socially useful work?"

Yet Sir John Hill's views on many environmental topics are practically indistinguishable from those of his strongest critics. For example, on democracy[4].

"Only the public can decide what sort of society and lifestyle they want. If the public feel that we have moved too far away from nature and that they would prefer a society that uses, for example, less energy, *it is right and proper that they should press these views upon the Government*" (author's italics).

and on energy growth.......

".......we recognise that the exponential growth in energy demand that we have seen for so many decades cannot go on for ever.......Many environmentalists....... argue that we have already gone far enough in standard of living. They see a wasteful society all round us, a vast consumption of energy, of metals, and a carelessness with the world resources. They argue that if we are to have a stable society in the future we must limit out demands on the planet, limit our material demands to something which can be sustained. *In this one cannot but agree with the environmentalists*" (author's italics).

Compare this with two contributions in the April 1979 issue of Whole Earth:

".........the insane technological acceleration of western urban society often caused its drawbacks to outweigh its benefits. We no longer fear plague, smallpox or famine, but heart disease, psychological stress and obesity". (5)

".......no worthwhile enterprise ever begins or should begin with a balance sheet or analysis of the economics involved, or the material benefits which are likely to accrue to oneself. The spiritual end is the end at which to start; and it ought only to be embarked upon when, having searched one's soul, one is satisfied that it is completely justified on moral and social grounds.......the question at the forefront of my mind has always been, not 'will it pay?' or 'what's in it for me?' but 'is this something which ought to be done?' " (6).

The discussion on energy forecasting is now continuing on an open basis, with the Department of Energy announcing in April 1979 that it was providing funds to examine the implications of the future energy supply and demand patterns outlined in studies by the Friends of the Earth and by the National Centre for Alternative Technology(7). Amory Lovins has published a remarkable matrix(8) shown below:

Forecasts of United States primary energy demand in the year 2000
(Units: QUADS)

Year of Forecast	"Beyond The Pale"	Heresy	Conventional Wisdom	Superstition
1972	125 (Lovins)	140	160 (AEC)	190
1974	100	124	140 (ERDA)	160
1976	75 (Lovins)	89–95	124 (ERDA)	140
1978	33 (for year 2050)	63–77	96–101	124

He comments that the current (1978) United States Department of Energy forecast for the year 2000, with a high oil price, is 95 quads - the figure which was greeted with "howls of derision" when he published it some two years earlier. Note this is also a diagonal matrix. Similar trends in forecast figures could probably be found for most Western countries.

But some sharply contrasting beliefs in the future were described by Cotgrove[9] in a recent article in "New Society". From a survey of 550 members of Friends of the Earth and the Conservation Society and 350 businessmen and engineers, he selected replies from 175 of those who thought environmental problems were extremely serious ("catastrophists") and 123 of those who saw them as only moderately serious or not serious at all ("cornucopians").

Their views are summarised in the table as follows:

The rival views of the future

	catastrophists	cornucopians
Environment	Many and serious environmental dangers: respect for natural systems.	Fewer and manageable environmental problems: nature available for conquest and control.
Science and technology	Too much faith in science and technology to solve problems	Science and technology can solve problems of energy and resources.
Society	Opposition to industrial society: artificial wants, large impersonal cities, unsatisfying work.	Positive attitude to industrial society: role of market, experts, advertising, achievement.
Values	Material values criticised: need for shift to spiritual/ post-material values.	Primacy of economic goals: growth and efficiency.
Utopia	Community, satisfying work, participation at work and in government decisions.	Individualism, rewards for achievement, expertise, differentials.

Communications

The conventional technology of alternative methods of producing energy is, in general, well covered by the media. But there are too many cases when, in the words of His Royal Highness Prince Philip:

"Truth, reality and exactitude are gradually being swamped by dogma, illusion and vagueness".

For example, a leading national daily published a review about a solar energy

publication in which the first half of one sentence in the publication was joined
to the second half of another sentence, completely altering the meaning of the
passage. After considerable pressure, they agreed to publish a letter putting the
record straight. Then the key sentence in the letter was completely wrecked by
the omission of the word "not"! This problem is not confined to alternative
energy, however, as this example from the nuclear industry shows:

"A Harwell scientist said yesterday: ....*By the year 2000, when nuclear power
would supply about half the nation's energy,*.......

(Report in National daily, March 1979). This seems to be a straightforward factual
statement. But "Energy Policy", HMSO, February 1978, states that the United
Kingdom Energy Demand (Primary Fuel) for the year 2000 is estimated to be between
450 and 560 million tonnes of coal equivalent (mtce) and paragraph 14.15 stated:

"A prudent view of the maximum of nuclear contribution that can be provided in
2000 is about 95 mtce *if it is competitive in price* (author's italics). If no
nuclear power plant were built after the completion of the reactors currently
under construction and those for which orders are being placed, the nuclear
contribution would be about 25 mtce at that time".

At best, 95/450 represents 21 per cent, while 25/560 represents 4.5 per cent. The
paper's energy watchdog was clearly asleep that night!

The Department of Energy's work in the field of alternative energy sources is the
subject of regular press releases. There are probably very few people who do not
appreciate that the United Kingdom is among the World's leaders in Wave Power
research, that we have embryo Geothermal and Wind Power programmes and that a
major feasibility study of the Severn Barrage is being undertaken, while the use
of solar energy for both water and space heating is already beginning to create an
appreciable market, both at home and overseas. Solar energy and, more recently,
wind power have learned societies associated with their applications. Solar energy
applications have also attracted its own trade association.

Many of the professional engineering institutions have taken considerable steps to
encourage new attitudes towards energy resources and conservation. For example,
their joint body, the Council of the Engineering Institutions, has formed a special
energy committee, known as the Watt Committee, which makes direct recommendations
to Government. Among individual institutions, the Institute of Fuel were given
permission by the Privy Council to change their name to the Institute of Energy in
February 1979 to reflect their widening role in energy matters, both nationally
and internationally. The Institution of Mechanical Engineers had the subject
"Energy and Environment" for its 1978 Thomas Hawksley Lecture. The Institution of
Chemical Engineers published a major review "Materials and Energy Resources" in
1976, and, reflecting the theme of the previous section, paragraph 217 is as
follows:

"Whilst we obviously have to make our economic assessments as best we can to allow
us to compare different energy sources, in the end, if we _must_ have the energy,
the exact price is no longer of over-riding importance. It may be worth paying
more for an energy source that is long-term, non-polluting, not subject to the
risk of political interruption, free from serious socio-political implications,
and probably progressively cheaper as time passes".

The Alternative Technology movement has a large number of decentralised information
sources, some of which are listed in the Appendix. One major reference source is
the Alternative Technology Directory, by Horace Herring[10]which contains hundreds
of varied reference sources, including a guide to ecological organisations,

magazines and books. Among the magazines, one of the best known is "Undercurrents" which gives a good coverage of energy topics and communications. Issue No 5, published in Winter 1973, gave an excellent history of AT, while Issue No 30, October - November 1978, brings the picture up to date. "Resurgence" has a philosophic approach to environmental problems, "Practical self-sufficiency" gives more information on rural crafts, while "Whole Earth" is published by a Brighton based cooperative group and has an emphasis on community living. "Appropriate Technology" is published by the Intermediate Technology Development Group and concentrates on Third World development. A common feature among many of these magazines is the difficulty of getting sufficient subscriptions to keep the enterprise alive. Very few have more than a few thousand subscribers. Distribution is a major problem. From time to time a key figure feels that he or she can no longer devote the time (and money) to provide the driving force and sometimes this causes a magazine to cease publication e.g. "Towards Survival", a very professionally presented conservation magazine, had its last issue in March 1975. Many of the contributors to this particular magazine are still active in other sectors of the AT movement.

The dilemma is apparent. To get a sufficiently broad base to support a fully professional editorial team needs a much larger circulation than the present decentralised individual groups can achieve. Yet this decentralisation and small-scale operation is also their major strength, providing the inspiration for much innovative thought.

Summary

Alternative Technology, as outlined in this paper, attracts a very emotional response from all sectors of the community. The business community, including professional engineers and industrialists, are on the whole amazed at the views expressed by the "catastrophists".

Yet, as Amory Lovins puts it[8], the 'soft path' or AT approach can offer simultaneous advantages for almost every on.

"It offers.......jobs for the unemployed, capital for the CBI (otherwise the capital goes mostly to energy and they never see it again), savings for consumers, chances for small business to innovate and for big business to recycle itself, environmental protection for conservationists, better national security for the military exciting technologies for the secular, a rebirth of spiritual values for the religious, world order and equity for globalists, energy independence for isolationists, radical reforms for the young, traditional virtues for the old, civil rights for liberals, local autonomy for conservatives".

But an increasing frustration is apparent among those who have very considerable reservations about the pursuit of growth, as they face political institutions dominated by the vested interests of unions, industry and government alike.

The problem facing communicators is to develop an understanding of these broader issues, so that the technological issues are not divorced from value judgments and 'quality of life' considerations.

References

1.   SCHUMACHER, Dr E F. (1974). The Age of Plenty. A Christian view.
           St Andrew Press, Edinburgh.

2.   HARPER, Peter. (1973). In: *Undercurrents, No 5.*

3.   DAVIS, John. (August/December, 1978). Appropriate Technology for the UK.
            In: *News Exchange*.

4.   HILL, Sir John. (March, 1978). In: *Atom,* 257, p.55.
                       (December, 1977). In: *Atom,* 254, p. 351.

5.   BALDWIN, Malcolm. (April 1979). In: *Whole Earth,* No 15, p.13.

6.   THOMPSON, Matthew, A. (April, 1979). In: *Whole Earth,* No 15, p.21.

7.   TODD, R.W. and ALTY, C.J. (eds). (1977). An alternative energy strategy
            for the United Kingdom. National Centre for Alternative Technology,
            Machynlleth, Powys.

8.   LOVINS, Amory. (January-February, 1979). 'Safe Energy".
            Resurgence, No 72, pp. 17-26.

9.   COTGROVE, Stephen. (March 1979). 'Catastrophe or cornucopia'.
            New Society, pp 683-684.

10.   HERRING, Horace. The Alternative Technology Directory. Pebble Press,
            P.O. Box 28, Brighton, BN2 1RZ. (1978).

Acknowledgements

While it would be impossible to list all the individuals whose ideas and comments
have influenced this paper, the author would particularly like to mention Dave
Elliott, Harry Frost, Gerald Foley, Gerald Leach, Amory Lovins, Diana Schumacher
and Robert Todd.

Appendix: Some additional reference sources

Books: Review article.
        J.C. McVeigh. Alternative/Renewable Energy. British Books News.
        pp. 954-961. The British Council, London, December 1978.

        A general article in which some 60 titles are reviewed.

        E.F. Schumacher. Small is Beautiful. Blond and Briggs, 1973,
        Sphere, 1974.

        R.C. Dorf. Energy: Resources and Policy. Addison-Wesley, 1978.

        Gerald Leach *et al*. A low energy strategy for the United Kingdom 11ED
        and Science Reviews, London, 1979.

        Amory B. Lovins. Soft Energy Paths. Pelican-Penguin. 1977.

        Gerald Foley with Charlotte Nassim. The Energy Question. Pelican
        1976, and, with index, 1978.

        J.A. Bereny and Y. Howell. Engineer's guide to Solar Energy.
        SES1, P.O. Box 204, San Mateo, CA 94401, USA, 1979.

Magazines:
        Intermediate Technology Development Group. A wide range of
        publications. 9. King Street, London WC2E 8HN.

Practical Self-sufficiency. Broad Leys Publishing Company, Widdington, Saffron Walden, Essex, CB11 3SP.

Resurgence. Pentre Ifan, Felindre Farchog, Crymych, Dyfed, Wales.

Undercurrents. 27 Clerkenwell Close, London EC1R OAT

Whole Earth. 11, George Street, Brighton, BN2 1RH.

Newsletters:
    Future Studies Centre, 15 Kelso Road, Leeds, LS2 9PR. West Yorkshire. Annual subscription currently £3. It gives a very wide range of forthcoming events and reviews many AT activities at home and overseas.

    News Exchange - Appropriate Technology for the UK - John Davis, 10 Grenfell Road, Beaconsfield, Bucks.

Organisations:
    Conservation Society. 12a Guildford Street, Chertsey, Surrey KT16 9BQ

    Council for the Protection of Rural England (CPRE) 4 Hobart Place, London, SW1W OHY

    National Centre for Alternative Technology, Machynlleth, Powys, Wales.

    Friends of the Earth, 9 Poland Street, London W1V 3DG

    Natural Energy Association, 2 York Street, London W 1

    Socialist Environment and Resources Association (SERA) 9 Poland Street, London WLV 3DG

Communications Network:

The Network for Alternative Technology and Technology Assessment. (NATTA), c/o Dr Dave Elliott, Faculty of Technology, Open University, Milton Keynes, Buckinghamshire.

The Role of the Media

Charles Cook

Energy Correspondent, "The Guardian"

The most popular song in the United States in recent weeks has been 'Cheaper Crude or No More Food'. Sung by a country-and-western band from Phoenix, Arizona, it has caught the mood of the people of America - at a time when that mood ought to be undergoing a fundamental change as a result of President Carter's energy-saving measures. What has gone wrong with the Presidential initiative, that such a song should sweep the States?

The problem is not just America's, although so profligate a user of raw materials of all sorts is she that her consumption is the most crucial to reduce. Despite other leaders' efforts - not always accompanied by such memorable phrases as Carter's 'moral equivalent of war' - conservation is failing to catch people's imagination.

I suggest part of the problem is caused by those trying to put across the conservation message not being basic enough. Carter's nicely-turned phrase makes good headlines, but what does it mean? Not much, apparently, to singers in Phoenix - or to quick-quipping East Coast intellectuals, who turned the 'moral equivalent' into a witty little mnemonic - Meow.

We need to be more down-to-earth in our approach to the problem; the equivalent, if you like, of putting a blonde nude on Page Three of the mass circulation newspapers. But how do you do that with the prosaic problem of the oil shortage, or the coming freshwater supply tightness, or the need to reprocess spent nuclear fuel to release the energy therein?

For a start, we should try to emphasise the advantages of cutting consumption, rather than concentrating on the gloom and doom to come if we fail. People are tired of being told the coming difficulties; they want to hear some good news.

On oil, for instance, we need to say more loudly that fuel bills can shrink dramatically if insulation and conservation are combined; that driving can be more relaxing at 50 mph; and that life in offices is in fact happier at 65 degrees instead of 75.

We need also to consider a basic human characteristic - greed. People are being offered insufficient rewards by those organisations wanting to upset their life-styles in order to construct vital resource-related projects. Before the nationalisation of the British coal industry, the local communities in coalmining areas benefitted by a penny a ton of output, a royalty paid by the coal-owners to those who helped make their fortunes. If a similar royalty was levied today on the massive new Selby 'supermine' in Yorkshire, for instance, it would benefit the area by about £100,000 a year - a relatively small cost for a ten million tons-a-year mine complex, but a reasonable recompense for the cost of higher rates needed to build homes and schools for the coming influx of miners.

If the coal industry in this country is to stay on target with its expansion plans, it needs to open a new 'supermine' every year from the mid-80s onwards. Already it is facing severe opposition, as instanced by the coming public inquiry over the Vale of Belvoir project. Might not this opposition take a more pragmatic view of the nation's needs if it could clearly see that the benefits were local as well as national?

A successful example - although some might disagree - of this policy could be said to be the Sullom Voe oil terminal project in Shetland. In return for allowing the oil industry to overturn their isolated way of life, the islanders have gained a payment on every barrel of North Sea crude landed at the terminal. By the end of the century the 20,000 Shetlanders will have accumulated some £50 millions. It will not compensate for everything that has happened there in the past five years - or will happen in the next two decades - but if you can put a monetary value on the quality of life, then it can be said to be reasonable compensation for the disruption.

Some people would call such a policy bribery, and in some ways perhaps it is. Certainly the oil companies were very much against the payment idea at first. But I feel such opposition was misplaced - as is the National Coal Board's dislike of the 1p-a-ton concept. The state of the energy industries in particular, and the natural resource companies in general is sufficiently strong today for them to pay reasonable compensation to those most directly affected by major new projects without destroying their financial viability. The sooner this is more generally accepted, the better for all of us - for we need the resources more than we need to defend the principle of being allowed to develop them as of right.

Of course, there are other ways of changing the public's attitude towards the developing natural resources problem. The media have their role to play - and the increasing number of energy specialists on the major papers and radio networks show a growing interest. But they need directing, and this is where there is great scope for an improvement in public relations within the resource companies.

In the past, the resource companies have been very bad at explaining to the public the vital role which their products play in modern society. As a result, coverage of commodities in general by the media is often bad or very limited - the commodity column in a newspaper usually languishes between the stock market share prices and the racing results.

If public appreciation of the tightening supply situation is to be increased, this must be changed. Those responsible for publicising esoteric and outwardly boring products like the famous copper wire bars so beloved of the BBC's commodities reports need to enlist the media's help in explaining the significance of these bars. Do people realise that central heating installation costs, for instance, are directly and surprisingly rapidly affected by events in Zaire and Zambia, the prime copper producers?

If you are handling such subjects, forget about your company's basic product - the one which is sold only to other manufacturing companies - and turn instead to the retail end-product. Approaching it the right way, and even the dullest commodity can become a potential centre-page feature subject. That is what I mean by putting natural resources on Page Three - and that is what President Carter has so far patently failed to do with the energy crisis in the United States.

DISCUSSION

In opening the discussion, Philippe Carvallo commented briefly upon the situation
in France. Communicators in France had been faced with extreme difficultity in
convincing an unwilling public of the realities of diminishing natural resources
particularly in the field of energy. This process had suffered greatly from the
fact that government policies were frequently seen as antagonistic to the
attitudes of those concerned with posing the problem and finding practical
solutions to it. The more informed a body was on the facts of the situation; the
more liable it was to be regarded as a target for political criticism. The entire
process and difficulty associated with it was constantly reinforced by political
debate where the emphasis appeared to be upon adversary confrontation rather than
a calm and fair examination of the facts.

An active discussion developed on the points raised in the presentations. The
attitude of the media, particularly in the United States, was strongly criticised.
Rather than reacting to circumstances and setting out the problem in the wider
context of its social, economic and political implications both nationally and
internationally, the opportunity was normally seized to arouse resentment and
conflict of interests rather than attempt to resolve these. If these prejudices
within the media and among the public were to be overcome those involved in the
resources business must indulge in strong selling of their ideas with a clear
commitment on their own part to a solution of the problem.

There was no simple answer. Each nation, community and individual had a distinct
and distinctive interest. The size of the problem was so great that it required
an involvement comparable with that achieved in time of war. Few countries -
particularly the United States of America - could now contemplate happily such
extreme action but if such a commitment were achieved those with a capacity to
solve the problem could indeed 'take off'.

Although the hope of many organisations and speakers had been to attempt to
achieve a mass transformation in public attitudes, the effect had been limited.
Despite this there was great value in continuing to discuss the problem and
putting forward positive solutions to it. Victories might be small but were very
well worthwhile.

The most important centres of opinion and significant action were seen to be
government. There was still a considerable job to be done in persuading them of
the nature of the problem and its solution. Only if the solutions were seen to be
positive and not restrictive were politicians and the public likely to alter their
attitudes. Both were equally interested in development and growth. Some of this
development might well not be along traditional lines but involving social change.
This could and had been presented with considerable success, particularly by those
who believe that "small is beautiful". Perhaps in technique and approach the
large organisations could learn much from the small pressure groups.

12

Changes in the Working Environment

Michael C. Pocock, CBE

*Chairman, Shell Transport and Trading Company Limited and
Senior Managing Director of the Royal Dutch/Shell Group of
Companies*

My subject must be set against the backdrop of economic and social change
affecting companies. I guess we could agree together quite a list of problems
facing business internationally – low economic growth; an industrialised economy
thrives on four motors of growth – private investment, public expenditure, world
trade and domestic spending. But today we see the first three stumbling, only
domestic spending is buoyant and that is scarcely healthy, certainly not in
isolation. There is little drive from new technology (except microchips, which
is an opportunity rather than a problem). No push from the economies of scale
because the limit has already been reached or even exceeded. There is efficient
new competition from the newly industrialised countries (NIC), blessed with up to
date plant, relatively low wages and a driving work ethic. This means a constant
shift in the balance of world trade and it exacerbates existing problems of
monetary imbalance and exchange instability.

We now see another massive transfer of money from oil-consuming countries to OPEC,
and either we accept this as a fact – as a transfer of wealth with deflationary
effect in our economies – or we try to compensate for it by printing money to hide
the effect. The first hits employment, the second fuels inflation – not an easy
choice.

So the world is in economic flux and structural change is continuously essential.
Yet there is resistance to change – immobile work force, unflagging wage demands,
unions both too powerful and too weak, sometimes squabbling amongst themselves,
and the unrelenting popular demands in the "entitlement state", all driving
inflation upwards. Investment is weak because of lack of confidence, because we
shy away from risk in the no-risk mentality of our societies, because of the
stopping power of small groups, consumerism, over-regulation in response to vocal
pressures and the general over-burden of state sectors which employ one-third or
more of our total workers.

It is a catalogue of woes which can lead – and indeed does – to persistent under-
performance of our Western economies, worrying bouts of inflation combined with
persistent pockets of unemployment and thus to social conflict, alienation of
youth, despair of the unskilled, break-down of authority and the threat of
political disruption.

In our Shell scenarios, we call this "World of Internal Contradictions" (WIC).
Perhaps the "Revolution of Rising Frustrations" would be another way of describing
it. No wonder that confidence is fragile and we live in perplexed insecurity,
and yet:

(a)   There are new ideas and successful sectors.
(b)   There are new markets in countries which have money to buy.
(c)   There are developing countries which organise for success, and
       I do not mean just the handful of six newly industrialising
       countries.
(d)   There are great opportunities for effective private enterprise,
       to work even in the government sector, there are jobs to be
       done – many thousands of them, if citizens have money in their
       pocket to buy and entrepreneurs feel it is worthwhile doing the
       job.   The answer to unemployment must be to widen job
       opportunities rather than to protect the out of date.

So our WIC scenario is inherently unstable. A corrective swing will come, but I
am afraid not yet, so my bet for trends in the 1980's is:

(i)   The Decade of Energy Challenge. After Iran and after Camp David we
cannot expect willing cooperation from key producing countries.   This holds out a
prospect of tight oil supply, which means higher prices, which leads to low
economic growth, and to a certain degree the cycle can be recurrent, leading at
some stage to deeper production restrictions.   The vulnerability of consuming
countries is obvious and dangerous because we should not believe that Iran will be
the last "accident".   It may take ten years for us to move to a new energy balance
but we must act now; first on conservation, which means belt-tightening; second,
on energy efficiency, which is a positive concept (it means new investment and new
jobs); and, third, on the great investment opportunities in coal and in nuclear.

(ii)   The Decade of the NICs or the "New Japans".   There will be dynamic
growth in the Pacific Basin and parts of Latin America.   This shift in world trade
challenges even the efficient industries of Japan itself.   In OECD it can lead to
new opportunities or to protectionism, to new employment or to structural
unemployment, the choice depends on our flexibility.

(iii)   Probably, but I think not certainly, this will be the Decade of
Conflict with the Less Developed Countries.   They are not a homogeneous body.
Some have already developed outstandingly, others are organising themselves to
meet the world.   Others of course – and I mean the poorest 30 of them – are in dire
trouble.   Their needs are obvious but how to meet the needs in a perplexed world is
not, nor is their own capacity to absorb help effectively.   I believe there is too
much generalisation about great principles of global economic justice, too much
argument about who is to blame and too little concentration on the areas where real
progress has been made and is still possible. Here again, there remain great
opportunities for private enterprise to contribute to their development on a basis
of contract, not of status, but contracts require dialogue, not slogans, and
contracts are meant to be kept.

Conclusions

1.   We will muddle our way through, not in a recession but not in $3\frac{1}{2}$ per cent
growth either. The question is, will our social and political fabric stand the
strain for so many years?   Above all, we must recognise new facts, and I quote
from a paper by Walter Hoadley of the Bank of America:

"A large part of the private sector's uncertainty," he says, "can be traced to the
failure to distinguish between cyclical or recurring change and structural or more
permanent change."   He gives these examples of structural changes in progress.
"slower real growth, persistent inflation, rising expectations of a better life,
massive pressures for more equality, effects or rising education challenging the
status quo, shortages of energy and other resources, higher standards of ethics

and human rights, and entrenchment of consumerism and environmentalism. The problem", he says, "is that too many businesses are waiting for conditions to return to normal when, in fact, what we are seeing today is the new normal. The good old days are gone. We have two choices: we can adjust to these structural changes, make the most of them, find new opportunities and keep moving forward, or we can retrench, drift and wait. One's not easy, the other unthinkable."

2.   So the threats are obvious and it is also obvious that industry cannot wait until the climate improves. We have to live and prosper now. Of course we would find it easier to achieve the necessary structural change if there were decent growth, but we still have to make these changes in a climate of little or no growth. A company, like a country, has two choices: it can hunker down and wait for the storm to pass or it can organise itself to overcome the threats and find the opportunities. Let us consider how we can set about doing this, under three headings: relationships with government, with the community, and with the work force.

3.   Industry and Governments

I have little time for those who say to governments "leave us alone, get off our backs". Too often those same people are the first to look for government help at a moment of trouble - special subsidies, injection from public funds, protection from unwelcome imports. Perhaps I am over-influenced by my background in oil, which is - has to be - very much "government business", but I believe as a general proposition that industry has a *high need* of government support, first obviously to provide an efficient physical infra-structure. But we also need government:

-     to set a sensible economic climate where endeavour and skill are rewarded, where the fruits of long-term investment bear proper relationship to the risks;

-     to support long-term research and development, which is often beyond the proper capcity of industry;

-     to carry out international trade negotiations, which are the necessary web of an interrelated trading world, in a way that helps - or at least without harming - our business.

And I believe that this calls for a close dialogue with government, not only by the industry confederations and trade associations but directly by companies where they have a special contribution. I believe that this dialogue should be reinforced, ideally by the interchange of staff, which proves not easy in practice; certainly by joint training courses and seminars - not perhaps seeking a tie as "incestuous" as the French interlocked establishment but surely more can be done to establish a close understanding of the different decision processes of the parties.

The links should be forged not only with civil servants but with politicians too. Our time horizons are different but usually there is a fair understanding. Where we can and must object is when the government, in pursuit of its social/economic aims, creates systems which seem damaging to the economy - price controls, wage freezes, the squeezing of differentials, job protection rather than job creation, immobility of housing - all of these demand a sharp riposte.

It is tempting to say the same about *regulation* on industry - planning controls, environmental curbs and so on - but I have little faith that in the event these will go away because the vocal pressures in a democratic system are too strong. Indeed we often welcome official standards just because they are universally applied. I believe the practical answer is to understand the system and to mitigate its worst effects by enlisting the counterbalancing forces - those whose proper interests are harmed by excessive regulation.   Why not pro-nuclear demonstrations?

There are occasions too where we can and must fight openly, where government seeks to change the rules of the game arbitrarily.   Nationalisation is an obvious example;   sometimes the managements themselves may not have a stomach for the fight but the corporation as an entity must.   Being asked to play the competitive game with loaded dice is another example, for instance in the unfair advantages accorded to the British National Oil Corporation ((BNOC).   Governments and their politicians must expect us to fight back on such issues because it is our duty. In fact they are probably surprised at how rarely we do this and how ineffective we are at prosecuting the war of speeches and press conferences.   Often our public relations efforts are fairly reported, but maybe we suffer from too little follow-up, too little of a sustained drive.

So there are occasions when we must adopt an adversary role, but for the most part industry and government are "partners in progess".   No government in a mixed economy can risk damaging the industry on which its policies depend, even though it may have different ideas of the contribution that industry should make; our job is to ensure that government understands us and consults us where we have a special interest.

The main rub comes from dirigiste governments who sincerely believe that you can "plan" industrial life.   They take their examples from monopoly industries like power supply and apply these to competitive activities like making motor cars, and then they wonder why we cannot sign meaningful planning agreements.   The truth of course is that in an open trading world the belief that you can live up to firm forecasts is a delusion, constantly upset by the whims of customers and by the raw facts of competition.   We in Shell certainly <u>invest</u> long-term, looking ten years ahead or more, but in our trading life we live with the 70/20/10 rule - 70 per cent of our attention is to "crisis" management, at a short term, 20 per cent is real planning for what may happen in the market in the next two years, and 10 per cent of our time is planning aimed at the longer term.   We would not expect it to be any other way.   Governments may not like it, but they have to calculate the same way.   Perhaps by now real life has tempered their ambitions, and we can revert to a quiet dialogue between government and companies which recognises the reality of the industrial market.

4.   Industry and the Community

I now turn to an area where the public relations influence is paramount - the relationship of companies with the community - both national and local.   The public relations job is to encourage the acceptability of business in society, no less, but <u>acceptability</u> must come first.   Good behaviour without good publicity is decent but unconvincing.   Good publicity without good behaviour is not only immoral, it is self-defeating.   You may build a reputation over many years but you can lose it by one stupid action.   To regain your reputation is a long, patient discipline, much more difficult than regaining a triple A status in the market, and it has nothing to do with "image".

So the first public relation task is internal, to help get the company's rules right and widely known inside (and maybe outside).   A code of conduct or statment of business principles helps, provided it is checked against practice and kept up to date.   In Shell we produced ours a few years ago, despite the doubts of many sceptics, and now we wonder how we lived without it.   Once you have identified your principles you have a base for dealing with the community.   But it does require continued good housekeeping (audits and check-lists).

It is difficult - maybe pointless - to generalise about societal values. The
climate for business in Japan is quite unlike that in the United States, yet the
value of wealth creation is broadly recognised in each of these societies. In
industrialised Western Europe, on the other hand, suffering as it does from
economic under-performance and social tensions, the traditional business values
are no longer accepted as automatically beneficial. Not surprising, perhaps when
it is evident that business values have not solved society's problems - persistent
unemployment, threatening inflation, unfulfilled expectations - all these seem not
to go away. So it is easily tempting to claim that it must be *business* that has
failed society and to seek some remedy by turning away from the creation of wealth,
forgetting that only a society made wealthy by business could presume to take such
a stance. The liberalism of the academic world has encouraged a hostile - or at
least cynical - attitude which indeed may be useful in academic discussion but
helps little with the imperatives of economic life. I do not think the doubts
will go away so I believe that business must tackle the doubters at their own game,
offer a dialogue, enlist the sympathetic voices - of which there are many - and not
duck the confrontation. We can shame the academics into friendly discussion. At
least they will know we are trying and they surely recognise that compared with
them we are amateurs at the dialogue game.

More difficult are dialogues with the environmentalists, who are dedicated and well
supported and usually by their nature not interested in growth, nor likely to be
persuaded by any economic argument. We must take them seriously and listen to the
argument, with a view to pressing the counter-arguments. We must get in early and
attempt to "manage" the dialogue towards the outcome we desire. An example is the
stymie-ing of new development. From many case-histories it is clear that we are
still woefully ill-equipped to win the battle of how to build new plant
particularly on greenfield sites. We have not learned enough about identifying -
and publishing - the damage caused by the stopping power of small groups. We have
not learned to identify the helpers, and build on these. Similarly, when there is
a serious accident, have we learned to step in and take the initiative, to bare the
facts and tackle the damage voluntarily before we are forced to do so by others?

The local communities around our plants are a special social responsibility. We
must accept entirely that they have a *right* to be involved, not just as to the
quality of the atmosphere but in the impact our establishments make on their
economic and social life. There are many methods - open days, information for
schools, work introduction for school-leavers, joint programmes with local
government, identification with local action committees, farming-out of services,
encouraging local firms - the list is endless. Improving the local environment is
good business sense, not just enlightened public relations.

A more difficult area is the responsibility of the individual firm to the public at
large. We now have no doubt that we must accept public accountability even if
public standards are constantly changing and society seems sometimes to be using
the corporation as a tool to achieve change which it has failed to achieve by the
legal process (the outlawing of bribery and of extortion - is an example). I feel
too that we must be ready with our response to wider national problems - ethnic
minorities would be one example, unemployment another - indeed probably tomorrow's
hidden time bomb. Of course we must rationalise our manpower and achieve internal
efficiency. Our own economic viability must be overriding. But yet we cannot
ignore the general impact of unemployment, so we have to ask ourselves what is our
duty to mitigate the impact.

Another area of public interest is disclosure of information. A lot has been said
about confidentiality, which I believe has been over-stressed as an excuse for doing
nothing. Usually it is clear enough what is really secret. The real objection to

disclosure is not that it gives ammunition to those who may use it against you – it is the cost, the confusion and the useless nature of the information. So we need to draw pretty clear limits of viability, but up to this point I believe that disclosure is a healthy discipline.   In the UK Clearing Banks, I hear, the requirement a few years ago to disclose their reserves educated them for the first time about what their real profits were. Of course we cannot bare everything, but the "need to know" philosophy is no longer good enough.

Moreover we have to live in the community. The standards by which we live evolve in society and society is bombarded by special-interest groups, so society needs to understand both sides of the argument.   Nowhere is the pressure seen more starkly than in the United States, which gives a perfect example of how corporations must respond to inform the public (myriad sectors of it) while there is still time, before damaging legislation overwhelms them.   We find that if we wish to see the need for a comprehensive community relations programme and the massive effort needed to sustain it, we send our national European and other executives to the United States for evidence.   (Not that it may seem to do much good!).

5.   Industrial Relations

So finally I come to the most pressing of our problems in the industrialised countries. How can companies achieve cooperation and maintain sound industrial relations between the work force and management, when they are pressed on three sides:

- first, by the unrelenting force of competition which demands flexibility and structural change;

- second, by the political force of parties which watch their votes, and of governments which demand democratic change; and

- third, by the protective force of workers' representatives who demand minimum change.

You all know the threat.   Voluntary sharing of information leads to a massive communication effort, this in turn leads to joint participation, this leads to co-determination at Board level and, for some, this in turn should lead finally to worker control.   The beguiling argument is that the more the employees know, the more they are involved and so, being reasonable people, the more they will act responsibly and cooperative in desirable aims.   It is difficult to deny this logic and difficult to describe where a halt should be called, but I will try. I believe, first, that we must distinguish two environments, which may merge in actual life but where the philosophy is in truth poles apart.

These environments have been described on the Continent (Netherlands) as a *Confrontation Model* (where union representatives confront management in an adversary role) as against the *Cooperation Model* (where employees in Works Councils sit together with management).   I think this is a simplistic dichotomy not normally recognisable in practice.   There are plenty of examples of cooperative industrial relations in countries where the Confrontation Model is supposed to exist (France), and there are many examples of bitter local confrontation, for instance in the United States, where the Cooperation Model of economic society is generally accepted.   I believe the problem is much simpler in psychological terms, and yet messier in its institutional mould.   The real dichotomy is "do your work force (and their professional representatives) agree with management that the health of the business is good for all, or do they ignore this?   And if they do accept it, will they put the health of the business above

their sectional interest?"   You might think that this is a fairly simple question,
yet case after case shows that the basic principle of economic health, of wealth
creation, of value added, is ignored and sectional advantage pursued as the over-
riding guidelines, self-defeating though this may be.

Our job therefore – and the public relations function has a prime role in this –
is to teach and persuade that we all have the same interest in the success of the
enterprise.   But let us start by accepting a few general principles:

- Employees are *entitled* to full *information* about developments which
  affect their jobs, and that means practically everything.

- Employees are *entitled* to *consultation* about changes which directly
  affect their working environment or conditions of service.

- Employees are *entitled* to expect that where they are so affected their
  views are *taken into account* and that these views will *influence
  decisions before* they are arrived at.

With an educated and knowledgeable work force it must be a blind management that
will not wish to take advantage of the benefit of this advice.   The problem is to
keep these areas distinguished and to establish :

(i)   where employees must be <u>told</u> what they must do, with appropriate
      explanation;

(ii) where employees must be <u>consulted</u> and their problems taken into
      account;   and

(iii) where the proper process is <u>bargaining</u> or <u>negotiation</u>.

There must be rules, there must be limits to disruptive action which are understood and tacitly accepted at any point in time, even though the boundaries will
no doubt shift over time.   You cannot, as we in Britain did through last winter,
tolerate chaos and pay wages for chaos also.

But there is a political element to it too.   We have seen in various countries in
Europe, and in the European Commission itself, several years of political endeavour
to bring a certain concept of "democracy" into industrial life.   It has been, and
in some places still is, a joining of hands between those political parties who
depend on union support with some – but by no means all – trade union officials who
seek to achieve control over industrial life via political action.   The aim is
cloaked in the reasonable terms of joint cooperation, and indeed it is easy to
point to positive factors in the proposals (for instance the Joint Representation
Committees in the British White Paper).   But the eventual aim has been made
clear: worker control – or, rather, union control – of much of the productive
process and eventually of planning and investment also.   Those who speechify
about "industrial democracy" by calling for the transfer of power to the workers
are sadly misinformed or, if not, they are trying to misinform the rest of us. The
workers in today's complex integrated industrial process already have power –
stopping power, that is, where just a few disgruntled or motivated people can stop
the work of thousands.

It is time that we stopped praising "industrial democracy" just because the word
"industry" is a good thing and the word "democracy" is a good thing in
representative government.   When the concept spreads to the work place it can
result in constant questioning, somewhat like daily referenda, about whether the
job shall be done, when and on what terms.   "Industrial chaocracy" would be a
better description; as Professor Dahrendorf has said, "total participation is

total immobility".

I see little joy in trying to apportion blame for bad industrial relations - is it the legacy of weak managements, unwilling to think things through or to take a stand on principle, is it unscrupulous competition, all too ready to sink thy neighbour, is it a fragmented union structure jealously guarding out-dated privileges? - all of these are no doubt true, in part and in places.   The real problem, if we reject the attempt to legislate in order to change attitudes, as I do, is what do we propose instead?   People talk of "participative" management, which has rather a woolly sound to it.   I prefer the term "open management".   It sounds good because openness exposes poor management, it sounds good because it it is open to discussion and influence, but it is still management.   I have no doubt that we will find it beneficial to enlist the participation of employees in constructive ways - setting work targets for instance, developing better working methods, optimising the use of plant and equipment.   I have no doubt that better educated employees will rightly insist on more autonomy, more self-starting, more self-motivation, a flatter organisation and less hierarchy.   Marx thought that in his ideal state all government would wither away.   I do not see much sign of that, but I do expect close supervision to wither away.

In this country (and I am sorry to finish on a UK note but it is a good example) we have a chance now to switch our attitudes towards the cooperative model, and I am sure there is a general willingness to move that way.   But just because the threat of legislation on industrial democracy has gone away for the moment in this country, it would be quite wrong to sink back into complacency.   I believe we must work hard at participation from the grass roots up.   If we let the matter drop the idealogues will be back in time with a new set of demands and we will richly deserve their attention.   In our Shell UK company they believe that participative endeavour should be concentrated at the grass roots level - plants, offices and installations - but should not be confined to nuts and bolts matters only. Employees and their representatives have a right, as they put it, "to have a shout" about changes that affect them, and this means that the UK Directors who authorise high policy must be seen at the work face and must join in the dialogue at that level.   Other companies may prefer a hierarchy of participation at different levels, even up to company headquarters, but in any event I hope that none of us will bend to tokenism and none of us will tolerate split Boards.

There are other initiatives and ideas that can greatly help - employee share ownership would be one (which we ourselves do not find easy), profit-sharing in the total company or part of it, a commitment to share with employees the value added arising from greater efficiency - there are many initiatives which may make sense in a particular environment.   There are also many gimmicks, and we need to turn a cold eye on these.

The key is working together for greater prosperity, which in turn will lead to job satisfaction and hopefully to stability of employment, which is not of course the same thing as job security.   It is said that the main difference between management in the UK and in Germany, say, is that our managers here spend up to 75 per cent of their time on industrial relations matters against only 25 per cent in Germany.   No doubt it would be nice if that differential slice of 50 per cent could be used on improving productivity, planning for the future, better quality and so on, but to my mind that is not really the problem;   the sad thing is that the 50 per cent is wasted on trivial argument.   If the same 50 per cent of management time could be spent on communication, seeking understanding and co-operation, how much better we all would be.

Let me finish on a hopeful note.   I do not expect to see S. Ramphal's Utopian new international economic order (NIEO) in my time. I do not even understand its consequences nor, I suspect, do most people who have worked at it. I do understand specific efforts in the area – commodity funds, income stabilisation plans, rescheduling of debts – there are many such programmes and they are of great individual significance; it is not helpful to ignore them.

No one serves an uneasy world by repeating heady slogans and I can assure you that country by country where we in Shell have joined in the dialogue of trade, investment or service with the governments of overseas countries, it is not done on the basis of United Nations slogans. We discuss together in a spirit of mutual benefit – what can we bring that you want and what are you prepared to pay for it (remember that brains and technical experience is about all we now have left) and may I say that in my experience the discussion takes place in a climate of mutual trust. That is the truth of the inter-change between the developing world and the developed, and I see no shame to it from either side.

So the challenge of this changing world in its relationships between the rich world, the very rich world, the fast-moving world and the emerging world is, as I see it:

- a willingness to understand the other party's fears, even where these seem irrational;
- a willingness to offer a flexible package in the mutual interest, even if such flexibility is not your ideal choice;
- a willingness to stand by deals honestly arrived at, or to renegotiate them on terms of equity;
- and on our part a willingness to help on proper terms because we have the skills, not only technical but – more important – the administrative capability and the integrated management which the developing world needs. For us this indeed makes economic sense and it fulfils our sense of decent duty too.

13

Public Relations in Action
How We Tackled the Problem

Introduction

The problem was to choose which six of the seventeen submissions were the most effective in demonstrating how a problem had been tackled or solved through public relations expertise. The problems, many extremely complex, ranged from internal relations within a building society, to community relations of a petrochemical company, a sugar industry, and in another study the timber industry. They included links between charities and the facilities offered by an hotel; links between Gerald Searle and computers; between the United Kingdom and the United States; case studies concerning the environment: domestically, related to Covent Garden, nationally (indeed internationally) related to conservation of a valuable material and the protection of the environment, or applied to classroom conditions. Others dealt with technological advances and their effect on a traditional industry; the importance of the individual within any organisation; the problems involved in arranging world-wide special events; in arranging visits for experts, and the need to use public relations techniques in training communicators.

To choose the most striking six case studies from this wealth of carefully prepared material from eight countries was the formidable task facing the panel of judges, all public relations practitioners with wide-ranging, penetrative knowledge of the art of public relations: Sir Fife Clark CBE FIPR, John Cole-Morgan DipCAM MIPR, James Derriman DipCAM FIPR, Peter Earl DipCAM FIPR, Denis Inchbald DipCAM FIPR and Margaret Nally DipCAM FIPR. Their work could have been made even more taxing had competitors availed themselves of the opportunity to submit entries in French or Spanish. In the event all were in English although originating from (among others) Belgium, Finland, Sweden and Turkey.

The six finalists, who agreed to give their ten-minute presentation in the special plenary session of the 8th World Public Relations Congress did so alphabetically by country. There were over 500 people attending this special feature on the last morning of the Congress - a very attentive audience who much enjoyed the presentations, most of which were augmented by amusing as well as artistically superb colour slides.

The texts of the six finalists' case studies are given below; each in its own way showed how a real life problem had been tackled and indeed overcome by the application of public relations techniques. When members of the audience were asked to vote which of the six presentations had impressed them most, the over-whelming number chose the meticulously prepared "Communication Festival", submitted and presented by Freddy Appassamy, Director of the Public Relations Office of the Sugar Industry in Port Louis, Mauritius.

The Chairman of the Session, Alan Eden-Green, in thanking the finalists for their valuable contribution to the Congress, stressed the indebtedness of the Congress not only to the six but to all those who had gone to considerable trouble to submit entries, a feature which had contributed so much to the enjoyment of all Congress participants.

Operation 200

Peter Mahon
Royce Public Relations

Operation 200 - a motivational communications programme was essentially designed for all the client and agency personnel responsible for the overall client performance rather than for its external consumers.

The Situation

Our client, Hotham Permanent Building Society became aware that its extraordinarily rapid growth over the past nine years had created management structural and communication problems at all levels within the Society which was reflected in its external performance.

By early 1977, the Society had slipped from No 2 position in the State of Victoria to No 3, the chance of a further slippage became a distinct possibility.

Staff morale was low, there was a general lack of incentive and there was a lack of effective inter-departmental communication.

The Objectives

The objectives of Operation 200 were very clear:

a)   To reverse the downward trend of the Society in relationship to its contemporaries and to seek a return to its rightful state as the No 2 Society in the State with an achievable goal of becoming No 1.

b)   To bring about a situation where there was clear interrelationship between all divisions within the Society on a divisional level, division to division and on a branch level, branch to branch, within divisions from head office to divisions and also from staff to staff.

c)   To reach a situation where all members of the Hotham Society from chairman to telephonist felt part of a growing organisation offering a distinctive service to the people of Victoria.

d)   Reactivating public confidence in the Society which would be reflected in an increased level of investment and savings accounts.

The Target Audiences

The target audiences for Operation 200 were clearly defined and were as follows:

Regional Managers

Branch Managers
Branch Staff
Head Office management and staff
Agents and Solicitors
Finally as a result of the above the public at large.

The Methods

To achieve the objective Royce Public Relations designed a programme titled
Operation 200. Its aim was to stimulate all marketing, sales and administration
staff into an over achieved position in a drive towards reaching a goal of $200
million in assets, within the forward 12 month period, a growth of almost 25 per
cent.

A multi-level competitive attitude was introduced amongst all staff. Awards were
offered for performance of staff against pre-set targets.

The Results

The target of $200 million in assets was reached during the period of the campaign
and the Society regained its former position as the second largest Society in
Victoria.

Operation 200 helped streamline internal communication and brought the Society
together as a total team.

The significance of Operation 200 was that it was a communications programme which
was essentially to internal publics, rather than the consumer.

The campaign whilst it officially wound up in March of 1978, is still having a
profound effect today with the Society enjoying record growth, improved
communication between staff at all levels and a high degree of enthusiastic staff
involvement.

Communication Festival

Freddy Appassamy

Public Relations Office of the Sugar Industry, Port Louis, Mauritius

The island of Mauritius lies approximately 1,250 miles off the east coast of Africa. It covers an area of 720 square miles and has an heterogeneous population of approximately 900,000.

The situation – The Objectives – The target audiences

Mauritius is essentially a sugar island and perhaps more so than any other island in the world. Sugar cane is cultivated on some 215,000 acres representing 47 per cent of the total island area. Sugar is produced by 21 mills and in a good year, production can reach 700,000 tons. The sugar industry is the largest employer of labour: 70,000 workers representing 36 per cent of the gainfully employed population. Sugar and its by-product molasses account for a-proximately 85 per cent of the country's visible exports, and for about one-third of its gross national income.

The sugar industry of Mauritius has always been known for its technical knowhow and efficiency. However, it was only in recent years that it started giving to its public relations the attention which it deserves. Indeed, it was not until 1968 that a central public relations office was created. Within three years all 21 sugar estates had appointed their own PRO's whose work was inspired and co-ordinated by the central office.

One of the priority assignments of the Public Relations Office of the Sugar Industry (PROSI) was to improve communications internally on the sugar estates (1,000 to 5,000 employees each), where human relations were anything but harmonious, and to make up for the communication gap which existed between the sugar industry and the population of the island at large. The industry was little known to, and misjudged by, the population and was always labouring under some form of socio-political pressure.

Something had therefore to be done to bring closer the internal public of the sugar estates – traditionally subdivided into three categories: staff, skilled workers, agricultural workers – and also to show the true face of the sugar estates to the population.

The method: "Sugar Time"

The local radio and television having readily agreed to cooperate in the joint production of a popular programme we took the opportunity to organise a song competition on sugar estates cultimating in a grand finalé on television. Briefly, this is how the competition was run:

Estates' PRO's invited entries from employees on their respective estates and held preliminaries to allow a short listing of competitors who qualified in one of three categories: European songs, oriental songs and the "Sega" (the local folk song and dance). A programme for holding the finals on individual estates, in turn, was arranged and these finals were broadcast on radio. After all the sugar estates finals had been held, the three finalists from each estate – one for each category – took part in an inter-estate competition which was broadcast live on television a few days before the official opening of the harvest, and lasted from seven o'clock in the evening until one o'clock in the morning. The whole exercise spread over five months during the intercrop season, i.e. from February to June.

The success of Sugar Time in Mauritius was quite outstanding. The competition took place in 1971, 1972 and 1973 and had the full support of the government, the press and of the population at large. The finals on the individual estates attracted crowds 20,000 strong at times and it is estimated that 80 per cent of the population watched the grand finals on television. Sugar time having achieved its main objectives, and because attention had to be given to other priorities, the exercise was not repeated after 1973.

The results:

Internally, the evenings on the individual estates, which had to be organised by the employees themselves, created a remarkable team spirit and boosted up considerably their sense of belonging. Members of the personnel – staff, factory and field workers – joined hands in making the finals on their respective estates a success, and they took great pride in their estates being on the local radio for an hour or so. Throughout the radio programmes, the commentator gave as much information as possible on each estate which thus benefited from a nation-wide coverage of its achievements.

Further, the Estate Managers went on the stage for the prize giving and addressed the audience. They thus had a wonderful opportunity of putting across quite a few messages to their employees and their families, and to the outside public. From a public relations point of view they did an excellent job.

On a purely personal level, some of the prize winners – most of whom simple workers – encouraged by their success, improved their talent and subsequently achieved semi-professional status. But to them, the achievement of their life-time remained the part they played one evening in holding the flag of their estate on television, watched by thousands of their fellow countrymen.

On the whole, Sugar Time marked a turning point in human relations on the sugar estates and started a communication process which has constantly improved since. Although the situation cannot yet be said to be satisfactory, there is no doubt that Sugar Time marked the beginning of a new era in the field of internal public relations on the estates.

On the external publics of the industry the impact of Sugar Time was decidedly positive. It gave an opportunity to all the residents of the various factory areas, "to invade" the sugar estates and to see at close range, a domain which they had always felt was out of bounds to them. For their first contact with the industry, they saw it at its best, and in a very festive atmosphere.

The evening performances on the estates invariably ended up in fiestas with every-body singing and dancing. To a rural population very much deprived of public entertainment these performances were looked upon as a real blessing, and the audiences gave full credit for it to the sugar industry.

It is also worth mentioning that, in spite of the huge crowds which gathered on such occasions, not a single incident had to be deplored. In fact it was officially acknowledged that Sugar Time had a pacifying effect on the population, at a time of the year when, because of seasonal unemployment, the atmosphere in the country was usually tense.

For the sugar industry, Sugar Time constituted a fruitful dialogue with public opinion thanks to the very wide coverage which the press gave to the event for three consecutive years.

The six-hour television broadcast which covered the finals was, as can be imagined, a real public relations dream. In a way, the sugar industry, in its Sunday best, visited almost every Mauritian home and was welcomed with open arms. Throughout the programme, information on the sugar industry, its socio-economic activities and the various ways in which it serves the nation, was given by the commentator and was particularly well received because of the happy circumstances in which such information was offered.

It can safely be said that the public image of the sugar industry changed with Sugar Time: the human aspect of the industry revealed itself, and people discovered the happy faces which had hitherto been concealed to them by cane fields and factories.

Having lived every minute of that wonderful human experience one cannot help being very enthusiastic about it. It was not only a successful exercise from the sugar industry's standpoint, but it also gave a new dimension to public relations in the island and paved the way to other much needed professional activities in that field.

Here now is an extract from the Prime Minister's Speech on the occasion of the official opening of the crop ceremony.

"And before concluding I cannot refrain from mentioning my joy, that this harvest ceremony should follow so close on the heels of the Sugar Time Festival. I realise, more than every before, that the bonds that keep all of us together have been forged on the anvils of the endeavours of the labourer, the docker, the artisan, the Trade Unions, and the millers, and that such a close association should be lasting and indestructible in our march towards ordered progress and prosperity. The sense of national belonging generated by the harvest season has found its authentic voice in Sugar Time and in this official consecration here today. In this season of the year when everything has reached fruition, when the cane stands tall and proud and thousands of arms are ready to gather the crop, it is as if the whole of Mauritius were standing at the end of a year of fulfilment, on the threshold of a new life and of fresh expectations".

Philanthropy Pays

Mrs Betul Mardin

A and B Public Relations, Istanbul, Turkey

The Sheraton Corporation added the Istanbul Sheraton to its hotel chain in August, 1975. Although the 18 storey de luxe building with a magnificent view of the Bosphorus was considered to be one of the finest examples of modern Turkish architecture and was the largest in the whole country, when it opened the hotel was not enthusiastically received, nor enough genuine interest generated to create a group of loyal friends amongst the local people. This was in fact extremely surprising for Istanbul had only one other de luxe hotel, the Hilton. It was apparent that the management had failed to use the Hotel's outlets and facilities to their full capacity.

After the opening, one after another their public relations managers resigned. In fact they were changed three times within the first year. Naturally, almost no relations were established between the press and the Hotel. During this difficult year there had been a strike as well, so that the Hotel was closed over Christmas and New Year holidays. Shortly after the dispute was settled, an earthquake brought tragedy to the East of the country. To top it all, a very unfortunate incident disrupted all community relations at the Istanbul Sheraton.

In order to assist the Welfare Associations in raising funds for the grief stricken people of the earthquake region, a luncheon was organised by the hotel's Public Relations Manager for the concerned ladies who were distinguished members and la crème de la crème of Turkish Society. Due to a misunderstanding at the end of the luncheon a bill was presented to the ladies, who had thought that they were the guests of the Hotel. The Management not only lost face with the Western Associations but also put under great strain their relationship with the pillars of society. The Public Relations Manager resigned following the unfortunate incident. After six months with no public relations officers, for there was no one to accept the job, the Management decided to approach us - a consulting firm. Since we were the only Public Relations Firm in Turkey, with only three years experience to our credit, we could not take the risk of being unsuccessful. As the famous Turkish proverb goes, "who needs a guide when one sees the village?" But the challenge was such that we accepted the account in October, 1976.

First we drew up a plan to better relations with the press and as this would take time and patience, we set about collecting 10,000 names and addresses of potential clients and celebrities. Besides these the ladies who were social figures were listed and filed. We scanned all society columns and were very careful not to leave anybody out even if one was only a debutante, thinking that very soon she too might use our premises for a wedding or an engagement party. Two mail shots to these 10,000 addresses were made to inform the public of the Hotel's facilities and to check the authenticity of these addresses. During July we planned our strategy concerning the Welfare Associations and the third mail shot was posted. This was a letter to all the members of the hundreds of welfare associations of Turkey. We knew that the best policy was to approach each member rather than the chairman. The fact that usually these philanthropic organisations did not have their own premises to meet together constituted the appeal to them of our Hotel. The letter explained that if an association would hold its regular meetings in our hotel, the room would be theirs free of charge except for the food and beverage they consumed. The letters were mailed during the first week of September, when we knew associations started planning their annual activities. Indeed there was an immediate vast response.

One week later we gave the coup de grace. We offered all Associations a package deal called, "colourful Thursday", which really meant Thursday lunches with mini fashion shows.

The deal had five objectives.

1.   to promote the hotel's high standard of cuisine
2.   to attract the distinguished members of society to the hotel
3.   to create an image of sophistication by featuring Turkish "haute couture" designers
4.   to establish and strengthen relationships with the charitable associations
5.   to get press coverage.

A specially reduced charge was offered enabling the charity associations to make a substantial profit and still be able to sell the tickets at reasonable price.

The bargain price covered a meal as well as the fees of our four models and a compère who would introduce the programme on behalf of the Management, interview the chairman of that Thursday thus promoting their charitable work, help coordinate the culinary demonstration and eventually present the fashion show.

The Hotel would supply the podium, taped music, lighting effects and even a new gimmick for each designer. All this meant that we at the Sheraton would find the designer, organise the fashion show, hire the models, think of a theme for the day, find the appropriate props, select the music, talk to the compère, invite the press, arrange the room and take full responsibility for the day. The only work that was required from the concerned association was to sell the tickets and for the chairman to stop for a moment to choose one out of the six menus on offer.

Upon the advice of the Food and Beverage Department, we decided to offer six different menus, introducing speciality dishes that would be a show case for the chef, as well as securing easy and smooth service for the Maitre D'Hotel who had to deal with 200 fastidious guests. To underline the importance of the Chef and to add colour to the day, we asked him to demonstrate one flambé dish each Thursday before the very eyes of the audience. Whilst he was mixing the ingredients the printed recipes were distributed amongst the ladies.

Before each event we sent press releases and invited reporters so that news appeared in the pages of the press and magazines continuously.

The first Thursday was on 17th October, 1977, 180 ladies attended and it was an immediate and tremendous success. When the last one was realised on the 24th April 1978, we had already organised 14 Colourful Thursdays and we had to move out of the specialty restaurant Le Mangal which could only seat 200 people to the Ballroom, in view of the rapidly increasing demand. In fact, the last Thursday saw us catering for 480 ladies who by now had become Sheraton fans.

The Hotel became trendy. The awareness of the immense possibilities this Hotel has started a flow of the local people to the premises. Consequently, the Sheraton became very much the centre of all important activities, which received extensive coverage by the Turkish Press.

As a result of the Colourful Thursdays, a new image was established for the Istanbul Sheraton. In view of the fact that some of these philanthropic organisations included projects to help solve various environmental problems the Istanbul Sheraton built itself a reputation of having a keen sense of social responsibility.

The designers were so pleased with the whole arrangement that the textile and ready to wear industry were made aware of the possibilities the Hotel offered. A new sort of business started: seasonal fashion shows, expositions for whole-salers as well as our rooms being used for travelling foreign and domestic buyers.

The Hotel is now working to full capacity. Meeting rooms have to be reserved a year in advance and the Ballroom at least three months ahead.

Yes, Philanthropy pays.

The British are Coming

Roger Fennings

Carl Byoir and Associates, London

In American Bicentennial Year 1976 Carl Byoir and Associates were appointed public relations consultants to the United States Travel Service. USTS is the National Government tourist office of the United States and is part of the Department of Commerce. Our brief on their behalf was to 'increase and encourage travel to and within the United States', and in so doing allay traditional fears of distance, expense, violence and difficulty of obtaining visas.

Ease of travel to and within the United States, inexpensive food and accommodation, variety of scenery and attractions, common language and hospitable people were all strong aspects of a product that had to be sold to a potentially vast travelling public, a public which was to include both the family holidaymaker and the businessman. And to convert the media coverage achieved to persuade the potential traveller into an actual ticket sale a substantial programme aimed at educating travel agents was also to be part of our task.

Our target audience was huge and media included radio, television, national and provincial newspapers, magazines and periodicals, both consumer and business - and the vitally important travel trade press. With a subject as varied and exciting as America the outlets were almost unlimited. To assist us in putting together an effective programme USTS in Washington together with Carl Byoir agreed on a number of methods to be used to achieve the most effective results.

The best of these has proved to be an intensive programme of journalists and agents visits, or familiarisation tours. On average, Byoir arranged some 200 journalists visits a year.

These visits fall into distinct categories. The first is the individual journalists visit where, with the authority of the US Government, Byoir request the granting of Civil Aeronautics Board waivers, with the concurrence of the airlines involved, to bona fide journalists or broadcasters visiting the US to produce travel-oriented material. Then, in conjunction with local state or city visitors and convention bureaux other facilities, such as local tours, are arranged

Another type of visit is the theme tour. As the name implies, USTS in Washington designs itineraries around certain themes - for example regional food, wildlife, national parks, and so on. These themes are developed from our input according to what we estimate to be the needs of our market. On these tours our expertise is required in selecting the best possible participants - participants who will be both productive and compatible with other journalists from around the world.

Thirdly, there is the industry-spnsored tour. A commercial enterprise such as BP or Disneyland might wish to sponsor a journalist visit - Byoir, on behalf of USTS, would select the most suitable participants and make all necessary arrangements.

But the most successful type of visit has been the post-Originated tour. Using a special budget allocation Byoir is authorised to design its own itinerary and select participants to provide outstanding coverage - and to set an example as to what represents a truly professional and productive travel media visit. This year's visit had four leading writers flown in a private aircraft for eight days through all the major national parks in the 11 states of the mountain west, an exercise which earned credibility and respect for both client and consultant - and produced massive coverage in the national and trade press.

In support of the familiarisation tour programme a number of other highly effective means have been used to get the message across. These include, for example, a wide range of feature packs on an enormous variety of subjects ranging from ancient American Indian civilisations to drag racing and the space shuttle. Features on food in New Orleans, the Kentucky Derby, or the Old Time Fiddlers contest in Idaho. These features and accompanying photographs are updated regularly and made ideal material for provincial press, or special interest magazines. They are all listed in our Feature Pack Directory, which is circulated to all appropriate editors.

Additionally, Byoir maintain an extensive black and white and colour photograph library on behalf of USTS - a full time job for our librarian.

The results, in the words of our client, have been "staggering". Travel from Britain to the United States has increased consistently over the past three years, and current US Government figures reflect an increase of 56 per cent which means that close on a million Britons travelled to America last year, and these numbers are expected to continue to rise dramatically.

I could tell you about the hours of television coverage which are the direct results of our efforts, but you have probably seen them. I could show you books of press cuttings from leading papers and magazines, but you have probably read them.

When evaluated, the millions of dollars worth of media coverage our efforts have produced show the public relations budget allocated to us by the US Government to have been a wise investment.

What is today's fastest growing travel destination? America. Everyone knows that.

And we at Carl Byoir are proud to know that we had something to do with it.

New Glass for Old

Denis Inchbald

Welbeck Public Relations, London

At 3.45 pm on Sunday 8th May 1971 an environmental group dumped a thousand empty bottles on the doorstep of a soft drinks manufacturer. And this was the start of the campaign against the Non-Returnable Bottle in the United Kingdom.

The Problem

The Group claimed that it was a waste to throw bottles in the dustbin. A credible claim and one that received support from many quarters with the media and politicians quickly jumping on what was to become a bandwagon of the seventies – Conservation.

The campaign grew rapidly to cause considerable direct pressure on the manufacturers of glass containers, represented by the Glass Manufacturers Federation. The debate spread; witness the numerous studies carried out all over the world.

In the United Kingdom, Welbeck Public Relations was brought in to advise the Glass Container Industry. Our evaluation led us to set the following objectives.

Objectives

Firstly, as ALL packaging was non-returnable, cans, plastics – even paper – would have to be brought into the debate (widening the issue would obviously benefit the glass container industry); Secondly, the case against non-returnable bottles was unproven: the Industry would need to seek out its own information and decide on its own case and present it to the various target groups; Finally, by definition, ANYTHING thrown away would be waste. If waste could be recovered efficiently this would be most desirable, especially in view of the various forecasts of 'growth' and the ensuing problems. The objective then would be to devise a method of salvaging glass.

Target audiences.

The main target audiences for the campaign were those normally described as 'opinion-formers' including: MP's, the media, consumer groups, government departments (particularly important); the EEC (and in particular the Environmental Protection Service); and the general public.

This is the background. Let us examine what has happened.

The programme and results

Firstly, how successful have we been in ensuring that all forms of container are

considered by the various Government bodies? The answer to this is clear. In the
United Kingdom an Industry Committee for Packaging and the Environment has been
formed and the Government has set up a Waste Management Advisory Council. This
latter body is carrying out a study of non-returnable containers of all types.

Secondly, how successful have we been in establishing the case for the non-
returnable bottle?

On the narrow question of non-returnable beverage containers, the Industry has
pointed out, with some success, that to consider environmental factors and ignore
social and economic consequences would be foolish to say the least. Studies in
the United Kingdom and overseas have since demonstrated that the case against non-
returnables, and in favour of the returnable bottle, is marginal if indeed it
exists.

The environmentalists in putting their case originally, not only exaggerated 'the
facts' as they saw them, but ignored totally the consequences of their call for
legislation.

The Glass Manufacturers Federation called together the Glass Industries from the
EEC to a seminar in Sheffield where the whole problem was debated at length and an
action programme was presented by Welbeck. The purpose of this gathering was to
ensure that the Glass Container Industry throughout Europe was well briefed and
able to present its point of view to the best effect to its own national
Governments.

This has proven to have been most important as the EEC in recent years turned its
attention to the problem and has also undertaken a study. Thanks to the GMF's
initiative the Glass Container Industry throughout Europe has been represented on
the various EEC Committees and has been most effective in presenting its views.

Thirdly, how successful have we been in reducing waste? This is clearly the most
interesting and positive aspect of the public relation programme. The problem was
the growing mountain of waste of all types; the GMF's answer was to rest in a GLASS
RECYCLING PROGRAMME.

The task we faced, together with our client, was to devise a method of recycling
glass. The method would clearly have to appeal to the public who would be critical
in ensuring the success of the scheme and the scheme would have to be self-financing.
Research was undertaken into finding ways of recycling glass either alone or as part
of a comprehensive reclamation project and the GMF's Environmental Manager visited
several overseas countries to see how they were coping with recycling glass.

After several false starts a successful method has now been developed in the United
Kingdom. It is known as the Bottle Bank scheme.

Bottle Banks are essentially skips, not too dissimilar from the types used by
builders. The skips are modified to give sections for the three colours of glass;
clear, amber and green. The public are asked to put their empty bottles into the
skips which are operated by the local authority which empties the skips at regular
intervals and stores the glass until a bulk load has accumulated.

Then the glass manufacturer collects the glass, takes it to its factory, and re-
cycles it by melting it down in the furnaces. From this molten glass comes the
bottles and jars.

The glass manufacturer pays an agreed price to the local authority for all the
glass collected.

The key to the success of the scheme is to gain the cooperation of local authorities and of the general public. And it is interesting to note that when the scheme was originally launched, some 40 local authorities were approached and only five could be persuaded to take part. Well now, the Glass Manufacturers Federation has a list of over 250 local authorities who are interested in operating their own Bottle Bank scheme.

As far as the general public is concerned it was essential, and still is, to motivate people within the regions of Bottle Banks to bring their bottles and jars for recycling. When the scheme was launched we pointed out in our press material that local authorities could save something like £11 million a year if the scheme was adopted throughout Britain.

We also indicated how savings could be made locally if Bottle Banks were operated and this publicity allied to the fact that a proportion of the public are concerned to save waste has helped make the scheme the success it has been to date.

After 15 months of operation, over 150,000 people are now depositing their waste bottles and jars at a Bottle Bank container every week.

Research we have carried out recently in two of the Bottle Bank towns established that something like 20-25 per cent of the local population used Bottle Banks regularly. This is a much higher figure than we had expected and one that makes glass recycling a viable and effective method of reducing waste and, indeed, making a small contribution to local rates or local charities.

The research carried out established that the main motivation for people using the Bottle Bank was to appease the guilt feelings they experienced when throwing bottles away. Glass is essentially an attractive material and people are far more emotional about throwing away a glass bottle than they are a can or a plastic bottle.

The market research company exmployed to carry out the survey commented in their report, "It is very unusual in our experience for a survey to show so few objections being raised to a new scheme or for such a scheme to be so widely accepted by all classes and age groups.

"It is equally unusual to find such very wide awareness, not merely of the existence of such a scheme but also of its purpose and the way it works".

To date we have launched over 30 Bottle Bank schemes with local authorities in the United Kingdom and plans are now being developed for the building of Cleansing Plants to handle the next phase of development for the scheme.

To summarise the campaign. The Glass Manufacturers Federation has made great efforts to communicate its faith in its own product.

It has held meetings and carried out presentations to the media, to consumer groups, to local authoriites and to MP's. It has been successful in convincing people who were in the early '70's wanting to press ahead with legislation that there was another way. Glass recycling has one massive advantage over any of the legislative options, and that is that it is capable of salvaging all types of glass container - not just non-returnable beverage containers. So potentially we have a solution to a problem and a solution that will ensure the continued prosperity of the Industry and, in a far wider context, make a contribution towards conservation of our environment.

The Renaissance of the Individual

Ronald Rhody

*Kaiser Aluminum and Chemical Corporation, Oakland, California,
United States of America*

For the past five years, we in Kaiser Aluminum and Chemical Corporation have been living through something of an industrial phenomenon. For want of a better description, it might be called "the renaissance of the individual". It has produced some remarkable changes in my organisation - changes for the better. And that is what I want to talk with you about today - about what can happen when real emphasis is placed on individual worth, and excellence, and initiative.

To put my remarks in context, it might be helpful to give you a little background on the kind of company we are, and what we do. We are a multi-product company that produces aluminum, industrial and agricultural chemicals, refractories, and additionally, we are engaged in major real estate operations and in international commodities trading. We are a multi-national company with approximately 100 major plants and facilities in 33 states in the United States and with operations in 17 countries outside the United States.

With that brief introduction, let me tell you about "One Person". A little over five years ago, things were not going very well for Kaiser Aluminum at all. We had just ended one of the worst years in our history. Morale was low and while the fortunes of the company were beginning to turn around, the only way that turn-around could be effected and sustained was if we received maximum effort and maximum contributions from the men and women who make up our corporation.

That was five years ago. Since then our earnings have been moving steadily upwards. Last year (1978) we completed the best year in our history. We are on our way to an even better year this year. Now, is all or even a part of this due to the "One Person Can Make A Difference" programme or to the attention that we have been putting on the importance of the individual in our company? I can not prove that it had, but I can say in truth that we would not have come so far, nor done so well, had we paid less attention to the importance of our people.

Almost immediately upon beginning the programme, we saw good things happen - good things that have benefited our company, our stockholders, and most importantly - our own employees. We saw costs saved, waste reduced, energy consumption cut, safety improved, additional contributions to profit made, and a special pride taken in the quality of our products and in serving our customers. These, and other beneficial activities on the part of individuals, and teams of individuals, within our company truly have made a difference.

We make no concerted attempt at the corporate level to keep track of such things as the cost savings or improvements in operating efficiencies that have resulted from the "One Person" programme, but the reports that come into corporate headquarters from individual plant managers indicate that the programme has, and is, producing a cost savings ranging from hundreds of thousands to several millions of dollars annually.

The programme is the essence of simplicity; for it is based on the very simple premise that one person really does make a difference. In order for the programme to be effective, however, it must be tailored to fit the individual objectives of the organisation using it. Typically, the programme is announced, or introduced, to all employees by either the location manager or the chief executive officer of the company. The introduction normally focuses on the problems or opportunities which face the organisation and defines the objectives which must be met in order to either solve the problem or take full advantage of the opportunities. All employees at all levels are invited "inside" the company – they are taken into the confidence of management – made a part of the team. The point is made that the objectives can be achieved only through the individual and combined efforts of people. The need for individual initiative and individual excellence is stressed.

Management then asks the support of everyone helping reach these objectives and encourages all who believe that one person does make a difference, and who have the confidence in their ability to reach the goals, to wear the symbol of the programme – a distinctive No 1. This symbol is made available in a wide variety of forms and is used in a multiplicity of ways to keep attention focused on the objectives of the programme. Simple slogans such as "One person can make a difference in efficiency". "One person can make a difference in quality, or in safety, or in production". Alternately, the No 1 symbols are used to help generate pride in accomplishment – to indicate that the plant or location intends to be No 1 in safety, or production, or efficiency.

Throughout the programme attention is constantly being focused on the objectives by the use of the slogans or the symbol, and by wide use of the symbol in a variety of ways – ranging from hard hat decals to posters.

In all instances, heavy emphasis is placed on personal recognition of individual and/or team achievement and accomplishment. Recognition of those who have made a difference is accomplished through such simple devices as short news-letter paragraphs, or bulletin board postings, or special posters that are used through-out the plants, etc. For the past three years, we have featured "No 1 employees" in our annual report – the company's most important external document.

There is no other "reward" other than recognition. The pride taken in a job well done, and a contribution made, seems to be enough.

It is, as you can see, a simple programme. That it has been so successful, has come as a surprise, an amazement, and a joy to all of us in Kaiser Aluminum. When we began the programme we felt it would be a success if it lasted two years. We are entering our sixth year now, and the programme seems to be getting stronger.

Having looked at the "how it works" part of the programme, let me take just a few minutes of why it works. First, and most importantly, we believe, we truly believe, that one person does make a difference, and our employees know that we believe it. Secondly, and perhaps equally as important, the programme is effective because it strikes a very responsive cord in these waning years of the century. And that cord resonates our of the sheer inadequacy that most people feel amid the problems and complexities of modern society. Wars, crime, violence, disease – everywhere one turns, things seem to be so large and so overpowering that the individual feels inadequate - unable to cope. More and more people feel they can do little about their situations.

But the "renaissance of the individual" contradicts all that. That is one of the reasons this programme has gone so well for us. There is a tremendous appeal in a large multi-national corporation like ours saying to its people - "You are important - you can make a difference - you do make a difference. You can and do make a difference in your community, in your state, in your country and you make a difference in this company by what you do. You are important". When things like that are said to people, they respond. They have responded, and they will continue to respond. They have gone that extra step. As I say, we have seen millions of dollars saved annually. We have seen much higher levels of morale throughout the company. We have seen a new interest taken by people in their jobs. We have seen a new pride generated by people in their work and in themselves.

As an adjunct to the "One Person" programme, we also launched last year a special programme for wives of our employees. In this programme, called "IRIS", we have invited the wives "inside" too. We have said we want them to know as much about the company as they want to know. We have told them we want them to understand our problems. And we have said that we would like their help on occasion in solving some of these problems. We hold special seminars and plant tours for the wives. We give them special training in such things as public speaking. We encourage them to be active in their own communities. We encourage them to be involved in helping solve the problems they are concerned about. We have said to them also "you are important, you do make a difference to this company". As I think you might imagine, the response has been excellent.

The "One Person" programme worked so well for us that we offered it to other companies in the United States. So far, we have had over 1500 requests for the programme and, while we have no definite count, we know that a number of companies are using the programme either in toto or variations of it suited to their special circumstances.

In closing, let me summarise in this manner: The fundamental reason that the "One Person" programme has succeeded so well in our company is because we have truly concluded that people are the most important resource we have.

We not only say so - we act so. Perhaps more important, though, all of us have grown to understand that if we hope to continue to succeed as a company, or in any company, we must recognise one basic fact. The basic fact is that in our company, or in any company, we are all mutually interdependent. Hourly, salaried, titled, untitled - at whatever level, the company succeeds only if all of us do our jobs as best they can be done - working together. In order for us to do that, we need to stimulate initiative, pride and excellence in ourselves and among those with whom we work. The "One Person" programme has given us the opportunity to do so. For the company it has been a phenomenon. For our employees it has indeed been the "renaissance of the individual".

14

Professional Practice and Ethics

Carlos M. Tomás

Director of Public Relations and Public Relations Studies, ESADE
(School of Management), Barcelona, Spain

1. Crisis - Credibility

"While most people are aware that a major revolution in communication techniques
has been going on for a number of years there are a great many thinking people who
are convinced that the content of the messages has been deteriorating. Truth,
reality and exactitude are gradually being swamped by dogma, illusion and vagueness."

I feel that it is highly pertinent to begin my talk with words taken from Prince
Philip's message to our Congress, a message which could have been written
expressly for this working session at which I am going to pose a few questions
which I feel affect us all. Perhaps after a mutual discussion we will be able to
find some ways to answer these questions.

First of all, I would like to stress Prince Philip's statement that "a great many
thinking people are convinced that the content of messages has been deteriorating".
We public relations professionals are daily in a position to observe the
deterioration of messages: we are constantly confronted by messages which lack
credibility for their intended recipients and which are therefore rejected by them.
This lack of credibility has spread from the messages themselves to the senders of
the messages. And among these senders of messages are corporations, institutions,
governmental agencies, etc. where public relations professionals are working either
as full-time staff members or as freelance consultants.

But is not this lack of credibility only a part - and a consequence - of a larger
crisis?

There are authors who unhesitatingly state that we are in a state of *global crisis,*
one of those crises which occurs from time to time throughout history. Erosion and
deterioration of the old order and emergence of the new. A quick look at the
different continents can give us an idea of the major changes taking place throughout the world: changes in politics, society, economy, religion, generations,
family structures, etc. and of the crises resulting from them, crises which cause
many people to feel a *lack of identity* or, as we say in Spanish, a *"crisis"* of
identity.

But it is precisely in times of crisis that we must reply to the new challenges
which face us and must reflect singly and in professional groups about what we can
contribute to this changing world. What contribution can we make here and now
which will give an immediate hope for correcting the lack of credibility of
institutions, corporations, systems, etc. and of the messages they transmit?

2.   Manipulation - Freedom

In the brief history of public relations many professionals in the field have already sensed the correlation between professional practice and ethics. We have all seen how the content of the messages we transmit is judged by the recipients and how these recipients find them more or less credible depending upon their opinion of the ethics of the sender. And, as all public relations professionals will agree, these messages are more than mere communications. In the recent First World Assembly of Public Relations' Associations, the Presidents of twenty-eight Associations, the FAPRA and FIARP Federations and the IPRA signed the Mexican statement on August 12th 1978 declaring that "Public Relations Practice is the art and social science of analysing trends, predicting their consequences, counselling organisation leaders and implementing planned programmes of action which will serve both the organisation's and the public's interest".

In order to exercise the profession thus defined, the majority of National Associations and Federations had already adopted a Code of Ethics. "In most cases they have taken the Code of Athens as it stands, or as a model with some local variation," Herbert M. Lloyd [1] tells us.

Today any mention of Public Relations Ethics is often synonomous with mentioning the INTERNATIONAL PUBLIC RELATIONS CODE OF ETHICS adopted by both CERP and IPRA.

The Athens Code is a moral Magna Carta of public relations, based on the *Universal Declaration of Human Rights* and, as such, can give rise to a second reflection: the historic confrontation of the concepts of FREEDOM and MANIPULATION.

I will base my thoughts on this subject on some quotations from Rahner [2]:

"The history of man continues to be basically a history of freedom struggling against manipulation, and not just a permanent history of other manipulations which are simply disguised as objectifications and possibilitations of freedom".

"As regards the task and objective of Society as such, freedom certainly does not mean the whim of the individual who does whatever he wants, thoughtlessly following his impulses. Freedom in this social sense means the best possible protection against manipulation of the individual and of Society by specific and anonymous social groups and forces; it means the greatest possible participation by the individual in the social process which should therefore - insofar as possible - be carried out in an open, rational and above-board way; and it also obviously means that Society will aid the individual to express his personal freedom".

While those Human Rights which we adhere to and defend have been a great advance in the conquest of freedom from all type of manipulations, it may still be asked if we public relations professionals are really working today - in those corporations, institutions, government agencies, etc. to which we offer our services - for a free and just social order which will silence the threat constituted by those who want to manipulate society and rob us of those freedoms expressly granted by the Universal Declaration of Human Rights?

3.   Dogmatism - Communication

Another point which might be considered is whether our personal attitudes actually make effective communication easier or more difficult in the agencies and corporations where we work.

If, as a working hypothesis, we admit that the *dogmatism* which is at the root of our tendency to judge, evaluate, approve or disapprove, is the greatest barrier to inter-personal communication, we could have a point of departure from which to examine the question posed in the foregoing paragraph, i.e. do we make effective communication easier or more difficult? If "communicate" means to "put in common", then when different, even radically different, ideas are measured against one another there are two opposing attitudes which can be adopted right from the start. One attitude is that of being disposed to judge, thus approving or disapproving, of whatever our interlocutor says. Our judgments are made from the point of view of the "dogmatism" acquired by each one of us throughout our existence.

The other attitude would be to try to verify whether we have accurately understood what our interlocutor is saying and if we understand it as he himself understands it. Once this is verified we can begin a dialogue in which we both express our points of view, no matter how disparate they may be.

We might well say that *the greater a person's area of dogmatism, the more difficult it is to communicate with him*. We might also say that *if we seriously consider the ideas and the background of our interlocutor, we run a greater risk of changing our own ideas*.

We could also state that *the fact that a person has a reduced area of dogmatism is not tantamount to lacking a system of values, to not having some idea for which in the most extreme of cases, he would willingly give his life*.

If our job as public relations professionals really is to capture the essence of our environment and interpret the existing signs of change which presage a different sort of future, then I would like to see us get together to analyse the best way to facilitate communication and cause the fewest distortions of its effectiveness. Our jobs are carried out within a specific economic framework. How do we capture and transmit criticism of this framework?

In order to examine our attitude of communication in this sense, I am going to quote now from Professor Sampedro[3] who writes: "We have developed a life style which is eminently artificial and destructive. But this deformative activity harbours the very weakness of the system and every day there is a growing awareness that this way of life cannot continue because, as is often said, *the model has its limits*. Not only is this awareness evident in the daily frustration of many or in studies - undeniably controversial - such as the first report from the Club of Rome, but also in more conventional texts such as the EEC environmental report from 1977-1981:

> 'Every day growing sectors of the population are rejecting
> the ideals and the hierarchy of values implicit in consumer
> societies while at the same time many phenomena of environ-
> mental saturation are becoming evident'.

"...this is a rejection not only of the current capitalist system but also of the socialist viewpoint which is equally technolatrous even though capitalism is consumer oriented while socialism leads to bureaucratisation".

"Different routes to reach an equilibrium"

"My reflections on this point lead me to conclude that, contrary to that pretence, expressed or otherwise, of the conventional Western economy, there does not exist a single path of development; instead, progress must be made by different routes, suitable for each case. I particularly see *two opposing orientations,* one for countries like those of industrialised Europe which have more than satisfied their material requirements and another for countries like India which still suffer from hunger and need".

"The former, whose development has placed exaggerated emphasis on externals should - if they act rationally - limit their material production and instead devote themselves more to the inner formation of man, which they have ignored for centuries now. On the other hand, the latter which have, in the case of India and other similar countries, maintained a rich inner culture, should make technical progress now in order to free themselves from the abject slavery of hunger and need. Thus, there exist two deliberately opposing ways to compensate for the currently existing imbalance. In the first case, inner progress to compensate for technolatrous excesses and, in the second, material development to give new bases to their inner culture. A distant future will see various adaptations of both routes (different versions for different societies) which would result in the convergence of industrialised nations with those of the Third World within a balanced area somewhere between outer- and inner- oriented development".

Here we could ask ourselves some questions on this subject: What is our attitude towards such visions of the future?   How do we transmit to our Corporations the future vision we capture, either the foregoing or another?   Are we really open to the signs of the times and do we try to keep them in mind when making decisions?

4.   The imperious need to live - Man's typical ability to maintain a distance

The European Code of Professional Conduct in Public Relations was approved in Lisbon in 1978 at the Meeting of the CERP Council and the CERP annual assembly.

The fact that a European Code of Professional Conduct has been approved gives me an opportunity to reflect about adhering to the values inherent in such a Code and to express my hope that, in the future, all of us gathered here today will collaborate in an attempt to present our differing points of view and explore possible response to the ever more insistent question of what the future holds.

Here, I would like to quote a few paragraphs from a recent work which impressed me greatly because of its serious approach to the subject matter and the high quality of the conclusions drawn. This work will, I think, aid us in our attempt to gauge the future's changes.

"What is typical of the animal impulse is the 'stimulus-response' circuit, i.e. the animal's interior is previously programmed in such a way that if a given object is perceived, the animal 'goes directly for that object'."

"Man, in turn, is a living being who speaks. Language transmits to the interlocutor a specific situation in which the speaker finds himself in relation to his environment and this situation is transmitted by the acoustic sound of the words. This means that language places the *experienced fact* in an acoustic sound - the word - in order to communicate it to the interlocutor".

"If the *experienced fact* transmitted by the speaker is an animal-type stimulus (as per the 'stimulus-response' circuit), the fact that he has been able to place this stimulus within a spoken word means that, even when the speaker is carried along by the current which leads him towards the object, he may simultaneously remain on the sidelines because he is capable of taking his own experienced fact as a whole and placing it within a word".

"This phenomenon of speaker extension means that he can be *experiencing his experienced fact* while simultaneously remaining *outside this fact*. It is the ability to be in the river and on the bank of the river at the same time. This is called 'man's typical ability to maintain a distance'. This distance is expressed in language and there is every indication that said distance is actually constituted by the language itself, i.e. by the fact of having found a place in which to put the experienced fact into an acoustic sound which is then transmitted to the interlocutor".

"This ability of man to maintain a distance explains the various human peculiarities. Thanks to this phenomenon, human behaviour has greater possibilities for innovation than does animal conduct".

"Even though man's 'imperious need to live' has its origin in his animal roots it is absolutely certain that this imperative and man's resulting behaviour are radically different from the imperatives and the behaviour of animals".

Thus, man's ability to maintain a distance permits him to stand on life's river bank reflecting and watching his life go by. He can live and reflect upon that life, and this is where he has the chance to establish a *set of values* which can serve as a guideline for living.

Here I would like to stress a point I made earlier. Even though we are disposed to die for a specific "cosmovision", this ideal must necessarily be constantly revised in the light of the changes taking place around us. And relating all this to the European Code of Conduct approved in Lisbon, I would like to say that the public relations professional's attitude towards the Code must be at once alive and reflective and that the Code must continually undergo the variations and adaptations necessary to bring it into line with new circumstances and social changes. This brings us to the need to delve more deeply and arrive at an *inner transformation,* i.e. to exercise the capacity to *maintain a distance* which is peculiar to man and which permits us to develop a profound and special sensitivity.

This inner transformation is by no means an ethereal and purely subjective thing. Inasmuch as we work together with other professionals with whom we meet in the various National Associations, we can discover some touchstone which will permit us to mutually probe to discover whether we are on the right path or if we have lost our bearings.

To conclude, I would ask that we think about and discuss the convenience of each Association of Public Relations Professional having a sub-group – which would at first be comprised largely of the persons present at this working session – to reflect upon a truly profound professional ethic and discuss the major ethical problems of the society and the profession in which we work while always *maintaining man's typical distance*. The questions which I have posed today could be the point of departure for contrasting subjective ideas with joint and objective action, questions such as: Does our behaviour create greater expectations of credibility? Do we contribute towards achieving greater areas of freedom? Does our professional comportment facilitate improved communication? Do we think seriously and deeply enough about our professional conduct?

The fruit of the reflections made by these groups of professionals could later be contrasted with the opinions of other members of the Association. This could then be discussed at a regional level and within the various Public Relations Federations and could be a permanent matter for reflection and examination at the World Congresses.

This would give us an opportunity to contribute the results of our continuous reflections on these subjects and I have no doubt that from these interchanges could come a greater hope in a future that will be more human, more free, and more profound.

References

1.   Lloyd, Herbert M. (1973). *First Report on Standards and Ethics of Public Relations Practice*. (London, Gold Paper n. One, IPRA.

2.   Rahner, Karl. (1978).   *Tolerancia - Libertad - Manipulación*. (Barcelona: Editorial Herder, 102-3. 104.

3.   Sampedro, José L. (1979). *La Crisis de los setenta*. (Barcelona: ESADE, 7.9.

4.   Corbí, Mariano and Comas, Carlos. (1979).   *Discours religieux, discours transmettant des valeurs a un groupe humain, et discours scientifique. Une clé pour leur étude*. (Barcelona: Instituto Científico Interdisciplinar, 43-44.

The European Code of Professional Conduct (Code of Lisbon)

James P. Derriman

President of CEDAN

The European Code of Professional Conduct in public relations was compiled by CERP (The European Federation of Public Relations) and agreed at the CERP General Assembly at Lisbon in April 1978 for adoption by all member associations. It has already been adopted by the national public relations associations of: Belgium, Finland, France, Italy, Portugal, Spain and the United Kingdom, and all their members are thus bound by it. Thirteen years earlier, in 1965, the Code of Athens had been adopted by CERP and subsequently by IPRA. It has now been incorporated into the new Code of Lisbon by reference.

Why then a new Code? There were two reasons:

1.   The Code of Athens is an admirable statement of ethical principles relevant to the practice of the public relations profession. It was not primarily, or perhaps at all, conceived as a piece of legislation which could be applied by the disciplinary committees of professional associations, with penalties for its contravention.

As the public relations profession has developed, the need has come for organisation and discipline of a kind which the older-established professions have long possessed. As public relations practice has become better understood, more sophisticated and more widespread, entering into fields as delicate as those of finance and government relations, the need for its integrity to be visibly maintained has become ever more apparent. Paradoxically the reputation of professional bodies has gained rather than suffered through the occasional mis-behaviour of their members, when those members have subsequently been reprimanded or expelled.

It is, therefore important that every professional body has a code which can be fairly applied in this way. The European Code was therefore compiled to serve this purpose, and to provide an enforceable code of professional conduct for any association which did not have one.

2.   The national associations of 13 European countries (by the time of the World Congress this number may have increased to 14) are linked by a federal committee within CERP, known as CEDAN – Conference des Associations Nationales des Relations Publiques. CEDAN is now well advanced on a programme to harmonise standards for the public relations profession on a Europe-wide basis. The object is to reach a position by the end of 1981 in which every full (i.e. public relations professional) member of any of the 13 associations (2) has an agreed minimum experience in the profession;   (b) is bound by an agreed common Code of

Professional Conduct, made effective by agreed common principles of fair and just disciplinary procedure.

If this position can be attained, in whole or even in large measure, it will represent a great advance in the public relations profession in Europe, enhancing its reputation with the public and those who use its services.

Establishment of a common Code was clearly necessary as part of this harmonised programme.

How was the Code established?

Throughout the Harmonisation programme, including establishment of the European Code, we have worked on two principles:

(a) We are not, and should not attempt to, impose standards from the centre. Through CEDAN, the national associations can agree upon common standards, which are then submitted to their members (the practitioners of the countries concerned) for formal adoption nationally.

(b) In setting standards (including, for instance, the Code), we must take the highest common factor - the best which all associations are prepared to accept. If certain associations do not feel able to accept any item, that item must be dropped or amended. Once an agreed common standard is accepted by all, it can be steadily improved as occasion offers.

In the case of the Code, every European association except that of Spain (which used the Code of Athens) had its own national code of conduct. These naturally varied considerably in detail and effectiveness. To have asked each association to have abandoned its own code in favour of a common European text would have been to court failure. At the least it would have caused intolerable delay in the harmonisation programme, and at the worst it would have raised opposition and possibly resentment in some countries. We decided therefore that our highest-common-factor Code should be intended for adoption alongside existing national codes. If, later on, any country wished to drop its own Code in favour of the European one, so much the better. Meanwhile, the members of the national associations would be bound equally by both.

A first draft Code was prepared by CERP in 1976, and subsequently adopted by Belgian professional body UPREL with slight amendments. The then President of CEDAN, M. Henri de Bruyne, and the Secretary General of CERP, M. Fernand Lekime, played a major part in the pioneer work.

The UPREL Code was then amended to be suitable for use by any European national association, and each clause was presented to representatives of the 13 member associations for comment and amendment. The agreed text resulting from this process - prepared in English and French - was finally adopted at Lisbon in April 1978, and issued as CEDAN Paper No. 2 (Harmonised Principles of Disciplinary Procedure, compiled by a similar process on the basis of procedure used by the British national association, the IPR, were also agreed and issued as CEDAN Paper No. 3; they have been adopted by those associations which have adopted the Code). (Appendix 1).

The code has 19 clauses, in sections covering general professional obligations, and specific professional obligations towards clients or employers, towards public opinion and the information media, towards fellow-practitioners, and towards the profession. It also incorporates an obligation to observe the International Code of Public Relations Ethics: The Code of Athens (Appendix 2).

European Code of Professional Conduct in Public Relations
(Code of Lisbon)

Adopted on 16th April 1978 at Lisbon by the General Assembly of CERP (Centre European des Relations Publiques, the European Federation of Public Relations) for use by all member national associations.

With the object of harmonisation and coordination at the European level, the professional members of (national association) are required to comply with the rules of professional conduct set out below, they are likewise required to observe the International Code of Public Relations Ethics known as the Code of Athens, the text of which is annexed to the present Code, of which it is deemed to form an integral part.

SECTION I

Criteria and standards of professional qualification of practitioners bound by this Code.

Clause 1

Every professional member of (national association) duly admitted as such in accordance with the rules of (national association) is deemed for the purpose of this Code to be a public relations practitioner, and to be bound by the Code.

SECTION II

General professional obligations.

Clause 2

In the practice of his profession, the public relations practitioner undertakes to respect the principles set forth in the Universal Declaration of Human Rights, and in particular the freedom of expression and the freedom of the press which give effect to the right of the individual to receive information, within the limits of professional confidence.

He likewise undertakes to act in accordance with the public interest and not to harm the dignity or integrity of the individual.

Clause 3

In his professional conduct, the public relations practitioner must show honesty, intellectual integrity, and loyalty. In particular he undertakes not to make use of comment which is misleading or information which is false or misleading. In the same spirit he must be watchful to avoid the use, even by accident, of practices or methods incompatible with this Code.

Clause 4

Public relations activities must be carried out openly; they must be readily identifiable, bear a clear indication of their origin, and must not tend to mislead third parties.

Clause 5

In his relations with other professions and with other branches of social communications, the public relations practitioner must respect the rules and practices appropriate to those professions or occupations, so far as these are compatible with the ethics of his own profession.

SECTION III

SPECIFIC PROFESSIONAL OBLIGATIONS

Towards clients or employers

Clause 6

A public relations practitioner shall not represent conflicting or competing interests without the express consent of the clients or employers concerned.

Clause 7

In the practice of his profession, a public relations practitioner must observe complete discretion. He must scrupulously respect professional confidence, and in particular must not reveal any confidential information received from his clients or employers, past, present or potential, or make use of such information, without express authorisation.

Clause 8

A public relations practitioner who has an interest which may conflict with that of his client or employer must disclose it as soon as possible.

Clause 9

A public relations practitioner must not recommend to his client or employer the services of any business or organisation in which he has a financial, commercial or other interest without first disclosing that interest.

Clause 10

A public relations practitioner shall not enter a contract with his client or employer under which the practitioner guarantees quantified results.

Clause 11

A public relations practitioner may accept remuneration for his services only in the form of salary or fees, and on no account may he accept payment or other material rewards contingent upon quantifiable results.

Clause 12

A public relations practitioner shall not accept for his services to a client or an employer any remuneration from a third party, such as discounts, commissions or payments in kind, except with the agreement of the client or employer.

Clause 13

When the execution of a public relations assignment would be likely to entail serious professional misconduct and imply behaviour contrary to the principles of this Code, the public relations practitioner must take steps to notify his client or employer immediately, and do everything possible to see that the latter respects the requirements of the Code. If the client or employer persists in his intentions, the practitioner must nevertheless observe the Code irrespective of the consequences to him.

Towards public opinion and the information media

Clause 14

The spirit of this Code and the rules contained in preceding clauses, notably clauses 2, 3, 4 and 5, imply a constant concern on the part of the public relations practitioner with the right to information, and moreover the duty to provide information, within the limits of professional confidence. They imply also a respect for the rights, independence and initiative of the information media.

Clause 15

Any attempt to deceive public opinion or its representatives is strictly forbidden.

Any form of blackmail, corruption or exertion of undue influence, especially in relation to the information media, is forbidden. News must be provided without charge and with no private understanding or hidden reward for its use or publication.

Clause 16

If it should seem necessary to maintain the initiative in, and the control of, the issue and distribution of information, within the principles of this Code, the public relations practitioner may buy space or broadcasting time in conformity with the rules, practices and usages in that field.

Towards fellow-practitioners

Clause 17

The public relations practitioner must refrain from unfair competition with fellow-practitioners.

He must neither act nor speak in a way which would tend to depreciate the reputation or business of a fellow-practitioner, subject always to his duty under Clause 19b of this Code.

Towards the profession

Clause 18

The public relations practitioner must refrain from any conduct which may prejudice the reputation of his profession. In particular he must not cause harm to his national association (name), its efficient working, or its good name, whether by malicious attacks or by any breach of its constitution or rules.

Clause 19

The reputation of the profession is the responsibility of each of its members. The public relations practitioner has a duty not only to respect this Code himself but also:

    a)   to assist in making the Code more widely and better known
          and understood;

    b)   to report to the competent disciplinary authorities any breach of the Code which comes to his notice, and

c) to take any action in his power to ensure that rulings
    on its application by such authorities are observed
    and sanctions made effective.

Any practitioner who permits a violation of the Code will be considered as having himself breached the Code.

International Code of Ethics
(Code of Athens)

Adopted by IPRA General Assembly at Athens on 12 May 1965 and modified at Tehran on 17 April 1968.

Considering that all Member countries of the United Nations Organisation have agreed to abide by its Charter which reaffirms "its faith in fundamental human rights, in the dignity and worth of the human person" and having regard to the very nature of their profession. Public Relations practitioners in these countries should undertake to ascertain and observe the principles set out in this Charter.

Considering that, apart from "right", human beings have not only physical or material needs but also intellectual, moral and social needs, and that their rights are of real benefit to them only in so far as these needs are essentially met;

Considering that, in the course of their professional duties and depending on how these duties are performed, Public Relations practitioners can substantially help to meet these intellectual, moral and social needs;

And lastly, considering that the use of techniques enabling them to come simultaneously into contact with millions of people gives Public Relations practitioners a power that has to be restrained by the observance of a strict moral code.

On all these grounds, the undersigned Public Relations Associations hereby declare that they accept as their moral charter the principles of the following Code of Ethics, and that if, in the light of evidence submitted to the Council, a member of these associations should be found to have infringed this Code in the course of his professional duties, he will be deemed to be guilty of serious misconduct calling for an appropriate penalty.

Accordingly, each Member of these Associations:

SHALL ENDEAVOUR
1. To contribute to the achievement of the moral and cultural conditions enabling human beings to reach their full stature and enjoy the indefeasible rights to which they are entitled under the "Universal Declation of Human Rights".

2. To establish communication patterns and channels which, by fostering the free flow of essential information, will make each member of the society in which he lives feel that he is being kept informed, and also give him an awareness of his own personal involvement and responsibility, and of his solidarity with other members.

3. To bear in mind that, because of the relationship between his profession and the public, his conduct – even in private – will have an impact on the way in which the profession as a whole is appraised.

4. To respect, in the course of his professional duties, the moral principles and rules of the "Universal Declaration of Human Rights".

5. To pay due regard to, and uphold, human dignity, and to recognise the right of each individual to judge for himself.

6.   To encourage the moral, psychological and intellectual conditions for dialogue in its true sense, and to recognise the right of the parties involved to state their case and express their views.

SHALL UNDERTAKE

7.   To conduct himself always and in all circumstances in such a manner as to deserve and secure the confidence of those with whom he comes into contact.

8.   To act, in all circumstances, in such a manner as to take account of the respective interests of the parties involved: both the interests of the organisation which he serves and the interests of the publics concerned.

9.   To carry out his duties with integrity, avoiding language likely to lead to ambiguity or misunderstanding, and to maintain loyalty to his clients or employers, whether past or present.

SHALL REFRAIN FROM

10.   Subordinating the truth to other requirements.

11.   Circulating information which is not based on established and ascertainable facts.

12.   Taking part in any venture or undertaking which is unethical or dishonest or capable of impairing human dignity and integrity.

13.   Using any "manipulative" methods or techniques designed to create subconscious motivations which the individual cannot control to his own free will and so cannot be held accountable for the action taken on them.

PANEL DISCUSSION

The Panel first considered: In what circumstances may a public relations practitioner decline an assignment which he is capable of undertaking? Are there products or philosophies which he should decline to promote?

No one was in doubt that some clients or assignments must be declined, nor that the decision in any individual case must ultimately be a personal one for the public relations man concerned. No universal rule could be laid down.

Hugh Samson suggested that there were two criteria: the dictates of one's personal conscience, and one's own professional judgment on whether an assignment is or is not in the overall interests of one's own organisation.

A public relations man could not, he thought, communicate effectively if he had his tongue in his cheek: - You have to believe in the cause or product, and if you do not you should seek alternative employment".

He himself would not handle second - or third-hand information which he could not check; only that week he had declined to issue a statement which had reached him from a reputable organisation in South Africa because (although it happened to accord with his own views) he could not verify it.

The extent to which the interests of one's employer were at variance with those of society had to be a matter for individual judgment. Public relations men were never likely to agree about individual cases, because they themselves were a cross-section of society, covering the whole political and ideological spectrum from Left to Right, differing on what was healthy for society and what was not. Some, for instance, believed that multinational companies were beneficial, others believed that they were harmful. Only if a person were true to his own beliefs and conscience could he do his job honestly and efficiently.

Rene Rohner agreed that it was a matter for the individual. He himself, as a consultant, would decline to work for a totalitarian regime, whether of Left or Right. He would not work for an arms manufacturer, although he served in the Swiss Army; nor would he act for a subversive organisation within a country. He himself smoked, but he would not accept an assignment for a tobacco company.

Willy de Cat reminded the audience that the Declaration of Human Rights was referred to in the Code of Athens, the European Code of Professional Conduct, and indeed in that of his own professional body, UPREL. This provided an important guideline on which everybody can agree and rely upon.

James Derriman pointed out that not every case was clear-cut. He drew a parallel with the legal profession, where there was a tradition that everyone had a right to advice and to have his case fairly presented. The public relations adviser could sometimes lead a client to bring his policies into line with the needs of society.

The same point was taken up from the audience by Professor Anne van der Meiden, Professor of Public Relations at the University of Utrecht. There were two methods of approaching an ethical problem, he said: the "deontological" one, where conscience, Christian education, etc were the starting points; and the "teleological" one, where the question was whether the goal was good or bad. Using the first of these approaches, a practitioner might decide it was against his conscience to serve a tobacco company; using the second, he might take the view that he would serve society better by full engagement, to 'convert' the client. Fr. Thomás felt that there were objective ideas of humanity, such as those in the

Declaration of Human Rights, on which professionals could agree independently of other criteria. It was necessary that they should do so if they were to have credibility.

The public climate of opinion at the time was necessarily one factor, James Derriman suggested. There was a parallel here with laws on censorship and obscenity - what was considered unacceptable at one period could well be in accordance with a later view of morality.

The Panel next discussed the enforcement of codes of professional conduct. Members of the audience agreed that it was of little value to adopt codes if there was no check on whether or not they were being applied. How many members, for instance, had been expelled by IPRA since its code was adopted 14 years ago?

James Derriman pointed out that when CERP invited its member associations to adopt the European Code, it also asked them to adopt harmonised principles of disciplinary procedure.

Goran Sjoberg of Sweden, the new Chairman of the IPRA Professional Standards Committee, said that a series of methods for dealing with breaches of the IPRA code was being drawn up and would be announced during 1979.

It was accepted by members of the Panel and the audience that the disciplinary powers of any association were limited to its own members. It was possible almost everywhere for people to practise public relations uncontrolled. As Willy de Cat said: "We must begin with what we have". He added also that disciplinary decisions, even if they are limited to the members of the public relations body, can possibly have a moral impact on non-members provided they are made known.

James Derriman explained that when the Institute of Public Relations in the United Kingdom made an important disciplinary decision, resulting in suspension or expulsion of a member, it was the practice to announce this publicly through the Press. Some countries found it difficult legally to adopt this course. The IPR was also considering seeking statutory registration of public relations practitioners, but before this could be done it would be necessary to define the profession so that it was legally clear who was within the profession and who was not. This problem was being tackled within CERP, in relation to application of European standards.

Rene Rohner said that the Swiss Relations Society provided for any decision to exclude a member to be published, but only internally to its own members.

Finally came a question on whether it was ethical for anyone to practise both journalism and public relations at the same time. The chairman suggested that this question might be widened to consider the ethical problems which could result from public relations people belonging to trade unions, such as those for journalists and for local government people.

A Spanish member of the audience was emphatic that a journalist could not simultaneously be employed in public relations.

The union problem had been met by two practitioners. One, from Australia, said that she was a member of the journalists' association but was employed in public relations. If journalists went on strike, public relations members of the union were not required to do so. A Swedish practitioner said that he was a member of both the journalists' association in his country and also the public relations association. When the journalists went on strike, he was expelled from the journalists' body, though since reinstated.

15

Communication Needs of Ethnic Minorities

The Chairman, David Lane, introduced himself, the speaker, Pranlal Sheth, Deputy Chairman of the Commission for Racial Equality; and Sean Browne, Senior Information Officer at the Commission, who acted as Convenor.

Mr Lane said: "The Commission is pleased to have been invited to participate in this important international event by focusing attention of the communications needs of ethnic minorities.

Today we hear more about ethnic minorities than ever before, perhaps because of the increasing flow of news and information. Only last Saturday, for example, "The Guardian" carried a report of a plea by the leader of the Iranian Kurds for solidarity among Iran's Arabs, Baluchis and Turks in their fight for autonomy. He was quoted: "We want freedom for all political parties and a government that both defends civil liberaties and respects the demands of Iran's ethnic minorities for autonomy".

Similar calls are being made by ethnic minorities in many other countries. The question facing us here today is: "Can we afford to continue ignoring the plight of these minorities, not only in the Third World but in industrialised countries also?"

In Britain we have large and vigorous ethnic minority communities. They, and other groups, face problems. But our British problems seem relatively small when we compare them with similar problems elsewhere (for example, in India).

I welcome Mr Sheth particularly warmly, as my friend and colleague and a Deputy Chairman in our Commission. As well as his very distinguished career in the law, in business and public relations, he has already made an outstanding contribution by his work for race relations in Britain. He is widely travelled and familiar with developments in other continents and there will be much for all of us in his message.

Understanding the Communication
Needs of Ethnic Minorities

Pranlal Sheth

Executive Director and Group Secretary
Abbey Life Assurance Company Limited and Deputy Chairman
Commission for Racial Equality.

To understand the *communication* needs of the ethnic minorities, we must first develop a proper grasp of the social and political environment in which ethnic minorities lead their lives. Only by so doing will we be able to understand their needs, their aspirations, their frustrations. Without such grasp we can hardly appreciate the depth of their feelings generated by the degradations, humiliations and hostilities they encounter in their daily life. Such understanding explains the tensions and conflicts retarding the progress towards establishing a just and human social order. It is therefore my intention to deal with the subject of my talk by first attempting to sketch broadly a picture of ethnic minorities not only in this country but in several other parts of the world.

In so doing I would also like to spotlight the problems of Third World countries as I believe that, in the context of the enormous wealth and exceedingly high level of technological superiority of the Western world, their position is analogous to that of the ethnic minorities who suffer from deprivation and disadvantage.

Let me therefore begin by saying that when we speak about the needs of ethnic minorities, we are really talking about minority rights. And when we refer to minority rights, we are really talking about human rights: the right of every individual to dignity and equality of opportunity and to justice before the law of the land in which he happens to live, and the freedoms of person, speech, association, worship and movement, regardless of his race, colour, nationality or ethnic origin.

Today, the struggle of minorities for their human rights is a dominant feature of the international scene. With the balance of terror among the superpowers, the threat of nuclear war has receded over the past few decades. The violent assertion of minority rights has now taken its place as the major source of anxiety and tension within and among nations. This affects our daily lives and the future of our children. The effects of the struggle of the Palestinians is the most dramatic example of that. Its reverberations have left no country untouched. The black-white violence which gripped American cities a few years ago, and that from Ulster which spills over the Irish Sea and claims unfortunate and innocent victims in England from time to time are other vivid reminders of volcanic forces which continue to smoulder.

Are we really justified in regarding them as if they were natural catastrophies which will unpredictably overwhelm us from time to time? Would it not be more rational to recognise and understand minority problems and defuse them before they

178

explode in violence?

That seems to me to be one of the major challenges facing us today. Minority
rights are everybody's business. The conflicts stemming from their suppression
constitute one of the greatest destabilising forces in our world. Those working
in public relations, like all who work in the media and therefore influence the
formation of public attitudes and public opinion, have particular (and, may I say,
inescapable) responsibilities in this matter. The discussion of this subject at
this conference is itself testimony that you regard yourselves as professionals
and are fully conscious of these responsibilities.

The Institute of Public Relations in this country defines public relations
practice as "the deliberate, planned and sustained effort to establish and
maintain mutual understanding between an organisation and its public".

The Institute adds that such a definition implies two-way communication and
thoughtful and intelligent assessment and planning. It has now become widely
accepted that advertising or publicity campaigns do not in themselves constitute
public relations.

Such a definition of the role of public relations means that you discharge your
responsibilities to your clients within the framework of your perception and
understanding of the total context within which you operate and with full
recognition of your own wider social responsibilities.

An informed awareness of the origin and nature of minority needs is now therefore
essential to the effective discharge of those responsibilities.

There are today few countries without an ethnic minority of some sort. They have
often sprung up in foreign nations in the wake of wars or persecutions. French
Protestants came to England in the late sixteenth and late seventeenth centuries.
Jews found a refuge here from pogroms in Russia and Eastern Europe in the late
19th and early 20th centuries.

Slavery has created the black minority populations of the New World. Arbitrary
map-drawing during the scramble for and partition of Africa by European powers in
the nineteenth century has left behind a legacy of minority problems. The most
tragic example perhaps is of those stripped of their natural rights and made out-
casts in their own lands: native peoples like the New Zealand Maoris, Australian
Aborigines, and the American Indians, turned into minorities by the arrival of
foreign colonists. Indians and Chinese were carried to many parts of the world
as 'indentured labourers' - a new slavery, as a recent English historian has
called the system. Since World War II, the need of cheap skilled and unskilled
labour within industrial Western nations has drawn immigrants to Britain from the
Indian sub-continent and the West Indies and from Turkey, North Africa and
Mediterranean Europe to other Western European countries. The oil-rich and
affluent states in the Middle East, Saudi Arabia, Kuwait, the United Emirates and
Qatar have attracted over two million migrant workers, principally from the
Indian sub-continent to help these states with the development of their economies.

Why are minorities considered to be 'problems'?

Probe beneath the surface and you will invariably find that the presence or
existence of a minority does not constitute a problem. A difference in race,
colour, culture, or religious affiliation is not sufficient to generate conflict.
It is rather the circumstances in which the minority is placed by the majority.
Human beings, alas, have appeared at their most selfish and greediest in the
treatment they have meted out to minorities. The sad truth is: there is no

minority problem. There is only the problem of the majority, and its treatment of the minority.

Take an issue which continues to haunt life in this country. For years we have been told that the problems in Ulster spring from the fact that there is a minority of Catholics, outnumbered by British Protestants who have settled there for several hundred years. That there is such a religious difference is not to be disputed. But the crux of the problem is not really religion. It is the denial of equal opportunity to that minority in terms of jobs, housing and so on.

As a minority awakens to the denial of its full potentialities for self-development and for a full share in life, conflict begins and blazes with increasing ferocity.

That is an important but uncomfortable fact which most of us, I fear, are very unwilling to recognise. For it means that each of us has to assume a personal share of responsibility for situations where minority discontent erupts into violence. It is far easier to blame them on cultural, religious or racial differences - as if the mere fact of diversity inevitably breeds conflict - or to blame them on 'agitators' or 'extremists' or the sinister hand of foreign powers - as if they could incite peaceful men and women, habituated to docile deference, if there was not a great deal to 'agitate' about.

Facing up to reality means, I submit, not only recognising such situations as symptoms of a much deeper malaise but working actively to remove its root causes. It means giving priority to consideration of minority discontent long before it erupts into open conflict. The communication needs of ethnic minorities must therefore be viewed in this light.

The problem cannot be ignored because minorities will no longer passively put up with manipulation and exploitation by majorities. They have found a new voice. They demand their rights as human beings. They want an equal share in the wealth they create. They are more and more willing to take to the streets to demand their rights. The voice of the dispossessed grows louder every day. It is a voice we cannot afford to ignore. Under severe pressure from liberal opinion in the country and to preserve its moral stature internationally and more particularly in the interests of its most vital and profitable strategic, economic and political relationship with its Commonwealth partners - more than 90 per cent of whom are of Afro-Caribbean-Asiatic origins - the British Government has by statute made it illegal to practise discrimination on the grounds of race, colour, nationality or ethnic origin, directly or indirectly, in any sphere of her national life.

In Britain, a great many minority organisations (both white and non-white) now exist to lobby for a better deal and to end discrimination in its many and varied forms. Members of the minorities are learning how to stand up for themselves. They demand a full voice in the community and in national affairs. They make fuller use of courts and of industrial tribunals and other statutory processes to fight the obstacles that are placed in their path.

On the other side of the Atlantic, the black minority has struggled bravely to win a better life for itself and its children. Public sensitivity to their needs and attitudes to their treatment have undergone a veritable transformation. Civil rights legislation guaranteeing America's black citizens full and unfettered enjoyment by them of all democratic rights has released a powerful regenerating force which will, if it is not already doing so, contribute significantly to a healthy social order, create new wealth, open up vast consumer markets and contribute enormously to the already enhanced prosperity of the country.

But despite these important developments in Britain and the USA, the battle is far from over. Last year what has been described as one of the most significant pieces of media research was undertaken in the USA through the efforts of Dr Carl Jensen, a sociologist who runs seminars in mass communications. A list of the 'Ten Best-Censored Stories' in the US press was compiled. The list is headed by: 'The Myth of Black Progress'. Number ten on that list is: 'The Exploitation of Illegal Aliens'.

So, while the picture is changing, it is by no means changing as fast as we may easily be led to believe. The response of governments is still predominantly to regard such situations as law and order matters. That is, to meet them by strengthening the machinery which will ensure the maintenance of a *status quo* based on inequality. But that is merely suppressing symptoms, while leaving the deeper malady to fester. It will not work. The basic requirement is not merely enacting laws or more laws, but the provision of decent housing and jobs, ensuring of unalloyed equality and social justice in the administration of law and bureau-cratic practices, not ever-greater numbers of policemen and soldiers to deal with the discontent of the deprived.

Race Relations are part of the much broader picture I have tried to sketch of the struggle of minorities for a better deal - whether at the corporate or the national level.

Good race relations are good for business and good for the nation as a whole. A disaffected minority of workers in a factory means that the efficiency and productivity of the entire plant suffers. Similarly, a nation with one or more disaffected minorities suffers a check to its advance unless it responds positively to the problem of minorities and gives them a sense of equal participation in the life of the Community. We now have a depressingly long list of examples of the dislocations these sources of conflict can inflict on communities and nations. To ignore them would be to earn the censure of future generations for our unforgivable blindness.

Checking the Facts

We must therefore further our awareness of the facts: that means cutting through the fog of half-truths, myths, and prejudices that almost always surrounds popular discussion of minority problems. In this country, for example, it is still usual to talk about 'immigrants', although by now more than about forty per cent of the non-white population was born here. The focus tends to be on checking non-white immigrants, although that is now strictly confined to wives and young children of those already settled here. Immigrant birth-rates are highlighted although every study shows their continuing and rapid adaptation to the family pattern of the majority. 'Immigrants' are largely limited to low-paid, unattractive, dirty and the least begrudged jobs which confine them to inner city areas. They are then blamed for the squalor in which they find themselves. This is a vicious circle well known to those who have worked on minority problems anywhere.

Indeed, research shows that the major cause of alienation among young blacks in British society is the frustration they experience because they are denied work on equal terms with their white fellow school-leavers. They have to try far harder to land their first job. An incessant round of futile job interviews leaves them with a deep sense of grievance, planting seeds that may one day yield a bitter harvest. Managements are not always aware that discrimination is being practised within their corporate field, nor of its wider significance.

The lesson of the American experience is clear. You cannot alienate one section of the community on the basis of their ethnic origins, and yet expect them to behave as good citizens. Those engaged in public persuasion, like yourselves, have a vital role in convincing your clients that it is in their best interests to eliminate any traces of ethnic minority discrimination that may exist within their organisation.

You also have a positive responsibility in renouncing and discouraging the exploitation by others of national and racial stereotypes. Those stereotypes too are symptoms of a deeper incomprehension. They express a selective denial of the range of one's human sympathies. As long as we are trapped by distorted representations of each other, we cannot respond fully to each other as human beings.

It is relevant to recall the guidelines which the National Union of Journalists in this country has set for newspaper and broadcasting journalists when considering a story with a 'race angle'. The questions are: Is it going to worsen race relations in a multi-racial society? Is it going to stir up the consuming fires of race hatred?

Does this mean that they consider that journalists should treat race issues differently from other issues? The answer, it has been said, is both yes and no. Yes – because race as an issue is different from other contemporary group relationships. No – because it does not restrict the journalist's freedom to tell the truth: rather to tell more of it, to tell it as it really is, not merely to present selective bits that chime in with a dominant view which simply perceives non-whites as a problem.

The International Association of Business Communications, based at San Francisco, have published an extremely useful 'Guidebook for Non-Discriminatory Communication' which warns about the power of language to reinforce bias and stereotypes. So powerful is the hold of stereotypes that they are unaffected by our personal knowledge of friends and of public figures. Yet they cloud the fact that all kinds of attributes are to be found distributed in all groups and individuals.

False Stereotypes

How difficult it is to give up the image of the fiery Spaniard, the hearty German, the inscrutable Asian, the conservative Briton and the exuberant Italian. Worse, we may think of snobbish, arrogant and condescending Anglo-Saxons; lazy, voluptuous and argumentative Mediterranean natives; cunning, clannish and menial Asians; clowning, unmotivated and ungrateful Africans.

Truly professional communicators would seldom ignore the advice that those working in the field of public relations should guard themselves against words, images and situations which imply that all members of a racial or ethnic group are the same. Qualifiers that reinforce such stereotypes must not be used. Racial or ethnic identification when it is not essential to communication must be avoided. Ethnic clichés must also be avoided. It must be remembered that patronising or displaying tokenism towards minority groups is deeply offensive and resented. A simple test is to substitute the identification of the majority community whenever tempted to do so for the minority: that is, imagine the sentence with the word 'white' in place of 'black'; or substitute an Anglo-Saxon surname for a Chicano or Asian one.

Those engaged in public relations can make an important and genuine contribution towards the peaceful resolution of one of the most potent sources of conflict in our time. It is in this context that the communication needs of ethnic minorities require to be evaluated. By recognising and understanding the challenge of minority rights, they can make their client-decision-makers more aware of the facts.

Even looking at it from a purely parochial self-interest point of view and not idealistically, can public relations consultants ignore the immeasurable reservoir of economic power and markets for consumer goods, which social justice and economic upliftment would release as the deprived and disadvantaged ethnic minorities start climbing up the ladder of material betterment?

Within national societies we each have an obligation to understand minority discontent and persuade others to remove its root causes if we are to build a stable and secure future for ourselves and our children. It is fitting that at an international conference like this we should equally recall our responsibilities as members of an international society. There is an important analogy here. Just as the last few decades have marked the eruption of minorities onto the stage of national politics, so have they equally witnessed the effective emergence of Third World nations onto the stage of world events to influence our everyday life.

According to a recent estimate, the Third World has 70 per cent of the world's population and yet it commands no more than 12 per cent of the gross world product. In 1974, one-fifth of the world population appropriated two thirds of the world income. Nearly a third of the world lived on barely three per cent of the world income and had a per capita income of not more than 120 US dollars. Some 800 million human beings live in absolute poverty. In the words of the World Bank's World Development Report this condition is "so characterised by malnutrition, illiteracy, disease, squalid surroundings, high infant mortality rate and low life expectancy as to be beneath any reasonable definition of human decency". The correction of this gross imbalance will doubtless form a major theme of international relations for a long time to come. The present world economic order is suffering from malstructure. Willy Brandt, ex-Chancellor of West Germany and currently Chairman of the Independent Commission on International Development Issues, has repeatedly emphasised that this malstructure "needs to be fundamentally restructured on the basis of social justice, equity and fair play".

The countries of the Third World do not, of course, constitute a minority. In terms of world population they are the majority. But only a tiny share of the world income is available to them, and like national or ethnic minorities, they, too, are deprived and disadvantaged and are struggling to realise their full human potential. The analogy, on a national basis, is more with small minorities, as say, Rhodesia and South Africa, monopolising for themselves the benefits of their exploitation of the human and natural resources. If we are to regard that as inequitable and dangerous, can we refuse to draw similar consequences for the world community itself?

It is not many years ago that such thoughts were either dismissed as hopelessly idealistic or received only polite acknowledgment. Now this is no longer possible. Command over strategic commodity resources, especially oil, has given Third World countries a new consciousness of their importance. Oil is not the only such commodity. Rubber is a sellers' market and is expected to remain so for many years. Depleting mineral resources in industrial countries, too, increase their dependence on Third World countries. The most recent military intervention in the Third World, significantly, was the Franco-Belgian one in the cobalt and copper rich areas of Zaire. A conflict is now looming up on the exploitation of the mineral resources of the ocean-bed, between industrial nations who consider it part of the freedom of the seas, and developing countries who press for an international regime to regulate the use of that area.

In their bid to win greater recognition of their own development needs, Third World countries are thus beginning to wield far greater influence through the 'producer power' given to them by natural resources which they have in abundance. But does

our understanding and acknowledgment of their needs have to wait so tardily upon
what are regarded as unforeseeable events? Our response, surely, should be more
consistently sympathetic, understanding and informed.

A greater responsibility rests, I believe, in these matters on those working in
public relations than others involved in the media. The media are generally
concerned with information and entertainment, and incidentally instruction. Public
relations men and women are far more positively involved in the formation of
corporate opinion. Their advice to clients must base itself on a deeper and fuller
assessment, which takes account of all relevant aspects of a situation. They must
think through clearly their positive responsibilities, too. That is what marks out
a profession from a mere occupation. In the long run - and I do not mean the
Keynsian long-run in which we shall all be dead - there is no incompatibility
between the real interests of their clients and those of society at large.

The Role of the Churches Today

That is clearer if we compare their role with that of the churches today. Once it
was simply seen as that of preaching the Gospel and of conversion. The social,
political and economic order, or patterns of inequality within it, or the
distribution of power, were not regarded as its business. As colonial inhabitants
used to bitterly remark, "before the missionaries came, the colonisers had the
Bible and we had the land; now we have the Bible and they have land". The church is
now having to rethink its place in the Third World as well as the role it must
assume in the fields of race relations and human rights. There is a widespread
feeling that the meaning of Christianity must be "lived out in love and concern for
their fellow citizens". Its implications for oppressive social and economic
conditions must be fully worked out so that the Church can no longer remain silent
about poverty and oppression. If it is to retain its credibility, the Church has
to avow that Jesus's teaching about love and charity is irreconcilable with
suppression of human rights, or with disregard of the needs of the majority by their
rulers or the needs of ethnic minorities who originated from these countries.

Those working in public relations must, similarly, rethink how they can retain
and enhance their credibility. They cannot otherwise serve their clients at all.
The problem of credibility has recently been highlighted by the so-called
Muldergate scandal in the Union of South Africa.

That scandal showed clearly that promoting a favourable image of a Government and
its policies cannot simply be regarded as a cosmetic exercise totally disregarding
the facts of the situation. Otherwise it is bound to be exposed as a hoax. It will
backfire both on the Government concerned and on the public relations agencies
involved. Public relations personnel engaged in such public or private promotion-
alism are not ultimately acting to the advantage of the clients they serve, nor
fulfilling their responsibilities as professionals. In all such cases, public
relation personnel must have careful regard of their duties when they advise clients
if they are not to be discredited together with their clients whom they will have
then badly served. They must go beyond the newspaper headlines and snap judgments
in making up their own minds about the facts.

Only by relentless probing and in depth study of the situations which you are
called in to deal with is it possible to avoid continually being caught out by
events. You need not then find yourself so often having to change and reshape
your image of individuals or even whole nations, only when the pressure of
necessity suddenly and unpredictably compels you to do so. Let us only recall
some of the more dramatic of such refashioning of images: How Mahatma Gandhi,
dismissed contemptuously as a 'half-naked fakir climbing the steps of the
Viceregal Lodge', has become recognised as the father of his nation and a world-

respected apostle of non-violence; or how the late President Jomo Kenyatta
described not so long before as a 'leader to death and darkness' was mourned by
Western royalty, Presidents, Premiers, Foreign Ministers and other dignitaries at
his recent funeral. Remember, too, how the attitude towards Arabs changed almost
overnight since the oil crisis. Or how the rules of apartheid have been bent in
the Union of South Africa to accord to the Japanese visiting that country the
status of honorary 'Europeans'. Nor can we forget how Presidents and Premiers and
royalty descended to court the Government of Mexico after its sensational new oil
strikes, so rapidly effacing the memories of electric fences to keep illegal
Mexican emigrants out of California.

The Lesson of Tanzania

Let me give an example, also drawn from Africa, about what I mean about going
beyond bold headlines and snap judgments. It is about what is really going on
today in Tanzania. Being in the City and continuously in touch with banking and
financial circles, I am very conscious of the almost total lack of understanding
of that country's brave attempt to work out an indigenous self-help approach to
the development of its human and material resources. It is an experiment which
must be seen against the background of the much-vaunted foreign aid programmes in
the Third World since the end of the War. The most recent figures show that
between 1972 and 1976, per capita income increased by 25 per cent in industrial
countries. It actually declined in developing countries by 33 per cent. The
Argentinian economist Paul Prebisch has pointed out that poor countries are
trapped in a vicious circle of low productivity and low savings followed by more
of the same. Tanzania has tried to break out of that circle, by devising an
alternative to the dominant strategy of export-led growth whose benefits accrue
largely to a small upper-income élite. It has aimed at more rounded development
whose fruits are spread over a wider part of the population. After all, the
developing countries require substantial aid from the industrial countries, not as
charity or handouts, but in order to achieve self-generating growth. It is in the
interests of the industrial world to promote that growth as rapidly as possible.
The British Minister for Overseas Aid in the previous Government had sensibly
argued against a World Bank idea of putting the satisfaction of the 'basic needs'
of Third World countries as the purpose of Western aid. That would be, as she had
said, to regard them as welfare cases, instead of aiming to make them capable of
self-sustaining development.

It is not handouts they seek.

A New York Times journalist, writing in justification of the world's economic
inequalities, recently commented "Forget about hard work, forget about generations
of development. The 'have-not' nations want equality with the 'have' nations now,
WITHOUT GOING THROUGH THE PROCESS OF DEVELOPMENT".

Which process of development? One is entitled to ask. The colonisation of
other countries? And exploitation of their precious raw materials and natural
resources? Or slave labour from Asia or Africa for hundreds of years which
brought so much affluence to the countries of the Western World?

There still persists in the Western countries the 'lazy natives' image of the
people of developing countries - dating from the colonial era. But, it is rightly
asked how many citizens of America or Europe could match an Asian or African
farmer's day of water-carrying, wood-collecting, field-digging or harvesting by
hand? Are these Asian or African nations really as lazy as they are made out to
be.

Incidentally, in 1977 the International Bank of Reconstruction and Development granted aid to the Third World amounting to 2.6 billion US dollars. But 1.9 billion US dollars of this was immediately recovered by offset in interest and amortisation. The net aid provided was therefore only 0.7 billion US dollars. Statistics like this make it painfully clear the meaning of what the British Minister of Overseas Development has said.

What is happening in Tanzania may have great significance for other developing countries, and demands at least some understanding of what it is trying to achieve. We only have to consider what lessons are to be learnt from recent events in Iran, although it is a very different economy in terms of its command of oil resources. The real lesson, I believe, is not that rapid economic development is destabilising and to be avoided. Rather that strategies to achieve it must be carefully tailored to the real needs and aspirations of people and that its benefits must be more widely spread. It cannot be blindly modelled on Western examples. The lesson, then, is that our approval or disapproval of regimes cannot depend simply on whether they copy Western models and provide markets for Western exports in the immediate future. That would lead to short-sighted judgments which must result in wrong choices and wrong policy decisions, and leave a legacy of hatred and bitterness.

It is, of course, the seeming lack of understanding and the persistent failure of Western news media to give attention to 'something other than coups and typhoons' in the Third World that has given rise to the demand from developing countries for a 'new information order' that would break the news monopoly of Western news agencies. They want more attention to their silent revolutions. They wish their aspirations and dreams, and what they are doing to achieve them, to be interpreted. They want sympathetic understanding of their struggle, after suffering under their own despotic rulers, under colonial subjugation, and after the post-war experience of being no more than pawns in international politics. We are rightly very conscious of the dangers of allowing governments to determine the flow of news from their countries.

Surely we should equally recognise the trivialisation and, in the end, gross distortion resulting from the maxim that only 'bad news is news' - especially when applied to distant countries still largely perceived in terms of the stereotypes of a vanished imperial era.

The most conspicuous of such failures is perhaps the Western press coverage of the incursion of Islam as a powerful third force in international affairs. Floggings, hand-chopping, and executions display its harsh contrast with professed Western ideals and receive headline treatment. But it is deeply misleading to regard them as exhausting its sum content. Islam is one of the world's great religions. The flowering of Islamic culture in the eleventh and twelfth centuries has left a deep imprint, especially on the emerging culture of Western Europe, through its influence on science, philosophy, and religious thought. The full significance of the present Islamic revival is far from clear. But at least we can maintain a sense of historical perspective. Let us reflect on how short-sighted to us seem those contemporaries who saw in the beginnings of the European Reformation of the sixteenth century nothing but a futile attempt to remodel society on the literal word of the Bible and certainly did not perceive in it one of the roots of an 'Age of Reason' which was to follow.

CONCLUSION

My brief today was to discuss the communication needs of ethnic minorities. I trust you will not feel that I have strayed too far from it in discussing many global problems. I have tried to show you that the needs of ethnic minorities are no different from those of others, who, numerically, constitute the majority of the world's population, but, in terms of access to utilisation of resources and receipt of world income, function as a minority.

In the end, it is a question of human rights, of giving every individual in the world community the opportunity of developing to the full his or her best human potentialities. Once this seemed an idealistic dream. Now deprived minorities within nations have found ways of making their voices heard. And 'producer power' has made it possible for the underprivileged majority in the world to put a formidable power behind the demand for equal opportunity. There is no escape from this demand. We live, in one interdependent, interacting world with transportation and communication which are swift and instantaneous. Individuals, corporations or nations cannot afford to remain isolated or self-centred. They must take a longer view in terms of this interdependence and interreaction.

Those involved in public relations must therefore penetrate deeper into the heart of such situations. They now wield enormous influence on the formation of public opinion. Only last month, commenting on a poll which showed that US public confidence in business leadership had halved over eight years, a Senior Vice-President of the Bank of America told *Business Week:*

"A public relations problem today does not simply mean loss of good will, it threatens a corporation's ability to achieve its business goals".

Public relations personnel are in the business of securing the best publicity and most favourable image for their clients. But they must continually be aware of the relation between image and reality in discharging that function. If the image is wildly at variance with the facts of a situation, it will boomerang and discredit both client and the public relations industry. The phrase, "It is just a public relations exercise" is still used all too widely and automatically. When that phrase is expunged from popular speech, public relations will really have come of age as a profession. There is only one way of achieving that.

All of you, who have assembled here, must be providing your specialised professional services to hundreds of thousands of clients — clients whose multifarious interests and activities are spread in many countries across all continents. Most of these countries must have ethnic minorities among their populations, or are themselves minorities in terms of their retarted economic development and their technological backwardness.

Your duty and responsibility to your clients would demand that you present to them most dispassionately and sympathetically, the true picture of these minorities and their great potential, given the right and equal opportunities.

You must not lose sight of the fact that the news that informs and shapes opinions is based on reports frequently ill-informed, sensational and utterly biased, often reflecting prejudice and ignorance.

By your in-depth assessment of the facts, your expert advice and with the aid of your particular professional skills you can promote democratic ideals of equality and justice for all, regardless of race, colour, nationality or ethnic distinctions. By doing so you not only discharge your social and moral responsibilities or act as guardians of democratic liberties, but you best serve your clients' interests — material and otherwise.

There is a need for public relations men and women to remould, reshape and re-sharpen their clients' attitudes and their thinking — which still clings to out-moded ideas despite unprecedented progress in the fields of technology and science — regarding the emerging power of ethnic and other minorities.

As Willy Brandt once said: "There still lies power in the word if it is formulated in the right way".

By explaining to your clients the needs, problems and aspirations of the minorities - whether ethnic or otherwise, in a way which promotes genuine under- standing of their relevance to economics or political philosophy, it is possible to influence your clients' decisions for the betterment of mankind.

Achieving Maximum Credibility

You must constantly seek to attain the maximum of credibility through your work, the advice you proffer to clients, and the concepts you promote. You cannot afford to ignore the human aspects of situations with which you must continually concern yourselves. You cannot ignore the violation of human rights: whether it is of Jews in the Soviet Union or of the Africans in what until some weeks ago was Amin's Uganda, or of the Biafrans in Nigeria, the Christians in Southern Sudan, or the tribal repressions taking place in a dismayingly long list of countries, or the evil of racial prejudice practised against ethnic minorities in the USA, Great Britain and several other countries of the world.

You may have to suggest solutions, or courses of action which may clash with existing prejudices, or with what are really short-sighted conceptions of client interest. But you will then really be contributing to the genuine uplift of countries and the cause of world peace, and thereby promoting the best interests of your client, as viewed from a truly professional standpoint.

Let me end with a simple message, in the words of Sir Bernard Braine, MP:

"It is the right of people in the industrialised nations to work and enjoy a reasonable standard of living. And for them and their children to be able to live in an ordered and peaceful world depends essentially on those same rights being enjoyed by all who dwell on our planet. We cooperate and grow together or we perish together. There is no other way".

DISCUSSION

During the discussion period <u>Victor Osinowo</u> pointed out that the conditions which prevailed in Nigeria during the civil war no longer existed and that Biafra should not be included among examples of places where basic human rights were being denied.

<u>Willis Player</u> said that Mr Sheth had given the impression that two-thirds of the world's population was being exploited by the other one-third. He would like it placed on record that the people of Germany, Sweden, the Netherlands and other developed nations had got where they were today largely through their own exertions.

<u>Frank Jefkins</u> suggested that the talk had dealt too much with effects rather than causes of racial tensions. There were, he said, both economic and psychological factors and these had to be fully understood.

Following comments by <u>William Greene</u>, Mr Sheth intervened to say he hoped he had not given a depressing picture of race relations in Britain. Many good things were happening and "we are moving ahead with courage and fortitude".

<u>Alain Modoux</u> said that he felt Western countries should not necessarily feel guilty. They had made many mistakes but they were not the only ones to have done so. It would be wrong to see it as one side being guilty with the other side the innocent victim. If this were to happen, it would harm constructive race relations dialogue.

Mr Sheth replied: "Britain must act properly and set an example to the rest of the world".

16

Consultancy Today and Tomorrow
What Consultants Provide and What Clients Need

Introduction

This concurrent session dealt with the problems and challenges of public relations consultancy today. The first speaker Jules M Hartogh spoke from the point of view of a "user" of public relations consultancies and he was followed by Bob Leaf, who described the way in which he thought public relations consultancies would develop in the coming years.

What Consultants Provide

Jules Hartogh

Vice President, Corporate Affairs, Philip Morris, Europe, Middle East and Africa, Lausanne and Switzerland

Today's changing scene

Traditional fields of public relations and corporate affairs are now outgrown and there is a dynamic emergence of new areas. We are no longer only concerned with information dissemination and promoting goodwill, there is a new emphasis on public issues – such as social responsibility questions, safeguarding workers' rights, the rights of women, consumer protection, and so on.

There is an increasing growth of government regulations in the market place – disclosure requirements, taxation, harmonisation attempts, anti-trust actions and measures designed to control competition. We have a proliferation of pressure groups with ever increasing influence – the environment lobby, the Nader followers, the legal brigades (particularly in the United States of America) out to exploit the product liability laws. The "Antis" are multiplying in various forms – in my own company's case, we are faced with anti-smoking forces that sociologists agree, present them with a fascinating case study in fanaticism with religious undertones.

There is the anti-nuclear movement – and here it is instructive to examine the public relations aspects of the handling, or the non-handling of the recent Harrisburg accident. There are those who are anti any kind of industry, the "back-to-nature" people – with conservative and religious drives.   Those who are anti private industry – less religious but strongly materialistic – who favour the benevolent all-powerful state, which is a *contradictio in terminis*. They feel that the state should take care of the individual from the cradle to the grave. This, in my view, poses a tremendous threat to the individual, to the possibilities for full development of human capabilities

Then, there is the professional "Anti" personality - these usually become the self-appointed leaders and "Correctors" of society and human behaviour. They pose a problem and a threat to democratic government and business, because they are out to eliminate private initiative and decision-making by consensus, with their passion to regulate and to restrict the freedom of the individual, trying to determine his own way of living. Their dream-world is like a bio-industry - we should all live like battery hens - instead of in our natural environment as free flying birds - facing up to certain risks - if we want to - because that is what makes our wings grow stronger.

These efforts by large powerful groups to suppress individual originality, have caused the build-up of tensions in society. They have created all sort of creatures with unnaturally marked characters such as the know-it-alls, the want-to-do-nothings, the involved and the uninvolved, the world-improvers, the power-hungry, the pessimists, and the optimists, the hypochondriacs, the live-it-ups, the excusers, the accusers, the self-appointed preachers, and teachers, harlots, zealots, and other idiots.

The mis-information dilemma

We are drowning in information. I wake up to the alarm clock and I hear that some fanatic has been executed because of some disagreement or other, or somebody has been shot or had his throat cut. And from that moment on, I am being informed about something, or other, whether I like it or not.

On the way to my office, I see the hoardings, the newspaper posters, and the radio is blaring in my car. Once in the office, I cannot avoid the mountain of newsclips that come in and the constant stream of information that people give me. At the end of the day, I am forced to switch on the television to watch the newscasts.

People, all over the world, are daily so bombarded with information, that it is difficult to take it all in and interpret the meaning.

Furthermore, this information has already been shaped, formed, summarised by a few individuals who each consciously or unconsciously add their own approach to it. And, therefore, it becomes distorted and leads to mis-information. The television reporter and cameraman make a conscious selection of what they show - and it has become fashionable to show a policeman beating a rioter and to omit the previous incident with a rioter first attacking the policeman. Radio, television and news-papers, all select what is recorded and shown, or written and, therefore, it is slanted to the particular point of view of their own that they wish to propagate. This system of mis-information puts enormous power into the hands of the media, who are often very cleverly manipulated by political groups or other powerful organisations in society.

So, just how raw is "raw news" today? Even the basic information supplied by REUTERS and the other wire services is often summarised - arbitrarily and subjectively.

The corporate affairs function - more complex than ever

In this climate, business is more exposed to external pressures than it has ever been before, and, therefore, more and more company decisions have public affairs and public relations implications. Next to their traditional concerns, such as research and development, finance, production and marketing, more and more chief executive officers are recognising that public affairs and public relations must have their personal attention and must be approached with the same professionalism as their other activities. The job of the Head of Corporate Affairs is to translate company policy into corporate affairs terms – employing in-company specialists for each of the main fields in which it is engaged: For example, editorial services/promotions: public affairs: management of issues. The objective must be to see that the company plays its due role in society and to anticipate and prevent problems rather than just picking up the pieces afterwards. To be the watchdog for corporate transgressions of the rapidly changing social mores, and, last but not least, to play a role in corporate planning by monitoring information supply and handling certain issues.

The consultants and services I need

Experience and professionalism are prime requirements. I am allergic to the "Hail fellow, well met" type of public relations man who exists still today on both sides of the fence. I take for granted that the basic mechanics will be efficiently carried out. I do not expect a single account executive operation – except in terms of continuity of contact. The consultant must have ready access to experts in many fields: Sociology, economics, political analysis, and so on. They should be aware of the political, social and economic situation in the country concerned. Also of the issues that are current, pending and developing. For example, in the areas of labour pressures, disclosure etc I expect them to provide me with reliable information, up to date and also with an analysis of possible developments in the foreseeable future in their respective countries. I expect a lot of information and input. And that information needs comment and interpretation.

My consultant must be almost as aware of the processes of government at the local, regional and national levels, as a parliamentary editor of a newspaper. He needs to have a thorough general knowledge of all the fields of my company's activities – and also of those of my competitors. He must be innovative. A sounding board. I expect integrity and honesty. He must never be afraid to criticise and be constructive. Essential that he knows who are the opinion leaders in all fields of endeavour – and how to reach them.

He must try to be the catalyst achieving common opinion with outside interests. Finally, he must be a businessman who professionally markets sound advice and good services.

The future

Increasing outside pressures will continue to affect companies' abilities to operate freely. More restrictions and regulations are to be expected – but, hopefully, these may be tempered in part by a growing awareness of their consequences and resentment manifested by public opinion. The basic argument being independent freedoms versus imposed regulation : The right to be responsible for oneself : The rejection of any type of Big Brother, be it government, a trade union or a religious movement as it has happened in Iran after the "cassette" revolution, (phrase used in the "Herald Tribune"). A feeling in the individual that says "Government stay away from me". Startling improvements in information systems (data banks) making more easily available information for early warning and interpretation. The mass of paper giving way to electronic information handling systems – stocking, retrieval, transmission – instant presentation on screens. Easier instant comparison possible of issues and experiences on an international basis. McLuans "Global Village", The spill-over effects of incidents will grow – witness Harrisburg – an urgent issue the world over in a matter of hours.

All this clearly shows that human problems and human factors, will become more important than ever. The automation process in industrial and agricultural production, as computers become more and more sophisticated and cheaper, will go faster and faster and will revolutionise our way of living. As, irrevocably we move down this path, we, workers, will have to adjust. This means that new fields of human endeavour must be found – creating more "software" than "hardware", and that the individual, in the future, must have the right to be educated and trained and retrained throughout life and private industry has a big part to play in this. It has made some mistakes in the past. It is still making them. But, a major task is to help motivate and educate people to be responsible for themselves.

Too often, we still put modern technology into the hands of people without sufficient explanation. There is, sometimes, a cutting of corners for financial reasons, take Harrisburg again, inadequate instrumentation, insufficient training, lack of motivation – and that is always a reason. The imperative for training in crisis management – how to handle a disaster – a difficult situation before it arises. If, in the future, we continue to allow that responsibility and initiative taken away from people, they become afraid to act on their own. They remain tucked in their niche in the hierarchy. Afraid of putting their head out for fear of having it chopped off.

Consultancy Today and Tomorrow

Robert S. Leaf

President, Burson-Marsteller International, London

If what consultants provide and what clients need is not identical there are going to be a great many people out of work since consultancies only exist to provide what the client needs.

I spend about 50 per cent of my time travelling. As a director of our United States company I go to the States at least four times a year for board meetings. Since my job makes me responsible for our European, Asian, South American and Middle Eastern operations, I spend a great deal of my time in those areas also.

I say this not to try to sound impressive but to build credibility for my observations.

The consultancy business has changed dramatically in recent years. These changes have affected both large and small consultancies. They have affected consultancies where the public relations profession goes back many years and those in countries where public relations is relatively new.

The consultancy business is getting more difficult. The reason is simple. Clients needs are becoming more complex as the world is becoming more complex. There is no consultancy in the world today which can fill *all* the public relations needs of any multinational client or many who can fill *all* the needs of a local client.

Unfortunately, though, for many years the business has been plagued by consultancies which continue to promise things they cannot possibly accomplish.

So the first thing a client needs from a consultancy is a realistic appraisal of what they can accomplish effectively. Can they handle a sophisticated industrial relations project? Can they provide support in fighting what the clients feels is unfair legislation? Can they provide support in dealing with the Common Market? Can they help fight off a takeover?

And if they themselves are multinational, can they do these things in each of the markets in which they operate?

The days are over when a dialogue like this between consultancy and a potential client can take place:

'I have a financial public relations problem, can you handle that?'

'Sure!'

'And we are launching both an industrial and a consumer product throughout this country and three others'.

'That'll be easy'.

'And we would like to launch a program aimed at the banks and security analysts'.

'Don't worry, we'll handle it'.

'We are also having problems at our plants at Lands End and John o'Groats'.

'We'll take care of it'.

'We'll need help in preparing speeches for our Nobel prize winner in molecular chemistry'.

'Send him round, we'll work on it'.

'By the way, how big is your operation'?

'We've three people including a secretary. But she's a smart secretary'.

This leads very easily to my next point. Changing clients' needs mean consultancies must provide far more sophisticated personnel than previously. This is true everywhere.

For example, we are getting far more difficult requests in our Kuala Lumpur office than we did two years ago. And while they might not be of the same nature as London or New York, they tax the resources of a market where public relations is relatively new.

A client needs people who are vitally aware of the world around them and who can relate the client's program to the various pressures being put on them by modern society. Who can plan a program effectively without knowing the position of various consumer movements or government legislative bodies?

How could you possibly represent a margarine high in polyunsaturated fats, without understanding the medical evidence regarding cholesterol and heart disease? It becomes even more difficult when you consider corporate public relations. What effect will the remarks by a chairman opening a new plant in one country have in another country where they have just released a number of employees engaged in producing similar products?

Public relations professionals are being required to know more and more. To read more and more. To delve deeper into problems and their ramifications.

This means that consultancies, regardless of size, have to do a better job at training their personnel and evaluating them. This is not just the job of large consultancies which can have formalised training programmes. The managements of every consultancy must make greater and greater demands on their personnel. They must encourage staff to attend outside seminars and courses and to engage in local community activities.

Consultancies must attract higher calibre personnel. This includes more people from industries or professions that previously did not go into our field. We must compete at universities and other institutions of learning for graduates that previously would look elsewhere.

We will have to attract people with marketing backgrounds, financial backgrounds, political backgrounds, etc. Public relations firms of the future will have executives with degrees in sociology, psychology and even law. Clients are seeing that it is impossible to staff internally with people with a diverse enough background to cover all their problems and are willing to purchase these skills in the market place.

What follows, as surely as night follows day, is that for consultancies to be able to attract these people they will have to pay higher starting salaries. And to motivate their staff to put in the intellectual and physical effort needed to keep ahead in today's environment they will have to provide greater increases and bonuses on a continuing basis.

Since consultancies are not charitable institutions with tax free status, to build the professional team of the future they will have to get the money to do this from somewhere. The only somewhere in our business is clients. That means the consultancies will have to be more profit oriented. They must charge fees that are realistic. That also means, as fees go up, that they will be under greater pressure to provide meaningful results.

Individual consultants must be business men and responsible for profitability on each account. It constantly amazes me when I interview some young account executive or supervisor and he does not know if the accounts he worked on were profitable or not and in some cases he does not even know the budget as that was a top management secret.

The consultancy of the future or even the present is going to be called on to provide more and more support services. If they cannot provide it from their own resources they are going to have to contract it outside. This means they are going to have to become more knowledgeable about whole ranges of suppliers.

Knowledge of the latest trends in audio-visuals is very important. Many specific programmes aimed at customers, the financial community, the local community, employees etc, are helped considerably by audio-visual support. These do not have to be super expensive extravaganzas combining numerous slide projectors and cameras electronically pulsed. Even simple slides can become twice as effective by knowledge of the latest techniques in slide production.

More client programmes will call for print work such as brochures, booklets, direct mail, etc. We now have clients where the out-of-pocket budget for material such as this is greater than our fee income. Clients are looking for literature that is more creative and better produced and the consultancy will have to provide it.

The same is true of photography. There is need for great improvement in the use of photography. As competition for space in media for news releases increases the picture will often be the key to successful coverage.

And the use of special lenses and other photographic effects can be the key. No one is expecting a consultancy to have on its payroll an ace photographer but more and more clients expect them to be able to come up with creative approaches to a photographic assignment.

There will also be the need for the consultancy to become more expert on the film as a public relations medium. The *right* film can provide tremendous impact but it must be the right film and come in at the right cost.

More public relations programs are going to be part of a total communications effort. Space advertising or direct mail can be integral parts of a corporate public relations program and practitioners must know how and when to use them. In promoting products, sophisticated brand managers are demanding that the advertising and public relations efforts be complementary. This means that public relations firms are going to have to work more closely with clients' advertising agencies in joint programs. Recently there has been an increase in advertising agencies and public relations consultancies making joint pitches for new business.

Public relations people engaged in this type of activity will have to understand demographics. In the joint program of the future it will not be inconceivable to have media schedules where certain publications or classes of publication are covered by space advertising and others by publicity.

Many of the public relations firms of the future are going to have to become more adept at what we call 'show business'. They will get more involved in sales meetings, distributor conferences, customer events. And the success of these can be the entertainment factor. And it does not have to be complex. For one Asian client, for example, for whom we were running a sales meeting, we took a competitive client's product that happened to be a marine engine and each salesman who entered the meeting had to hit it with a hammer. This emphasised very quickly to the sales force who the enemy was and set the tone for the whole meeting.

Sometimes the needs are far more complex. We have been increasingly asked to prepare programs for companies executives through various forms of role playing. We have re-enacted problems involved with oil spills, refinery explosions, executives being kidnapped, local communities getting hold of a secret company, memorandum containing damaging implications.

We have hired actors or had our own staff portray a South American terrorist, a student protestor and an irate housewife living near a cement plant whose husband had lung disease, politicians from a variety of countries, representatives of a wide band of minority groups, and representatives of all kinds of media.

Last year, while putting an oil company through one of these programs I played a Wall Street Journal reporter who asked relatively simple questions about output cost etc at a proposed refinery, and when the local chief executive answered what he thought was accurate I quoted the chairman of the company who had announced completely different figures that were quoted in the press six months previously. We had done our homework and it made crystal clear to the executive how important it was that he do his before having any significant interviews. Consultancies will have to work more closely with clients in preparing for public interviews.

This gets me into an area that more and more consultancies are becoming involved in and more and more clients want - speaker training. Executives are not only having to face both print and electronic media but they are facing an increasing variety of pressure groups. How they present themselves is important to getting the right message across. Throughout the world consultancies are training their clients with various degrees of sophistication. Some just listen at a rehearsal and comment. Others use videotape replays.

What is important is to be honest with clients, though tactful. There is no sense telling a client he came across like Winston Churchill when in reality he sounded like Donald Duck. These sessions must be carefully planned and the key to them is not only the criticism but how to improve the performance. We had one client who always had his hand in his pocket jingling change. It was highly disconcerting. We convinced him to have no interviews or to give no speeches until he removed everything from his pockets.

It is as important to teach clients awareness as it is techniques. Clients are often unprepared for the wide range of questions thrown at them by various groups in addition to media, and they have to be prepared for hostile questions.

Research is another area that will grow in importance. As budgets for programs get larger, clients will demand research to ensure the approach is correct and to measure results. There will be greater use of benchmark studies at the beginning of a program to see what the attitude is of the public involved so that later a second measurement can be made to judge changes in attitude.

Even more significant will be greater use of basic research before a program is prepared for a client. Too often programs are aimed at solving communication problems that a little research will prove do not exist. Maybe the local community is not really hostile. Maybe the consumer does not believe the competitive product is better.

I think that in the future most of the large public relations programs will have a research section costed and built into them. It is happening now. We have research departments in the United States and London and they are getting busier and busier.

Another client need is a greater effort to establish meaningful dialogues with supposedly hostile audiences. More communication is needed with militant unions, left wing student groups, consumer protection groups, etc. Often it is found that when there are intelligent programs aimed at explaining a position to groups like this they are not as hostile or inflexible as it originally seemed.

We must remember conditions change very quickly in this world. American multi-national companies were advised to take a low profile years ago because of the popularity of the book 'The American Challenge' by Jean Jacques Servan-Schreiber. It warned that the companies were a serious threat to Europe's independence and they would soon be taking over various countries through their economic power. Some companies, as a reaction, felt they had to pretend that their factories and warehouses were not really there. Now the reverse has happpened. The American multinationals have pulled back considerably and nearly all European countries faced by unemployment are actively welcoming them with open arms. You read much less today about the multinational octopus.

Those companies that kept up an active intelligent public relations program even during the period they were supposedly suspect are in better shape today than those who felt the need to be an ostrich and bury their public relations program in the sand.

Companies and consultancies will become more flexible in their approach. We recently opened six offices in the Middle East and I have been visiting the area. It is obvious that in countries like Saudi Arabia the use of press releases is different. Many newspapers there have not received many releases and some do not regard them in the same way as in this country. They see them as advertisements pure and simple. And sometimes they will print the release and send a bill. They are not being greedy or dishonest. It is just a culturally different outlook. This does not mean they will never publish any press releases. But it is much more difficult to get mentions there and clients must be aware of that. It might mean that direct mail or other corporate communications might have to replace a press relations program.

The Middle East emphasises a point stressed earlier. Consultancies will need staff that are politically and intellectually aware. Circumstances change quickly and dramatically. Public relations programs aimed at the Arab world now have to be modified because of the division between Egypt and some of its former allies.

For example, a company opening a plant in Egypt would automatically have planned to maximise publicity for that fact throughout the whole area. Now they have to look at the situation carefully before making the decision that this is a wise approach.

As consultancies become more involved in wide ranging problems they are becoming more privy to confidential client information.

In some countries the consultancy business was historically slow in developing because top managements did not believe in providing information to outside consultants when it was not positive. But this is changing. To provide the consultancy with an incomplete picture is like going to a doctor for an examination and not telling him where the pains are.

As a result of having greater knowledge of the client, consultancies of the future will become more involved in primary planning and be called in as part of a team.

For example, when selecting a country for a new plant site, questions automatically come up such as: are there adequate tax incentives, a supply of local labour, necessary transportation, a significant market for the product etc. Now equally important is: what will be the reaction of the public to having the plant in that particular locale. And who is better able to judge that than the public relations professional?

Similar valuable inputs can be made in the areas of product development or decisions regarding mergers or acquisitions.

Charles Dudley Warner wrote in 1870 'Public opinion is stronger than the legislature and nearly as strong as The Ten Commandments'. This is even truer today and the public relations consultancy will have to work closely with clients in trying to both anticipate and interpret public opinion before vital decisions are concluded.

Another area of increasing consultancy involvement will be in anticipating potential client problems and helping plan for them in advance. Any company can come up against a disaster such as an explosion, fire, etc. This does not just happen to refineries and tankers. How many companies have clearly defined programs to cover these eventualities? Are they prepared to act quickly to satisfy the needs of all the various publics, such as national government, local communities, employees, the general public, etc? More consultancies should be working with their clients preparing disaster plans that can be put into effect immediately.

Another area where consultancies must and will be active is the area of social consciousness. It is not charity but self interest to understand and alleviate the problems of the developing countries. Public relations consultancies must be active in programs that create meaningful dialogue between the haves and have nots.

All this means that the consultancy business is going to get more exciting and more rewarding, which is good for both clients and consultants.

Twenty-two years ago I joined Burson-Marsteller as their first trainee. We were a handful of people and we were engaged primarily in product publicity. We have seen tremendous changes in the business during those years. But it is not going to take 22 years for similar changes, or 15, or 10, or even five. Every year is bringing new and difficult changes.

Right now the potential business for consultancies appears limitless. In our field the worry is not where business will come from but whether consultancies in total will have the people and resources to cope with accelerating client needs.

I am optimistic. I see public relations professionals within companies or with consultancies achieving more status and having more personal satisfaction. I foresee more and more highly qualified people entering our arena to the benefit of everyone.

And most important I believe that in the future as the client's needs proliferate, the public relations consultancy's ability to handle these needs will expand accordingly.

17

How Will Public Relations
Practice Change?

I am Michael Rice and I have been given the privilege of chairing this final
plenary session. The reason I have been invited to take on this considerable
responsibility and great honour, is because I am the current chairman of the
Public Relations Consultants Association, which is one of the two organising bodies
of this Congress. And if it is not too late for me to do so, I would like on my
own behalf and on behalf of my 80 colleagues in the Public Relations Consultants
Association in this country and overseas, to greet you and to say how privileged
we have all felt to meet you here on this very notable occasion.

The topic with which this session deals is framed as a statement and not as a
question. It does not ask whether change will come to the practice of public
relations but rather <u>how</u> it will come. Public relations in the sense of a
professionally structured practice is a pheonomenon of our time. Indeed the
public relations man, I suspect, is himself a symptom of the sort of world in
which we live. That world and our human society is undergoing a degree of change
more radical it seems to me than any which has faced our species since Neolithic
times at the end of the long and dismal procession of the Stone Age when most of
us began finally to throw off the old ways of the hunting gathering societies and
to settle into communities which eventually, with the help of agriculture and the
management of herds, grew into the cities and societies around the Ancient World
from which today we descend.

Our society faces the dilemma of quantity on the scale which mankind has never
previously experienced. There are simply too many of us for comfort - or for the
sensible management of the sort of society in which most of us want to live.
Issues which were once local; famine, deprivation, aspiration, identity - have
now become global. And if we cannot communicate with each other through all levels
of society then we are lost. I found myself largely at odds with most of our
speakers during the Congress. For myself, I believe that we have very little
future as a species left before us. We are less the consequence, I believe, of
creation than of aberration. We are a new, and I suspect, a somewhat incompetent
animal. But we do have the capacity - so far as we know - for more complex and
subtle communications than any other animal on the face of the earth. And if I
could see any grounds for hope, it would be that before it is too late we might
find the way to use that phenomenal capacity in the interest of the species'
survival.

The panel who may well hold more optimistic views about our future than I do, will
put before you their concept of the ways in which public relations will need to
change to respond to the colossal opportunities - if such they see them to be -
and the undoubted hazards which the future has in wait for us. This congress has
heard a succession of variations played on the theme of change, with variety and

virtuosity which would have satisfied the most conscientious composer of the late Baroque. I am the impresario today of a quartet of four distinguished soloists, who will further embroider this complex theme.

The Pacific - the Sea of the Future

Paddy Shubert

Trade Relations Director
Shell Group of Companies, Malaysia

May I, Mr Chairman, through you thank the International Public Relations
Association for the invitation to be here today. Specifically, I believe I am
asked to peer over the public relations horizon of the 80's. I am no futurologist
and any resemblance therefore to Hermon Kahn is purely physical. I am further
asked to put the focus on my own country, Malaysia. We are a small country. We
are developing. We are very unpretentious and unassuming. My son tells me that
we are best known because we are one of three locations in the world favoured by
the leathery turtle when she wishes to lay her eggs. Having observed this species
I know that for the turtle at least the only way to make progress is to stick out
your neck. I am going to try to emulate the Malaysian species and indulge in a
spot of intellectual streaking for which I would ask you please to fasten your
mental seat belts because it will be exciting I hope but a little bumpy as we are
in a lesser known territory.

Malaysia does have a public relations profession. We have had visits from Alan
Eden Green, Harold Burson, Bob Leaf and Nigel Nielson. They were not seen as
Martians. We found we had sufficient common language. I wondered where I might
begin therefore to point to some of the differences of approach and practice.
Being a tropical country I thought there was no better beginning than with the
Eskimos. You see the Eskimo has fourteen different words for snow. Snow is the
dominant element in his environment. He has to learn to describe, to handle, to
deal with and to manage snow. And public relations likewise is situational. It
may derive from an international profession but it is also culturally and
environmentally determined and it will be differentiated in part by the particular
situation in which it is practised.

I would like to begin with the international spectrum a little because this
conference is dedicated to it, and Malaysia owes a great deal to the international
profession. But I would then like to measure against it the situation of our own
country. I say we owe a great deal; any developing country can do in a decade
what it took centuries for the advanced world to develop. So we have, fortunately,
the tools, concepts and techniques of a highly developed profession at our disposal
which we are trying to acquire by a conscious educational effort. We draw from all
societies. We have on the one hand courses of mass communications in the American
pattern at our universities and at the same time we have a professionally oriented
course much nearer to the CAM diploma. And we have adaptations in that there is a
corpus of case studies based on experience within the specifically Malaysian
environment. But we also inherit, along with the techniques, some of the problems
and pressures and the context in which public relations today is practised and of
which you have heard a great deal.

Business, it would seem is a crisis-ridden environment. We have many Chinese in
my country. Their idiogram for the word "crisis" has two components. One indeed
means danger but the other means opportunity. Unlike my chairman I am an unrelenting optimist. I believe that the crisis for business has spawned the
opportunity for public relations. It is true that never before has the corporate
sector come under such scrutiny, such fierce debate and such attack. The multi-
nationals are under siege from activist groups, the consumers, the environmentalists, the women's libbers, and all the other protest groups are there as part of
our environment and have to be answered. We live, I conclude, in a fairly
unfriendly atmosphere and under the threat of these external pressures I find there
is a sudden new enchantment with public relations. Because it is all the more
necessary to state your case, to stand up in public and declare yourself. And in
this sophisticated world of media it is necessary to reach out for the profession
that can handle this in the best possible way and which has always handled public
opinion and communication. And therefore public relations has come into its own
the more governments have begun to intervene in the affairs of business.

My title, which is the strange one of "trade relations", merely means anything
which impinges on the company's ability to trade. You can imagine I have had a
very busy time in recent years. But as these interventions increase, the corporate
sector is forced to the knowledge, however belated, that we live in a state of
public relations whether we like it or not. We have seen the power of the media
bring down the most powerful person in the world, the President of the United
States. We are up against the sovereignty of new nations and this is a particular
issue for the developing country. The framework of regulations increases around
our activities the whole time. The framework of reality is changing and there are
new demands of corporate citizenship and of social responsibility. It is the age
of accountability but it is also the age of disclosure and I see the profession
having developed round the world at an accelerated pace as a result.

I would like to think that this new status for the profession was hard won entirely
in the context of our battles to gain professional legitimacy but I think we must
owe part of it at least to the siege mentality of business. The ghost that ought
to hover over these proceedings is the ghost of Ivy Lee, he would find a very
different scene from the one he pioneered. He would find, for one thing, that we
have crossed a very significant threshold where we are no longer just a tool of
management but an integral part of management and as a manifestation of that we
have penetrated the board room and no longer is there the empty chair signifying
the man in the street whose viewpoint is not interpreted. That empty chair is now
occupied by a public relations man. If it is in the United States he is the Vice
President of the company and he will monitor social, political and economic change.
He will be there when policy is made and he will be counsel on the likely impact
upon public opinion of any major activity. We have also penetrated through to the
Chief Executive Officers. My task, when I began twenty years ago, my most
dangerous and delicate task, was educating the boss about the needs of public
relations beyond organising cocktail parties. Today he sees himself quite rightly
as the front line public relations practitioner for the organisation and he has
been translated from chief "executive" to chief "responsibility". He knows that
the company has been politicised whther it likes it or not and in addition to his
excellent technical head and his excellent commercial head he has now got to have
a third head which is a political one. The political head needs an advisor, and
that is I think the purview of the function that has always concerned itself with
looking to the external side and has always concerned itself with the environmental
role.

In the days of social audits and accountability we are the watch-dog for the
company's transgressions and the "buzz" words in America I am told are issue
analysis, and issue advocacy. In this situation of course the profile of the

practitioner has changed and has been enhanced. We have added an intellectual content and to my delight we have added a managerial one. We operate by objectives and budgets and work programmes, we are now managers not just technicians. How does this perhaps exaggerated rosy view of the profession apply in a developing country like my own. I would here like to let the turtle's neck protrude a little. I believe there is indeed a generic universal profession, concerned however with the science of public relations, that is, with its techniques and its tools and its methods, its ethics and its concepts. And these can be transplanted and are transplanted round the world. But there is an aspect of public relations not so susceptible to easy transplant where the environmental tissue may be rejected. By environmental tissue I refer to the cultural conditions in which it is practised and where attitudes of the local situation may be very different. A developing country may be very ready to accept a European who is peddling a new chemical product, but not so easily will they accept a style of behaviour or ideas that impinge upon behaviour and I think one area where we have to change and develop is where we apply the science of public relations to the particular way in which the local community acts and thinks.

Malaysia is in the fastest developing part of the world. The Mediterranean it is said, was the "sea of the past", the Atlantic the "sea of the present" and the Pacific, "the sea of the future", and this is where it is all happening with tremendous growth. And we have, therefore, to have a public relations profession that will accompany and accommodate economic growth. But what is the situation into which it is transplanted. We are a multi-cultural, multi-racial, multi-lingual community. Apart from the problems that poses in terms of communications and interpretations we have a multiple sensitivity that we have to deal with. Where you have races who are a minority they assimulate and in nearby Thailand they have taken Thai names and learned the language. In Malysia, we have 50 per cent of the indigenous Malaysia rural and – on the whole – poor and 50 per cent the immigrants who are town people, much more advanced educationally and economically. One group holds economic power, the other political power, conflict is endemic in this situation and has in the past caused race riots. One public relations result of this was when a very large international tobacco company was the victim of a false rumour – through poor communications rather than fact – that it was discriminating in its employment policies in favour of one race against the other and as a result there was a boycott on their products that reduced profits to 40 per cent for two years. It needed a classic public relations fire brigade rescue operation with one of the largest international consultants called in to advise. That is the atmosphere in which we live. We also have a massive programme of social re-structuring to bring the indigenous people level with the rest; a national economic policy which enjoined upon the corporate sector that they must radically change the racial balance of their work force and their equity structure in order to achieve this reconstruction. In other words, corporate citizenship is precisely spelt out in my country and becomes the judgmental area for corporate behaviour, no longer can we justify our role by economic contribution alone. We have to answer to the social and the moral and the political requirements in which we operate.

May I just say that in the art of public relations – which is what this is all about relations being the second word of our profession – we have a great deal to learn. Management has not done very well in the past. My part of the world coined the phrases: the ugly American and the ugly Japanese. Perhaps unfairly but you can see the area of sensitivity. We have a legacy of international business. You can have political self-determination but economic determination follows much later. Business is conducted at the international level, so you have the joint venture, the expert and the multi-national corporation. In public relations terms what ever happens in one part of the globe gets instantaneous publicity around the world – what was once a local problem becomes a world wide attack on credibility. In this situation I think relations are the keynote and if we look around for the profession that might best be left to handle those relations may I humbly, but optimistically suggest that that profession should be public relations.

Seven Pillars of Efficiency

Jacques Coup de Frejac

President, Information et Enterprise, Paris, France

T H Lawrence referred to 'seven pillars of wisdom'. From a European viewpoint I will try to forecast the seven pillars of efficiency for public relations in the years to come. It will be up to each professional to prove if this leads to wisdom.

Though I am French - and quite decided to remain so - let me also indicate immediately that my pillars are not going to be classical but Baroque, not material but psychological, not gilded but realistic.

Some people may believe that public relations is going to change because of new economic, political or social situations; others may consider that the pressure groups (ethnic minorities, consumers, ecologists, labour unions) will play a leading role in imposing new models.

I do not share these opinions.

We public relations professionals have always had to operate in changing economic, political and social environments. This will no doubt continue. As a consequence it is our capacity to adapt to evolution which is our main challenge. Our efficiency will only be measured by the excellence of our basic principles, by our will to apply them; in one word, by our professionalism.

What must be changed - and improved - is our professionalism. I am confident that it will, but I must admit that, today, with the development of public relations (public affairs, corporate relations, employee communication, press relations) we seem to be gaining in numbers but not always in density. Here lies the danger.

If public relations practice is melted down in a floppy protoplasm of fashionable communication, we will disappear. If public relations practice remains a hard nucleus of vigorous relations with selected publics, we will survive and prosper.

So, what are these principles of professionalism, these pillars of efficiency?

I have chosen seven. Each is as important as the other.

Shyless combativeness

In real democracies, in free enterprises (the only places where public relations can exist) the performance of the economy is second to none.

Corporations are the most extraordinary machine to generate economic wealth and social progress. We have a truthful story to tell. Let us shake loose the inferiority complex of management.

Let us be offensive, knowing that it is more difficult to declare peace than to declare war.

Rigorous discrimination

The worst inflation we suffer from is the inflation of information. We must deflate it or it will overcome us. Public relations professionals must only issue useful information, adapted to each specific public according to his desires, his needs and, above all, his intelligence.

We must always speak to the brain and we must keep in mind that brains seldom work well. It is the brains of the others that count.

Quest for dialogue

The most irresistible temptation in public relations is to speak and write; the most crucial need is to listen. It is only after you have listened that you know what you should say.

This is where communication takes over from information. It is dangerously wrong to pretend that the more communication you give out, the more communication you generate. It is the contrary that happens. Forcible feeding of information forbids communication.

We need dialogue. This is our superiority over the media. This is our basic challenge.

Astute far-sightedness

The most intolerable dictatorship is that of current events; it generates spleen, confusion, intolerance, loss of personality.

Public relations professionals must carry out continuous programmes of economic understanding in a world where it is almost non-existent.

Far-sightedness looks into the past as well as into the future. Here again we need to be superior to the media.

Creative research

This is today our weakest point and where the shoe pinches most.

We must engage in careful public mapping, in research for information motivation, for appropriate driving belts, for proper timing, for the duration of memorisation, for saturation thresholds, for knowledge application, for eye and ear availability. We must bring in scientific appreciation of media efficiency.

We must shake loose from any routine.

Plausible semantics

It is not only in public relations world congresses that we speak foreign languages. It is at every moment with anybody else.

Our semantics are not in harmony with the understanding of our listeners.

The most horrifying example is that of our press-releases which are worded in the same way for a wire agency, a mass medium, a technical magazine, a regional daily, a political bulletin, not to mention a radio station and a television desk.

Lack of readability can kill us. Readability is the must.

Intelligence

In the French 'Littré' dictionary, the definitions of intelligence are the following:

> capacity to understand
> power to reach general ideas
> action to penetrate the mind
> ability to choose the means to reach an objective
> communication with people.

This is really the nucleus of our responsibility and should be the pride of our profession.

Let us simply be a little more intelligent than the others.

After telling you that, in my mind, economic evolution will not play a major role in the changes of public relations practice and after putting the emphasis on the crucial importance of the improvement of our professionalism, let me say in simple words again that none of these factors will have as much influence on the future of our business and procedures as the extraordinary communication revolution that the American technicians call "compunication" and the French call "telematique".

The consequences of this revolution will make today's methods for press relations, for direct communication, for economic education, for the use of leisure time completely obsolete. We have no time to waste to incorporate into our public relation practice and techniques these new extraordinary communication techniques.

There are certainly other pillars of our efficiency, other factors which influence public relations practice. Whatever they may be, they lie with us, not with outside events.

As far as I am concerned I can only think of one more important aspect of public relations: Never run out of time.

I believe in the future of public relations as long as it remains - as General de Gaulle said, 'une ardente obligation', a 'fiery duty'.

Japan Needs Public Relations

Satoshi Sugita

Vice-President and Group Manager
Burson-Marsteller Fuji, Tokyo, Japan

Untangling Japan

In predicting the future course of our profession, it is easier and safer to draw a pessimistic picture. In fact, pessimism about the future of public relations prevails among my Japanese colleagues.

This inclination to expect the worst possible outcome is not peculiar to Japan, even though some of you may believe that the Japanese invented suicide. It is akin to the proverbial Japanese doctor in the days of shogun, who made it a policy to announce "It's too late!" every time he saw a new patient. Should the patient die as a result of his treatment, the people would say, "The doctor said it was too late and nothing could have been done". And if the patient recovered, it was due to the doctor's great skill, because he had said, "It's too late".

His policy obviously was wise and he won the respect of his patients. One day, an injured man was brought to him. He had fallen down the stairs and broken his leg. The doctor, as usual, started out, "It's too late, fellows". "But doctor, we brought him in as soon as he fell". "Maybe so," the doctor said with a thin smile, "but you should have brought him here before he fell".

You may never be accused of lacking in proper judgment by envisaging a gloomy future. Either you will be right or, if that is not the case, you can attribute the unexpected success to the exceptionally earnest endeavour of yourself and your colleagues. But it is not necessary to be always pessimistic.

The pessimists among my colleagues, of course, have their own arguments. To start with, they are quick to point out that public relations is still very backward in Japan and that it will be many years before there is a breakthrough. Indeed, a noted book on how to do business in Japan, written by an American, says that the present state of the public relations business in Japan, compared to the United States, is somewhere in the Middle Ages. It has also been said that there is no clear distinction in the minds of the Japanese between advertising and public relations.

Second, a popular belief, even among public relations practitioners, maintains that there is no inherent need for public relations in Japan. Unlike the United States or Malaysia, Japan is an extremely homogeneous country with a single race and a single language, and its people communicate fairly well without so many words - either spoken or written. An old Japanese proverb goes, "Eyes speak as eloquently as the mouth". In fact, the Japanese do not have the habit of writing business letters.

Third, to the Japanese his company is his castle and there is little willingness on the part of Japanese employees to share work with outsiders, thus inhibiting the growth of public relations consultants. Even though there may be no organised public relations staff in a Japanese company, the function usually exists, in the form of a general affairs department or the office of the president or whatever name it may be known as.

There is also in some quarters unwarranted suspicion toward western public relations firms, especially after the Lockheed and Grumman scandals involving public relations people. A major weekly magazine put out by Japan's largest daily newspaper some years ago said that most of the principals at American public relations firm in Tokyo are CIA agents. I regret to say that during all the years I have lived in Tokyo, I have never been approached by the United States agency.

There are other reasons, too: the Japanese never can equate public relations consultations with money; the cream of the Japanese labour market will always join major Japanese companies and consultancies will not be able to attract capable account executives; Japan is so different that western communications methods won't work. And so on and so forth.

I am an optimist, however, not only because it does not seem too much use being anything else, as Sir Winston Churchill once said, but also because public relations could accomplish so much in Japan.

Japan is really a publicist's delight, as it combines a highly literate population with probably the most sophisticated mass media in the world today. Let me give you some facts on the media. Japan's total daily newspaper circulation is 60,780,000 or 542 copies per 1,000 population, the highest ratio in the world.

There are three major quality national dailies with circulation figures ranging from 4.5. million to 8 million. The *Asahi Shimbun*, Japan's most influential newspaper with 7.2 million circulation and over 130 local editions, employs approximately 2,000 journalists. There are four industrial and business newspapers that are published daily. There are also over 3,000 technical and trade publications in addition to about 4,000 consumer magazines.

98 per cent of Japanese households own colour television sets and average television viewing time among Japanese housewives is four hours and 18 minutes a day, again the highest ratio in the world.

Dependence on the Mass Media

In general, the Japanese are most heavily dependent on the mass media. Japanese consumers were asked in a recent survey to name one item that was considered most indispensable to their life. Thirty-seven per cent listed television; 20 per cent said newspapers. In a similar survey carried out in the United States, 41 per cent listed the automobile and 38 per cent a refrigerator.

This domestic market is serviced by no less than 50 independent public relations firms of various sizes and two industry associations. The Public Relations Society of Japan, of which I am vice chairman, has about 60 individual members, both corporate and consultancy people. The Japanese Association of Public Relations Agencies has 26 member companies. Additionally, a couple of thousand people are considered to be employed by Japanese corporations in various public relations capacities.

Even though the pessimists may be fairly reasonable in their assessment of the basic weakness of the public relations market in Japan, no nation in the world is totally devoid of the problems that Japan has. The United States can claim no exception.

Rather I feel that the basic tools of public relations and communication are well nurtured in the Japanese society through the extremely intricate human relations. I believe that the greater challenges and opportunities for public relations in the next decade lie not in the domestic areas but in the international field. The gradual maturation of the Japanese market will be stimulated from outside, as more and more Japanese companies are using public relations overseas to compete with their western competitors, and they are becoming increasingly aware of its value.

There are ample indications that major Japanese companies are beginning to import their own favourable images abroad for consumption on their home grounds. Companies like Sony, Pioneer and Matsushita, among aothers, are publicising in Japan their overseas success stories to impress Japanese consumers.

Great demands exist for versatile and experienced professionals in cross-cultural communications. Japan needs a lot of untangling and uncomplicating to the outside world, and it must attain an international level of sophistication in its communications with people in other lands. More than a century after the end of the national isolation policy, Japan is still a closed society in many ways, and foreign companies find it a difficult market to tackle.

Japan is also a market of great contradictions. Despite the inundation by Japanese products of every market of the world, the Japanese are probably the least internationally minded of all people. They find it uncomfortable to mix with people from other lands, due partly to the language barrier and partly to their clannish nature. The Japanese, known as a "tension race", also bitterly lack a sense of humour.

It is also true that, though Japan may be the second largest economy in the Free World, its people still live in what apparently appear to westerners to be "rabbit hutches", as the confidential EEC document recently pointed out. Of the thousands of people you see travelling in a quasi-military manner, following a man with a flag in major capitals of the world, most of them probably live in "hutches" without flush toilets.

Here is another apparent contradiction. The Japanese did a great job in improving the image of their products after World War II. Before the war, Japanese products were synonymous with cheap prices and inferior quality.

The reputation of the Japanese has undergone a swift change from being the manufacturers of shoddy Christmas tree ornaments to the producers of the world's finest products at very competitive prices.

They first improved the quality of their products and then successfully communicated this fact to the rest of the world. This should be a classical case history in international public relations. Remember the old textbook that said public relations can bring about no miracle and the message must be backed by facts to be promotable.

But then the question is: why are they so poor as communicators when it comes to controversial current issues, such as whaling, low wages, import restrictions or non-tariff barriers?

A good part of the criticism levelled at Japanese business is caused by misconceptions based on mass psychology or simple fear, but the Japanese have been so terribly inadequate in responding to them. There are several reasons for this failure.

Japan has always been very eager to learn from the West, but it has done little in learning to communicate with the rest of the world, especially when Japan is on the defensive.The communications balance, at least, has always been in favour of the West.

There is, of course, a lot being said within Japan on the controversial international issues, both pro and con, but the Japanese never had the sophistication or experience in international communications to present their prima facie case to foreign audiences. This is the area in which public relations can be of great help.

Furthermore, the ability to think logically and to speak effectively and impressively - with occasional humour - has never been emphasised in the Japanese educational system. The need for speech clinics and debate training is being given belated recognition in Japan. By organising speaker training sessions and producing audio-visual aids, public relations professionals can make a great contribution to improving and internationalising the quality of communication by Japanese business firms.

Everybody recognises that the Japanese are diligent workers to be sure. But diligence will no longer be tolerated as a virtue if the outside world sees Japan as a nation of "workholics" who are willing to sacrifice good living simply for the joy of toiling. Equilibrium in trade is just as important as equilibrium in communications.

The Public Relations Professional
Must Equip Himself for His New Role

Arthur Reef

Director of Public Relations and Advertising
AMAX, New York, United States of America

The organisers obviously decided that in this last session the last speaker would
have the job of attempting to stimulate and provoke some discussion by picking up
some of the points that were made in this session and perhaps in a few others.
Either to agree or, preferably to disagree. Let me pick up therefore some points
made this afternoon. Paddy Shubert discussed the present role and the future role
of the public relations executive. His role with regard to the corporation and
government; his importance; the need for a proper relationship between the public
relations practitioner and the top echelon of either government or business or any
element of the community. Paddy Schubert also referred to the power of the media
and the need to understand the media and how to use it. Coup de Frejac said that
some people believe that public relations practice is going to change because of new
economic, political or social situations. Others consider that the pressure groups;
consumers, ecologists and labour unions will play a leading role in imposing new
models. Sanat Lahiri, the IPRA President emphasised the other evening that it was
not the change that is so remarkable but the frightening rate of change in these
modern times. The incredible degree of consumerism, energy problems, social audit,
social responsibility and all the other elements of social activism that have
impinged on the activities and functions, not only of the corporation but of the
individual citizen. It has meant a tremendous intrusion of government into the
lives of the average citizen and the average enterprise and this intrusion is
increasing at an ever greater rate.

Paddy Schubert indicated that in the current practice of public relations the ideal
situation is one in which the public relations executive shares the seat of opinion-
molding with the top echelon of the corporation or government. She said the ideal
public relations executive should be capable of interpreting future trends,
analysing them, reporting on them to the management, and helping management form
its policy in addition to communicating such policy to the various groups with
which the corporate or other entity must make contact. That is an ideal situation.
Unfortunately it does not exist in too many instances.

You can't have a meeting of public relations executives anywhere in the world,
without one of the first complaints being the fact that the public relations role
has been denigrated. It is not at the level at which the public relations
executive believes it should be. Why is this? Why is it, for example, that in a
great number of corporate entities in the United States and in other parts of the
world the role of chief executive in public relations or public affairs (call it
what you will) has been relegated to an increasing extent to lawyers or financial
experts who will then include in their departments public relations executives.
And the reason I think is that too many of us are not equipped to undertake the
responsibility of this major role that Paddy Schubert indicated. Not equipped

213

either through education, training, experience or even the ability to interpret. It does require an assembly of a large basket of capabilities: sociology, history, communications techniques, economics. The business world today is extremely complicated. Understanding a balance sheet is just as important today to the public relations executive as understanding how to write a press release and unfortunately too many executives who hold a public relations role are not equipped to undertake it. And if public relations practice is going to change in the future, the public relations executive has to equip himself for this role.

Understanding the Media

A second point that was made and I thought an interesting one - briefly by Paddy Schubert and also in the context of some other statements in the course of this congress - had to do with the power of the media and understanding the media. We all heard in the meeting two days ago a gentleman, a representative for the Dominican Republic, who I think voiced a complaint that has been voiced by a great many other delegates. Namely that the news media , the news agencies have emphasised the unhappy, the unfortunate, the disaster, and that when the Dominican Republic, for example, overthrew its dictator and a quiet revolution was taking place - a quiet metamorphosis - there was almost no reporting of that particular event. It is a common occurrence and the complaint is voiced often. All of you are aware of the problems faced by the transnational corporations, particularly the petroleum corporations and Dr Lall earlier in the meeting said that the trans-national corporation is the most powerful, single entity in the world economic scene. The largest TNC's dwarf most Third World countries in size and production and income. They have the most effective and widespread international communi-cations network that span our globe, and so on and so forth. I would submit that if you talk to the biggest of the transnational corporations, the petroleum companies in the United States, and in some others - you could easily substitute the complaint voiced by the delegate of the Dominican Republic with a similar complaint by the Head of a multinational petroleum corporation. The petroleum corporations have been unable to achieve understanding of the energy problem. They have been unable to get understanding so much so as a matter of fact, that many of them have undertaken very expensive campaigns. It is not as effective obviously because the identity of Mobil Oil as a spokesman immediately redounds somewhat to the credibility of the message in the eyes of the viewer. And yet, the trans-national corporation, the petroleum corporations are seemingly in the same boat as many of the representatives of the countries in the developing world in terms of getting a fair hearing in the press. Why? I think it can be summed up in perhaps a few brief comments. One, some of you may have heard of the unwritten law of television news editing which says if it does not light up, or does not blow up then we will not use it. There is a fascination among the news media with the unhappy, with the unfortunate, with the disaster because the media believes - and this is true of the news agencies and the newspapers which are competing in a commercial sense for readers - that if they are to gain their readers they have got to give their readers what they believe their readers want. The editors and perhaps the readers have influenced this selection of the news. This must be understood in order to make an impact with the media. It also is true that it is of no use in terms of an emergency situation to try to contact the news media on a last minute basis. A relationship has to be built up with the editors, with the writers, in order to ensure a hearing whether it is good news or bad. The availability to the media is terribly important. Unfortunately in a case of the transnational petroleum corporation for many years there was a degree of arrogance which inhibited some of this continuing fruitful contact with the media.

Investigatory Reporting

Finally the news media has changed. We are in an era of "investigatory reporting". It is unlike what it was 25 or 30 years ago when a reporter went out on a story and no matter where the news went his nose followed it and he came out with the results, the story, good bad or indifferent. Too often the investigatory reporter starts out today with a premise: I am going to do a story which will expose A, B or C., and I am going to uncover only those facts which support my premise – don't confuse me with facts that do not support my premise. And this is a concept that you must be aware of and which we must tackle.

I am going to tell you just one story in which I think some of you have heard which exemplifies this kind of bias in reporting. It is a story that supposedly took place during the Nixon administration when the press counsellor at the White House to President Nixon said that he had a very, very unhappy relationship with the press. We are all aware of that. And his press counsellor said that he ought to remedy that particular situation by meeting with them more often and more informally. And supposedly President Nixon agreed and the press officer organised a Sunday yacht trip on the Presidential yacht which went out on Sunday afternoon with a dozen of the Washington correspondents, primarily the *Washington Post, The Star*. *The Washington Post* particularly because as you know it was particularly antagonistic to Nixon. And the afternoon went extremely well. There was a relaxed give and take conversation and discussion. Cocktails and buffet. And as they headed back to the pier to end the afternoon about 100 metres from the pier, President Nixon turned to his aide and said I am getting rather tired, a bit bored, I think I am going to walk the rest of the way. And his aide looked at him in sheer horror and said, I beg your pardon, and Nixon said, I am going to walk, it's only 100 metres. I'll get off the boat and I will walk across the water the rest of the way – I can do that. And his aide said, No, Mr President, please. Nixon waved him aside, Good afternoon gentlemen, I am going to walk the rest of the way. He clambered over the side of the boat and walked on the surface of the water the hundred metres to the shore, climbed into his limousine, waved goodbye and was obviously taken back to The White House. And the next morning *The Washington Post* had a great big banner headline, "NIXON, CAN'T SWIM"!

DISCUSSION

Chairman: We have had a very profound and wide ranging analysis of some of
the prospects of Change with which we have to attempt to cope in the years to
come. I always think wistfully of the 18th Century British Member of Parliament,
Sir Cloudesley Shovell who is remembered for his remark: "All change is wrong".

Nemercio Nogueira (Brazil). I would like to add a few words to what has been said
by the panel. An international drive towards official recognition of the public
relations profession on equal terms with doctors, dentists, engineers, lawyers etc
should be our major goal in the forthcoming years through IPRA and through our
national and regional associations. Brazil was the first country to do it in the
whole world and to recognise and give official recognition to our profession back
in 1967, twelve years ago. And that is why we felt that our delegation, which is
relatively large to this Congress, could contribute a great deal to our colleagues
from other nations towards that end. The reason why we think that that should be
our main goal, our permanent struggle, is the fact that on this recognition
depends the professional relevance of public relations. On it depends the growth
of employment opportunities for young people. The incorporation of young people as
new professionals, the growth of our number and of our economic significance is
the only way for us to become a profession with a professional purpose rather
than just a mere practice, which clearly shows its own insecurity by over-defining
itself all the time.

I have prepared for this Congress a case study on the Brazilian law and how it
works and how it is working and copies of that study have been distributed. I
would just like to say that the law defines in Brazil that the specific public
relations activities are those concerning the institutional information between
the entity and the public through the communication media, the coordination and
planning of public opinion research for institutional ends, planning and
supervision of the use of audio-visual media for institutional ends, planning and
execution of public opinion campaigns and finally teaching of public relations
techniques. It is a very important struggle, Mr President, and that is why I
thought I should make the point.

Carroll Bateman (United States of America). I would like to present a view which
I believe is shared by many of our colleagues in the United States. And that is
that we have a great fear of seeking from government any kind of franchise for
the conduct of public relations activity where freedom of speech is so important.
What government gives – government can take away. And we feel that recognition of
public relations as a profession should come through the activities of
professional organisations at the national and international levels rather than
from any action of government.

Jolly Kaul (India). We are coming to the end of this Congress and I thought I
would like to refer to a phenomenon that has taken place in our country and I have
a feeling that this kind of phenomenon might be taking place in many other Third
World countries also and perhaps in other parts of the world too. I refer to the
fact that in our deliberations here we have been speaking about public relations
mainly in the context either of governments or of large organised corporations
whether they be transnational, multinational, corporations or large national
enterprises. But in our country there is a growing feeling that there should be
restrictions on the working of large national or transnational corporations both
because there is an apprehension that too much power in their hands might not be
good and also because in an over-populated country, they feel that a small
enterprise creates more employment and from that point of view it is desirable. I
believe even in the Western world, the slogan: "Small is beautiful", is gaining
ground and there is a trend that perhaps instead of large we should go towards

small. And definitely a lot of government action is taking place to prevent the growth of large companies in my country - and I believe in certain Third World countries. Now I think this has two implications for public relations. One is that public relations practitioners should try to think how they will cope with this change that is taking place and secondly, I think public relations practitioners and consultants are going to have to try and see how they can offer a range of services for the small and medium enterprises other than for the large enterprise.

Reef.   I would only like to make one point in regard to the discussion on licensing of public relation practitioners. I would amplify the comment I made previously. Recognition of the public relation.man must be earned not granted. He has got to demonstrate his capability, he has got to earn the respect and confidence of the people he is working with. That is the only way we are going to get real recognition.

Question from India. I think we have made a lot of points but we have left out one major point and that is sincerity to our public. I think that is a very fundamental point and we must make our management aware of this fact that whatever we give out should be sincere.

Ed. Murray (Canada).   I would like to qualify this question by stating that I am a feminist. I would like to hear a comment from the panel regarding the social phenomenon of feminism, not womens lib., but feminism. We have seen it in our own country in regards to the increase of members of the female gender in a profession as well as the second careers involved of married women. The increase of day care centres throughout our country and the various social problems that have brought possibly the break up of the family unit or a change in the family unit. Can any of the panel comment on this please?

Shubert: Yes, I think that it is a phenomenon that is shared in many other countries. We have many women public relations practitioners in Malaysia. Part of the reasons are wrong and part of them are right. For the wrong reasons I picked up my newspaper one morning and read to my horror that public relations is just a pretty face. This would have led to my resignation had that been the only reason. This is of course in the mythology that public relations is restricted to organising the chairman's social functions. But the other and the proper reason I think is that as a profession we are talent-based. It is a profession that is creative, it is ideas generating, and it is based on the ability to communicate. Now it does not matter what is the sex or gender of the hand that holds the pen. Proficiency in communication is self-evident. And this has opened up the doors and that is why I think we have so many women public relations practitioners.

18

Chairman's Summing-Up

Dennis Buckle

Before making my few closing remarks I would like to conduct a presentation which arises from the proceedings of the past three days. I would like to ask Paul Winner to come and present a silver cup, which he has kindly donated, for what you have voted the best presentation in the special event this morning, the feature on case histories. It was won by Freddy Appassamy from Mauritius.

We have been through a hard-working two and a half days and the last thing that you would want me to do is to try and summarise what has gone on. You have heard it all for yourself – and in any case we are going to publish the whole proceedings as a book as fast as we can. We have enjoyed having you. It has been a very good Congress and we hope that the programme has achieved what should be the objectives of any world congress and that is to provide a meeting place for public relations practitioners to listen to surveys of the world situation to open our minds to wider spheres and major world trends. And to enable us to learn about new thinking in our own profession and new technology in communications and I would like to refer here to that wonderful session on electronic communications which was organised by Alfred Geiringer and his colleagues. But also we learn how other people see us. And this I think is sometimes a very salutary lesson. None of us can pretend to work in a closed situation. Whatever the scope of our job – whether within or beyond national boundaries – what is going on in the world affects people, and we deal with the hopes and the fears and anxieties and ambitions of people. So in having our four distinguished international speakers and our two after lunch speakers dwell upon the broadest spectrum of human relations – I hope we will be encouraged <u>always</u> to look into the middle and the far distance and put a true perspective on the service that we provide to our principals and through them to the public at large. We have had many problems of the world of the future outlined to us. The East and the West, the North/South, the rich, poor, the industrialised and the non-industrialised relations situations. We have had pinpointed for us the outcome of the present failure to inject into decision processes full consideration of the confusion of mind, perplexities and sheer fear of ordinary people in the world, in terms of confrontation, apathy, and self-centredness often sponsored by increasingly rapid communications in what has become a global village.

The erosion of national confidence and stability created by international mis-understanding is a by-product of these failures. I recall a most telling phrase which all of us – as public relations people should have imprinted on our minds and on our hearts, and the phrase is: "That we are each other's guardians and each other's wards". There can be few better descriptions of the very serious responsibilities of a public relations practitioner today. Our involvement <u>cannot</u> and <u>must not</u> be solely that of a transmitter of other people's decisions and attitudes. It must be based on the needs of people in a new world which is with much pain and much philosophical chaos being created out of what is and what we are for the future of the whole of mankind. We have indeed had good discussions and good sessions.

Now what shall we take away from this world Congress? If I refer back to the theme of the Congress: "Challenges of a Changing World", I would answer my own question thus: Firstly that the well-worn phrase, "Changing world", is not a cliché, but a reality. And a reality in terms of the changing condition of societies and of human beings at an ever increasing pace. Secondly, that there are trends in international relations that will strengthen and proliferate and which on whatever time scale must be factors in a development of a profession as a whole and the contribution each of us makes to it. Thirdly, with the increasing complexity of political, trade and social exchanges within and across blocks of nations we will need to understand and use equally human and sophisticated bases for our thinking and planning and the highest professional art to achieve our desired affects in the public interests. Fourthly and lastly, quite simply the conviction that our profession has a tremendous contribution to make to the peaceful progress of the world and the benefit of all mankind and we must make that contribution.

Ladies and Gentlemen, may I say for myself and my colleagues on the Organising Committee, this Congress has been an unbelievably stimulating experience and you the delegates have made it so. Since we first met at the inaugural luncheon the whole thing has immediately jelled. There came an atmosphere instantly created of warmth and friendship, of eagerness to learn from each other, of conviction of involvement and it has made it a unique experience. It was more than we could possibly hope for in our wildest dreams. And now with the closure of the Eighth Public Relations World Congress, let us look forward to the Ninth in Bombay in early 1982 and an intervening tranquil and harmonious progress in meeting the challenges of a changing world.

Recommended Further Reading

BLACK, Sam. (1976). In: *Practical Public Relations*, 4th Edition, Pitman.

BLACK, Sam. (1976). In: *The Role of Public Relations in Management*, Paperback Edition, Modino.

CUTLIP, Scott M and CENTER, Allen H. (1978). In: *Effective Public Relations*, 5th Edition, Prentice-Hall Inc.

BERNAYS, Edward L. (1977). In: *Public Relations*, University of Oklahoma Press.

LESLY'S Public Relations Handbook. (1978). 2nd Edition, Prentice-Hall Inc.

NOLTE, Lawrence W. (1979). In: *Fundamentals of Public Relations*, 2nd Edition, Pergamon Press.

MOORE, H Frazier and CANFIELD, Bertrand R. (1977). In: *Public Relations - Principles, Cases, and Problems*, Richard D Irwin Incorporated.

PALUSZEK, John L. (1977). In: *Will the Corporation Survive?*, Reston Publishing.

ROSS, Robert D. (1977). In: *The Management of Public Relations - Analysing and Planning External Relations*, John Wiley and Sons Incorporated.

WATTS, Reginald. (1977). In: *Public Relations for Top Management*, Cromer Publications.

BOWMAN, Pat and ELLIS, Nigel. (1977). In: *Manual of Public Relations*, Heinemann (in association with CAM).

Name Index

Ansah, Paul, 47-51
Appassamy, Freddy, 146-8, 218

Bateman, J Carroll, 17, 216
Bateson, Gregory, 40-1
Bernays, Edward L, 44-6, 52
Black, Sam, 17
Bol, Jean-Marie van, 29-41
Braine, Sir Bernard, 188
Brandt, Willy, 183, 188
Braun, Professor E, 116
Bright, Roy, 105-7
Browne, Sean, 177
Buckle, Dennis, 1-2, 218-9

Carvello, Philippe, 116, 132
Clark, Sir Fife, 142
Clarke, Robin, 123
Cleverdon, Julia, 81-2
Cook, Charles, 116, 130-2
Cole-Morgan, John, 142
Coup de Frejac, Jacques, 206-8

de Cat, Willie, 175-6
de Kock, Jan D M, 101
Derriman, James P, 142, 166-8

Earl, Peter, 142
Eden-Green, Alan, 143, 203

Fennings, Roger, 152-3
Ferrer, August, 30
Fransen, Anna, 86, 91-4, 101-2

Gardener, John, 17
Geiringer, Alfred, 104, 218
Gram, Jorgen, 189
Greene, William, 189

Hart, Norman, 44, 52-6
Hartogh, Jules, 190-3

Hoadley, Walter, 134
Hollis, Nesta, 104
Horack, Sarah, 117-21

Inchbald, Denis, 142, 154-6

Jahn, Burkhard, 83-5
Jarratt, Alex, 81
Jefkins, Frank, 189

Kaul, Jolly, 44, 52-63, 216-7
Kozminski, Professor Andrzej, 84-5

Lahiri, Sanat, 16-18, 213
Lall, Sanjaya, 86-90
Lane, David, 177
Leaf, Robert, 194-200
Lee, Ivy, 204

McBride, Sean, 12
Mahon, Peter, 144-5
Mardin, Betul, 149-51
Marshall, Michael, 81
McVeigh, Dr J C, 116, 122-9
Meiden, Anne van der, 44, 73-7, 175
Modoux, Alain, 189
Murray, Ed, 217

Nally, Margaret, 142
Nogueira, Nemercio, 216

O'Brien, Dr Conor Cruise, 1-6
Osinowo, Victor, 189

Pandit, S, 101
Paulus, John, 13
Player, Willis, 189
Pocock, Michael, C, 133-41
Prince Philip, HRH Duke of Edinburgh,
    1-2, 25, 125, 160

Subject Index

Apartheid, 26, 185
Aspen Institute, 3
Audio-visuals, 196

Bateman-Cutlip Report, 62

CEEFAX, 106
China Syndrome, The, 14
Churches, role of the, 184
Churchill, Sir Winston, 210
Code of Athens, 161, 168, 173-4
Code of Lisbon, 166-72
Communication, 10, 13-4, 81-4
    global, 13
    in Eastern Europe, 84
    in Germany, 83
    in UK Welfare State, 81
    trade unions, 82
Communication Advertising and
 Marketing Foundation (CAM), 34, 56
Community Affairs
    local community responsibility, 137
Computers
    compatible with the press, 108-9
    computerised news, 103-15
    computerised news handling, 108-11
Consumer Affairs, 97, 135
    framework of rules, 93
    illegalities, 89
    interests, 91, 100
    protection, 102
    protection groups, 198
    The International Organisations of
    Consumers Unions, 92
Dialogue, 207
Energy
    cutting consumption, 130
    demand, 124
    next decade, 134
    problems, 117
Environment, 98
    achieving resolution of problems,
    117
    alternative technology, 123
    a third alternative, 123
    history, 122
    in differing societies, 122
    intermediate technology
    development group, 123
    opposing views on, 123, 125

American scenarios, 120
British scenarios, 120
coal industry, future of, 131
corporate priorities and the
 energy problem, 117
- need for research, 117
cutting consumption,
 communicating benefits of, 130
de-centralised information
 sources, 126, 128
defining the problem, 117
media, role of, 130-132
professional engineering
 institutions, 126
shrinking resources,
 communication of, 116
Sullom Voe Project, 131
UK department of energy press
 releases, 126
USA future energy demand, 124
Eskimo, 203
European Economic Community (EEC), 14
European Public Relation Centre (CERP)
 29-31, 38-9, 161, 163, 166-7

Feminism, 217
Foundation for Public Relations
 Research and Education, 29, 33

Gandhi, Mahatma, 184
Global Affairs
    effective management of change,
    22
    problems, 23
    Third World influence, 183
Global Village, 24
Government Information Services, 42-3

Harrisburg (Three Mile Island), 11, 13,
    14, 117, 193
Hitler, Adolf, 4, 6

Industrial Relations
    cooperation, 138
    dialogue with the
    environmentalists, 137
    diversification, 95
        and community, 136
    free enterprise, 85, 206
    industrial democracry, 139

DATE DUE

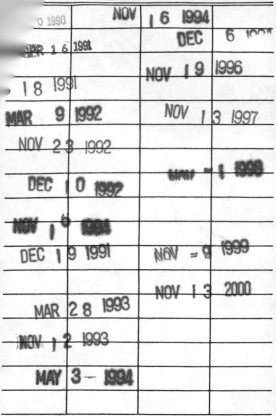

	NOV 1 6 1994	
0 1990	DEC 6 1994	
MAR 1 6 1991	NOV 1 9 1996	
1 8 1991		
MAR 9 1992	NOV 1 3 1997	
NOV 2 3 1992		
DEC 1 0 1992	MAY 1 1998	
NOV 1 6 1994		
DEC 1 9 1991	NOV 9 1999	
MAR 2 8 1993	NOV 1 3 2000	
NOV 1 2 1993		
MAY 3 1994		